A British Attaché

in the

Russo-Japanese War

Volume I

Sir Ian Hamilton & Genl. Kodama

A British Attaché
in the
Russo-Japanese War

Volume I

By Sir Ian Hamilton

Legacy Books Press
Military Classics

Published by Legacy Books Press
RPO Princess, Box 21031
445 Princess Street
Kingston, Ontario, K7L 5P5
Canada

www.legacybookspress.com

The scanning, uploading, and/or distribution of this book via the Internet or any other means without the permission of the publisher is illegal and punishable by law.

This edition first published in 2021 by Legacy Books Press
1

This edition © 2021 Legacy Books Press, all rights reserved.

ISBN: 978-1-927537-61-9

First published as *A Staff Officer's Scrap-Book During the Russo-Japanese War, Volume I,* by Edward Arnold in 1905.

Printed and bound in the United States of America and the United Kingdom.

This book is typeset in a Times New Roman 11-point font.

"One eyewitness, however dull and prejudiced, is worth a wilderness of sentimental historians."

– W. E. Henley.

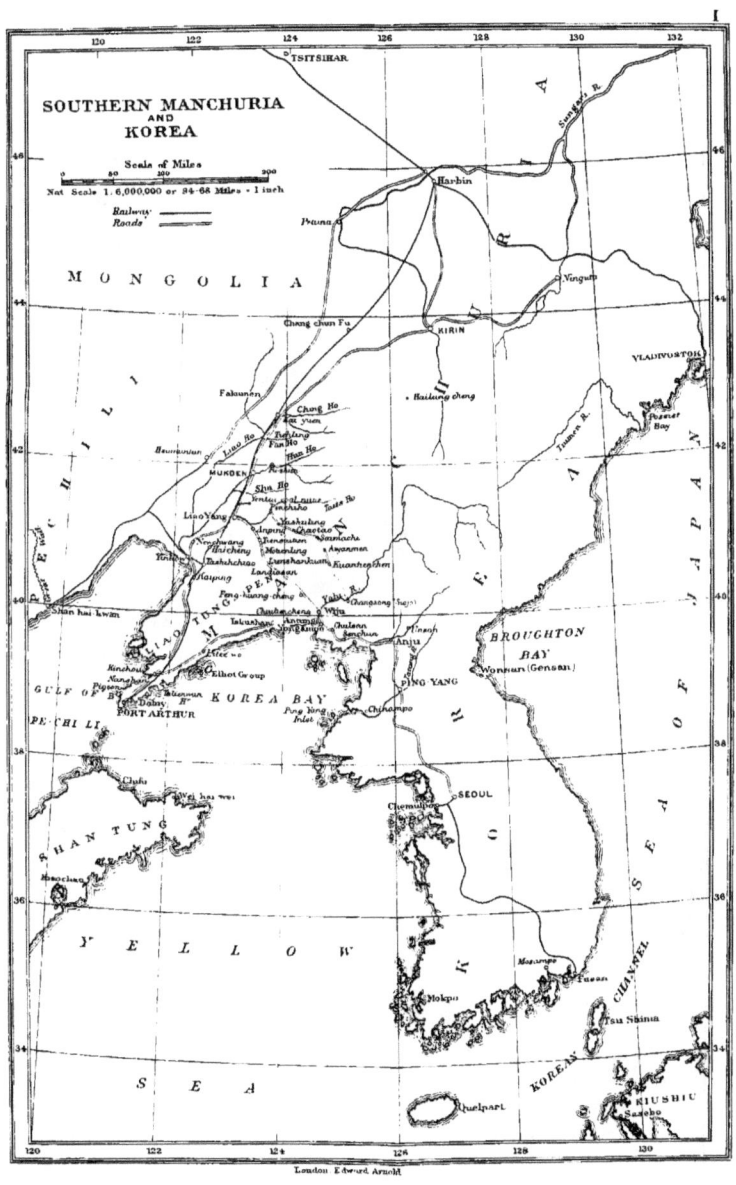

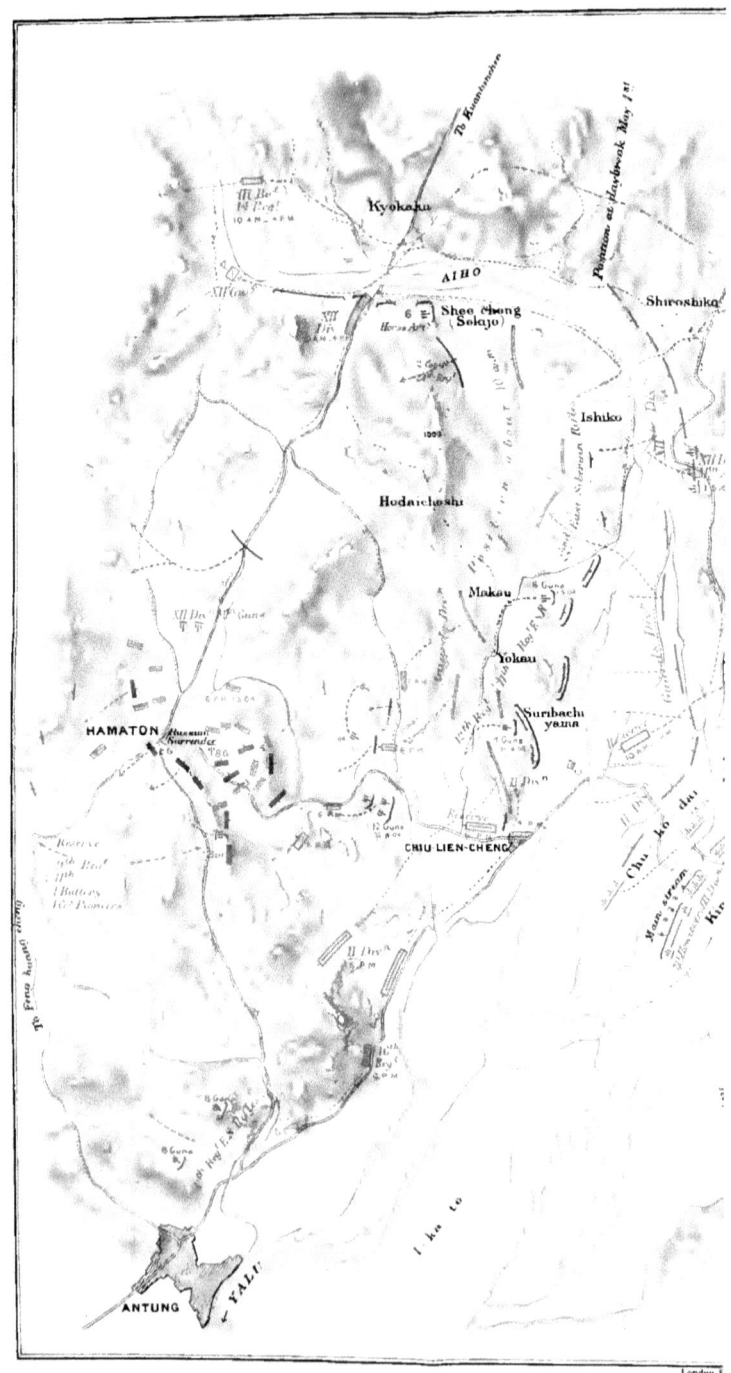

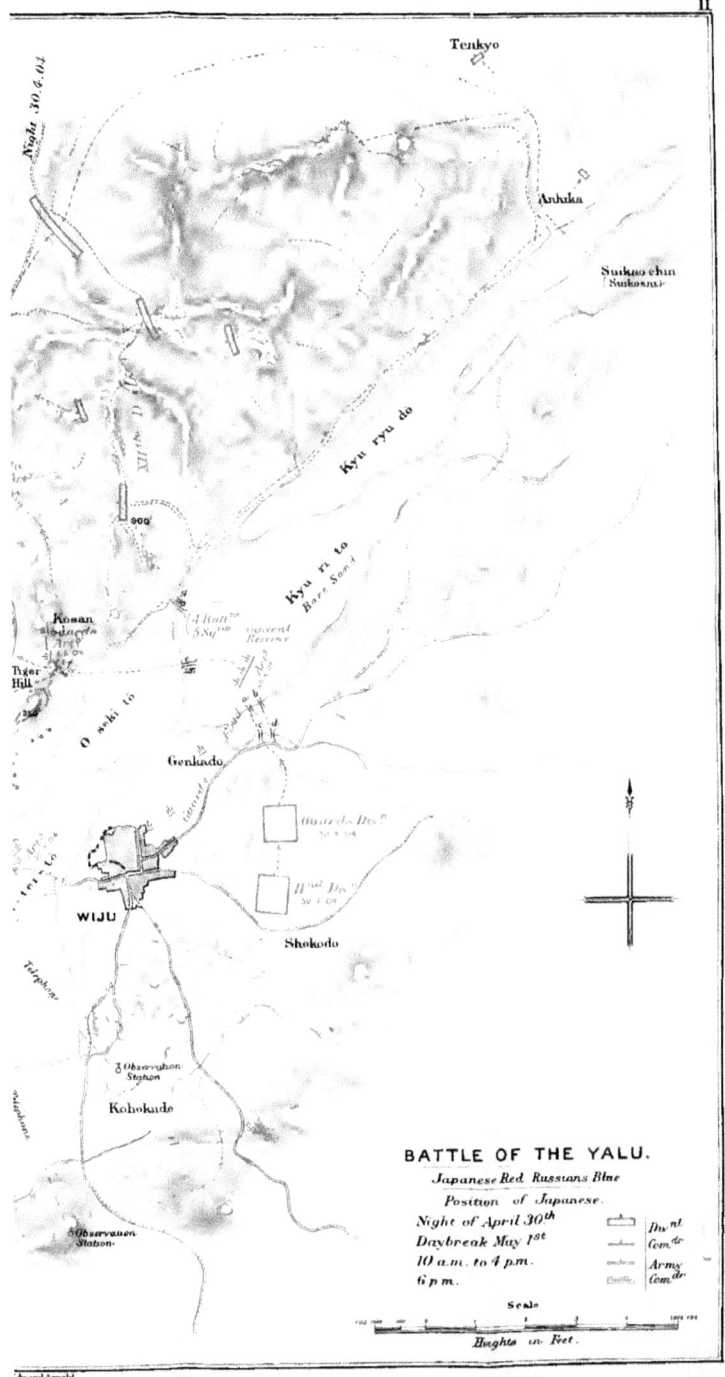

Table of Contents

Publisher's Note 3

Preface 5

Chapter I – First Impressions of the Japanese Army 7

Chapter II – Some New Acquaintances 21

Chapter III – Three Pleasing Traits..................... 35

Chapter IV – From Tokio to the Yalu................... 41

Chapter V – Fenghuangcheng......................... 58

Chapter VI – The Position on the Yalu.................. 65

Chapter VII – The Battle of the Yalu 84

Chapter VIII – The Attachés Are Entertained 120

Chapter IX – The Chinese General Pays a Visit.......... 136

Chapter X – General Fujii Talks...................... 153

Chapter XI – The Feast of the Dead 163

Chapter XII – On the March at Last 177

Chapter XIII – An Affair of Outposts.................. 194

Chapter XIV – The Battle of the Heaven-Reaching Pass.... 212

Chapter XVI – A Pause Before the Advance 257

Chapter XVII – The Battle of Yoshirei 267

Chapter XVIII – The Disastrous Retreat from Penlin 290

Index 313

About the Author 322

Publisher's Note

The original edition of this book contained a number of untranslated phrases and passages in languages such as French and German. Where it would aid understanding, translations have been provided in the footnotes.

Preface

It is difficult to convey to the peaceable citizens of Greater Britain a true picture of that glorious and impressive survival from heroic times, a nation in arms. The difficulty is enhanced by the fact that military history must be always to some extent misleading.

If facts are hurriedly issued, fresh from the mint of battle, they cannot be expected to supply an account which is either well balanced or exhaustive. On the other hand, it is equally certain that, when once the fight has been fairly lost or won, it is the tendency of all ranks to combine and recast the story of their achievement into a shape which shall satisfy the susceptibilities of national and regimental vain-glory. It is then already too late for the painstaking historian to set to work. He may record the orders given and the movements which ensued, and he may build up thereon any ingenious theories which occur to him; but to the hopes and fears which dictated those orders, and to the spirit and method in which those movements were executed, he has for ever lost the clue. On the actual day of battle naked truths may be picked up for the asking; by the following morning they have already begun to get into their uniforms.

If the impressions here recorded possess any value, it will be because they do faithfully represent the facts as they appeared to the First Japanese Army while the wounded still lay bleeding upon the stricken field. Further than this they do not profess to go.

The time has hardly yet come for a full and critical account by an ex-attaché of a war round which so many conflicting national ambitions have revolved. Meanwhile these scraps, snap-shots, by-products, or whatever they may be called, are offered to the public in the hope that they may interest, without hurting the feelings of either of the great armies concerned. If this hope should be realised, I shall be encouraged to advance with Kuroki through conflicts fiercer and bloodier far than any I have here attempted to set down.

My special thanks are due to Captain Vincent for the help he has given me, and for the maps, sketches and photographs with which the volume is illustrated. It is hardly necessary for me here to acknowledge my indebtedness to my kind hosts, or to other British attachés, for this will become patent to the reader as he reads.

Ian Hamilton

Chapter I – First Impressions of the Japanese Army

British Legation, Tokio, 11 p.m., March 16th, 1904. — Startled from sleep by the sudden stillness of the engines, I ran up on deck this morning and found our great ship gliding forward without effort, noiselessly, as if to the soft attraction of a magnet. She was heading due west, and made her final stately approach to the land of the Rising Sun, with the deep red rim of the sun rising directly in her wake. All around us stretched the bay, smooth and green as polished jade, and freckled with the sails of fisher-boats where the margin grew darker under the reflections of encircling hills. So much I saw, and then — incredulous at first as when some fairy vision is caught for one moment in the meshes of a daydream — I realised Fuji. Fuji uplifting a pale unearthly crown of purest snow far above ship, bay, town, and all the misty network of subordinate valleys and mountains! Unawares — too swiftly and unceremoniously — found myself ushered into the presence of one of the marvels of the world! Venice from the sea. The immortal Taj. My thrill of surprise and admiration had touched some sleeping chords of memory, for, unbidden, these wonders of days gone by rose faintly to my eyes, then fading away left me face to face with the stirring realities of the present.

The past was past, the future had never seemed so full of life and strange adventures. I breathed a short prayer for continued good fortune, whilst our Japanese reservists, summoned from Hong Kong to march through ice and snow and fire and blood for Emperor and Fatherland, raised a shout, unfamiliar as the landscape itself, to mark the accomplishment of the first stage of their journey.

I wonder sometimes, is it possible that the human soul has a power vouchsafed to it of moulding time and circumstance to meet a calm and confident desire? Is it not the case that things involving struggle are rarely worth obtaining, whereas all the best of drops, like the manna of the Israelites, from the skies? I moved heaven and earth with my importunities to get to Japan. But when I stopped struggling and simply believed I must arrive in good time, then the way was presently made straight for me. I no longer accept the theory of life which Dick Whittington evolved to the tune of the bells of London, but believe rather in keeping mind and body absolutely fit; doing whatever work happens to come to hand, and leaving the rest to Providence.

At a time when the last smouldering fires of the Boer War were reducing to ashes the political hatreds accumulated during the previous century, I had strained all that friends or credit could do to obtain permission, as soon as peace was concluded, to come home from South Africa via Japan, Korea, Manchuria and Russia. Thus I hoped I might get an opportunity to study not only the actors, but also the theatre, of an impending world drama; a world drama more fascinating than any staged since the Greeks put measure to another ambition which had known no bounds until the curtain rose on the plains of Marathon. My application found favour in the eyes of the War Minister and Commander-in-Chief. My belongings were mobilised — and, three days before starting, the conqueror of Omdurman signified that it might be more convenient if I accompanied him home! The convenience of a conqueror is not to be gainsaid, and thus, the mere expression of a wish shattered my glittering Japanese castle into its original components; the card pack of a gambler with fortune. Yet now — when the experiences I seek are ripening for the harvest — the

First Impressions of the Japanese Army

proverbial illwind has veered in my favour. Who could have foretold that the cutting blast which swirled through Pall Mall some six weeks ago, making a clean sweep of a venerated institution situated therein, would turn to the halcyon breeze that was to waft me to these happy isles. Out of the War OflBce into the realities of war; out of the English fog into the presence of Fuji, with all that Fuji now portends to a soldier!

The best qualification for success seems then to be not to desire it over anxiously, and certainly the best moments in life are not those in which a man sees success impending; still less, those in which he savours the dead sea fhiit of achievement with its sickly complimentary sauce of congratulations and applause. Are they not rather those moments in which it is borne in to a poor mortal that some immortal has clearly designated the field of action, wherein he has only to be true to his convictions and himself, and advance confidently by word of command to the accomplishment of some predestined end?

It is now midnight. There is nothing in this luxurious English room with its blazing coal fire and close-drawn curtains to tell me I am at last in Japan; yet surely this diary, commenced in a manner so foreign to my intentions, is evidence of the fact. So let me to bed, and may I dream of Fuji! Pale Fuji — touched into life by the strange dull crimson of this morning's rising sun. An emblem — a sign sent from the Heavens and sealed in the mountain — proclaiming the blood yet to flow before that sun climbs its full height up the sky.

"And blood, he cried, the chariots and the horses.
The noise of shout and thunder of the battle heard afar."

Tokio, April 1st, 1904. — I am not quite sure if it was William of Normandy or Julius Caesar who burnt his boats? Anyway, on this very suitable date for a foolhardy action, I have put a torch to the whole of my fleet, and I only hope I may be as well justified in the result as was the conquering hero with regard to whose performance my memory is a little shaky. To descend from my insecure historical platform to everyday life, I have posted my letters and I feel the same uneasy qualms about them as when about October 1, 1899, I had fairly launched from Pietermaritzburg a batch of futile warnings. To-day there has been nothing of the Cassandra spirit in my strain, hut I have taken some chances all the same. For in these letters just despatched the last poor shreds of my military reputation have been staked upon a forecast that the Japanese army will beat the Russian army wherever they meet them on terms even approaching equality. Further, I have fairly let myself in for the opinion that the Japanese army, battalion for battalion, surpasses any European army, excepting only the British army at its best (not at its second best, which is the state in which it usually finds itself). The diagnosis may be considered somewhat hasty, but experts with urgent convictions to express cannot afford to wait like amateurs until the course of events makes prediction fairly safe at the cost of nine-tenths of its value.* There is certainly no more thankless task than that of playing prophet. It is like betting with some one who says, "Heads I win; tails we stand quits." Loss is possible, profit is not. Still, it appears to me best to state my impressions frankly, and not to balance whether or no it will be expedient to do so.

And now for my reasons. It was not only because I had fought against the Boers in the year 1881 that it was borne in upon me how long and difficult would be the way to success in the year 1899. It was because of my conviction that up-to-date civilisation is becoming less and less capable of conforming to the antique standards of military virtue, and that the hour is at hand when the modern world must begin to modify its ideals, or prepare to go down before some more natural, less complex and less nervous type. The Boers furnished one example of those primitive peoples whose education and intelligence had just reached a stage at which they could avail themselves of modern rifles and guns. City-bred dollar-hunters are becoming less and less capable of coping with such adversaries as Deer-slayer and his clan. In situation after situation where our soldiers were helpless the Boers were perfectly

---

* These letters were delivered in England with the morning papers announcing the Japanese victory on the Yalu river.

First Impressions of the Japanese Army 11

at home. It was this which made one Boer equal to three freshly landed British soldiers in everything except those hammer-and-tongs fights which, in such a war, are quite exceptional. Even now the old civilised nations try to shut their eyes to this. They do so upon exactly the same principle on which mankind refuse to let their thoughts dwell upon the subject of death. It is more comfortable to blame the British War Office, to sneer at British officers, and to speak slightingly of the cost and bloodshed involved in defeating "a handful oi farmers," than to face the tremendous truth with all that it involves, this truth being that it is just because the Boers were primitive farmers that they were able to make so long a stand against troops who had not such an advantage. Had the war taken place a few years later, the overthrow of the advanced types of civilisation by the backward types would have been inaugurated with the disappearance of the British power, name and language from South African soil.

As it is, we have escaped that sad initiation, but we are not yet out of the wood. We have still to face the problem of Afghanistan which Russian and English jealousies now condemn to barbaric isolation. Such people as the Afghans and the tribes on the Northwest frontier of India must be resolutely penetrated and tamed within the next generation; or they will become capable of overthrowing and uncivilising India herself; just as Abyssinia, unless she is absorbed and educated within the next thirty years, may become capable of overwhelming North Africa, and as the Basutos, Zulus, and Herreros would make short work of South Africa if the white population were not fortunately convinced believers in the necessity of cultivating military ideals. Western civilisation must enlighten its eventual conquerors as Rome even dying enlightened the barbarians, lest when our modern world is finally defeated in the field Europe should be wrapped again in darkness. Is it not the old, old story? India is Gaul; Central Asia is Germany; Varus loses his legions at Maiwand.

This is no time for any civilised nation to play pranks with its army, or to gamble at confidence-trick games with its rivals at The Hague. Disarmament talk from the mouths of the masters of India would be supremely ridiculous were it not so dangerous. Have those who cry "peace" ever paused to consider the lordly Sikh, whose god is the sword and his religion war? What would he say, or do rather, for he does not say much, if the Sahibs tried to transform gallant armies into military police? Every thinking soldier who has served on our recent Indian campaigns is aware that for the requirements of such operations a good Sikh, Pathan or Gurkha battalion is more generally serviceable than a British battalion. If, for instance, a non-commissioned officer and a dozen men are required to picquet a mountain top two or three miles distant, until the column has passed, and are then to find their way back and follow on with the rear guard, no one in his senses would send British soldiers. They might lose their way; they might unseasonably exhibit a preference for fighting and require to be extricated; or, in some way or another, accentuate the anxieties of their general, even if they did not form the text for a regrettable incident despatch by getting cut up completely. For advance guards, rear guards, roadmaking, night fighting, escorts to convoys, and for everything in fact that takes place in these mountains except a definite attack upon a definite position, the best native troops, being more in touch with nature can give points to the artificially trained townsmen who now form so large a proportion of our men. I do not ignore the fortunate fact that the scouting and reconnoitring of the British army has vastly improved since the South African War. But even so we remain, and must continue to remain, a long way behind more primitive nations in these important warrior characteristics.

All this is supposed to be a secret; a thing to be whispered with bated breath, as if every sepoy did not already know who does the rough and dirty work, and who, in the long run, does the hardest fighting. Nevertheless, these very officers who know will sit and solemnly discuss whether our best native troops would, or would not, be capable of meeting a European enemy! Why — there is material in the north of India and in Nepaul sufficient and fit, under good leadership, to shake the artificial society of Europe to its foundations if once it dares tamper with that militarism which now alone supplies it with any higher ideal than money and the luxury which that money can purchase.

I have taken Nepaul as an example of the primitive State whose people are natural born fighters, and it is owing, I think, to my

First Impressions of the Japanese Army

knowledge of the gallant little Gurkhas that I have found confidence and courage to write home so early in the day giving an estimate of the Japanese army. From the standpoint of practical study, experience and knowledge of men and material, I have lees claim to express an opinion on that army than any civilian inhabitant of Tokio who has kept his eyes open and seen its officers, non-commissioned officers and men, march and drill and walk about the streets for the past twelve months. But imaginatively I carry a key which gives me the *entrée* right into the heart of the machine.

At intervals since 1879 I have fought alongside of Gurkhas — I have had the honour of having them under my command — have watched them long hours at musketry when the heart of the soldier very much reveals itself — know them in camp and on the march, in war and in peace. Nor must I forget the sport we have had together, my visits to Nepaul, or, above all, that glorious week in the southern jungle with 400 elephants and two battalions of Khas Gurkhas to help the great man I was with to his tigers. I ought to know the Gurkhas well, and, if so, I know the Japanese soldier also. He is a very old friend. Lord Roberts had a faithful orderly, a splendid fighting Gurkha, who watched over him jealously from 78 to '81, and is now a respected native officer retired upon his pension. We called him "Bullet-head." Behold, in one Japanese company, at least a dozen young "Bullet-heads," as small as life, and quite unmistakable in their resemblance to that splendid old soldier of the Afghan war!

Whilst I was looking at the company it was dismissed, and a number of the men having been freshly summoned from country districts hung around to enjoy a good stare at the foreigner. This gave me an opportunity of letting loose my interpreter at them, and we exchanged some sentiments. There was no doubt about it: the resemblance between Gurkhas and Japanese is more than skin deep. The same ready smile; the same jolly good-humour; the same independent manner, evincing, dearly but not offensively, the soldier's pride and his conscious superiority to any civilian, especially a foreign civilian. When I told them that I too was a soldier they became communicative, and we had quite a conversation. These were surely Gurkhas; better educated, more civilised: on the other hand, not quite so powerful or hardy. The majority of the company, perhaps two-thirds of it, conformed to the type of the Muggurs of Nepaul; squat and square: bullet-headed and pudding-faced. The remaining third were different; more slightly built; with a keen, grave, aquiline cast of countenance, they gave me the impression that they also would prove to be forward in the fight. In the whole of Tokio I have not seen a single soldier who is flat-footed, narrow-chested or slouching. The company officers seem businesslike and athletic; the staff officers, as a rule, do not. This Japanese army shows conscription at its best — a comparatively small number, picked out of several hundreds of thousands for physical fitness and aptitude at certain necessary trades. The army is the cream of the nation. "How different from us. Miss Beale and Miss Buss!"

The force of the Russian army, as against other European nations, lies in her private soldiers, who are peasants; still in touch with nature; robust, hardy, patient, and stolid. But they have neither the habitude of war, nor, except perhaps when fighting in defence of their hearths and homes, do they possess that inborn vital spark of martial ardour which will compensate in battle for many defects in character or physique. Least of all are they endowed with that independence of character and power of acting on their own individual initiative upon which modem war will henceforth make such high demands.

The Japanese soldiers are equally peasants, equally solid and unaffected with nerves. There the resemblance ceases; for our allies are warlike by taste and tradition; and upon the patriotism, which they have absorbed with their mothers' milk, their government has been careful to graft initiative, quickness, and intelligence. This is accomplished in the schools, which keep the soldierly virtues in the forefront of their curriculum. Here is a rule of conduct given by the head of the Otono clan to his retainers in remote antiquity, a rule familiar from his childhood to the Japanese private soldier: "You must die by the side of your great lord, and never turn your back on the foe. If you die at sea, let your body sink into the water; if you die on the hillside, let it be outstretched on the mountain grass." Since the Highland clans made way for the red deer, no woman in Great Britain would think of imparting such ideas or ideals to her child.

The Japanese and Russian armies denote the overlapping of two stages of civilisation. Apart from its great military forces, the one saving strength of our old Western world lies in its education and intelligence; and yet, in this case, the representative of the East is the superior in these very factors.

The one army is close to its base, the other hangs dependent at the extremity of a single line of railway thousands of miles long, like a soap-bubble at the end of a churchwarden. What reason, then, to fear that my batch of predictions will be falsified? None I It is not so much the idea that we may have put our money on the wrong horse which now troubles me; still less any fear that I may have made a false estimate of the new force which this army represents. But it should cause European statesmen some anxiety when their people seem to forget that there are millions outside the charmed circle of Western civilisation who are ready to pluck the sceptre from nerveless hands so as the old warrior spirit is allowed to degenerate. It is strange to read of conferences discussing the desirability of peace, and urging the repression of the military spirit, just as if there was no one in the world but themselves; just, in fact, like sheep discussing watchdogs, oblivious of the wolves. As if, indeed, Asia and Africa were not even now stirring uneasily in their sleep, and dreaming dim dreams of conquest and of war.

Unless I very much mistake, this small nation, Eastern to the backbone, is about to testily by the mouth of her cannon that the six Great Powers are not all the world but only a part of it, depending as a last resource on the courage of their fighting men for their money-bags and liberty, and all else they hold most dear. Providentially Japan is our ally, and not one, if I may presume to judge so early, who will prove ungrateful. England has time therefore — time to put her military affairs in order; time to implant and cherish the military ideal in the hearts of her children; time to prepare for a disturbed and anxious twentieth century. The first thing we have to learn, I am sure, is that neither pay, conscription, numbers, or equipment can compensate for any falling off in the adventurous fighting spirit of which the germs still exist in the souls of our race. What civilisation may have stolen, perhaps inevitably, from the old semi-barbarous warrior spirit, she should have surely made good by quickening a more enthusiastic patriotism, and giving the young generations an ideal for which they would lay down their lives. Is it too late to expect this? From the nursery and its toys to the Sunday school and its cadet company, every influence of affection, loyalty, tradition, and education should be brought to bear on the next generation of British boys and girls, so as deeply to impress upon their young minds a feeling of reverence and admiration for the patriotic spirit of their ancestors.

In England the War Office and the Education Department have not even a bowing acquaintance, and this is not altogether the fault of the Education Department. Government departments have no souls, no aspirations, no hearts. If Bushido was for sale in the market it might go hang as far as they are concerned. What a department likes is something tangible to show the taxpayer; a hobbledehoy, for instance, in a cheap red coat, so that answer may be made in due season, "You entrusted me with eighteen pence, see, here is a soldier!" Whether the poor child was starved into the ranks by the pinch of a hard winter or whether he was naturally attracted to an honourable profession is a matter of no consequence. He has a red coat and he breathes; Rule Britannia! If our military system and our educational curriculum continue to neglect cultivating the old natural warrior spirit which first made us a free people, then cowardice, followed by its antidote conscription, will soon be knocking at our gates. I do not envy the feelings of the head masters of public schools in England when they read extracts from the report of the Royal Commission on the war in South Africa, and recollect to what lengths they have gone in their time actively to discourage their best and brightest pupils from embarking in the career of arms. As for the teachers in Government schools, they are, according to their lights, an enthusiastic and patriotic class. But to how few of them has it ever even occurred that the soul of a greengrocer's boy might be fired with martial ardour, which might some day be more useful to his country even than the three great R's!

With our education anti-military, and our army organised on a basis of wages, we are marching straight in the footsteps of China, who one thousand years ago became so clever as to see that war was a relic of barbarism. So it is; but to neglect its precepts on that account is to band over the conduct of the world to barbarians. The Mandarins discouraged their best from adopting the military career, and thought their worst good enough for the army. Many, many years ago they faced the problems which now agitate our Western peace idealists, and thought they had solved them. Now, in 1904, helpless as Prometheus in the vulture's clutch, China sees a foreign war about to devastate her fairest province; a war of which she herself seems destined to be, indirectly or directly, the victor's prize. Never was the verdict of Ruskin better exemplified: "All the pure and noble arts of peace are founded on war; no great art ever rose on earth but among a nation of soldiers. ...There is no great art possible to a nation but that which is based on battle.... When I tell you that war is the foundation of all the arts, I mean also that it is the foundation of all the high virtues and faculties of men. It is very strange to me to discover this; and very dreadful — but I saw it to be quite an undeniable fact. The common notion that peace and the virtues of civil life flourished together, I found to be wholly untenable. Peace and the *vices* of civil life only flourish together. We talk of peace and learning, of peace and plenty, and of peace and civilisation; but I found that those were not the words which the Muse of History coupled together; that, on her lips, the words were peace and sensuality — peace and selfishness — peace and death. I found, in brief, that all great nations learned their truth of word, and strength of thought, in war; that they were nourished in war, and wasted by peace; taught by war, and deceived by peace; trained by war, and betrayed by peace: in a word, that they were born in war, and expired in peace."

It would be well for us if this extract could be taught by heart to every school-child in England. Here it would be superfluous. At military manoeuvres, when troops march through a district, all the children are given a holiday, and trot down to line the roads along which the soldiers will pass. In Tokio, whenever any especially stirring departure of troops takes place, the tiny mites of both sexes are brought to wish Godspeed to "our dear brave soldiers." In their schoolrooms are portraits of heroes and pictures of great battles. The Japanese have behind them the moral character produced by mothers and fathers, who again are the product of generations of mothers and fathers nurtured in ideas of self-sacrifice and loyalty. But they do not on this account trust entirely to heredity to produce them an army. If they wish to have every man in the nation a potential fighter they know they must begin at the beginning, and put the right ideas into the babies as soon as they begin to toddle. The parade march of the 5th German Army Corps impressed me far less than the little Japanese boys and girls I saw marching down in their companies to say good-bye to the soldiers. "There," I said to myself, "go the world-renowned, invincible armies of 1920!"

Now, just before I go out, I must try to fix on paper as clean an impression as I can of this Japanese people. The impression is probably absurdly wrong. Indeed, even a globe-trotter would hardly venture to. have a decided opinion at such short notice. Still I want to be able to look back later, when I know our allies better, and either laugh at my own mistake or admire my own acumen, as the case may be. Moreover, there is an undeniable value in the first impressionist flash. When I have got to feel like a Jap, as I dare say in time I may, then I know I must entirely fail if I try to convey any idea of his characteristics to a European. After all, I have already been here one week longer than the authoress of "Castle Daly" had been in Ireland when she wrote her classic on the inhabitants of the Emerald Isle. Let me then be bold to say what I think.

In my presumptuous opinion, the Japanese are just as civilised as would be the Black Prince and his army if, by some miracle, they could now be resuscitated, and have a thorough good German education grafted on to their unformed, mediaeval minds. Outwardly they are as civilised as we are, only, having got to their goal by a short cut, they have not had time yet to acquire the luxury, sensuality and nerves which, with us, have insensibly grown up *pari passu*^{*} with the refinements and mechanical facilities of life. It is as if the Japanese had possessed a virgin field, and for this, their first crop, had been able to exclude all the noxious and parasitic weeds which threaten to get the upper hand in the worn-out soil of the older cultivation. Most of the men seem to be slow thinkers,, giving the impression that their brains work

---

* "Side by side."

with an effort. This puts them out of court as conversationalists, but, on the other hand, they think accurately; their ideas are generally sound, and they never talk nonsense, except when they do so on purpose. It is only fair to add that my opinions have been formed by meeting some of their leading men.

Japanese women are not yet emancipated. They walk out of dinner after their lords and masters, and take the lower place both literally and metaphorically. If, however, Europeans and Americans wax critical on this point, the Japanese can make the crushing retort that the result leaves their women the most charming example of the gender feminine in the world. Looks may be a matter of taste, but charm is not. The smile of the Japanese girl is an enchantment. She looks exquisitely good, and I am sure those looks at least do not belie her. There is something childlike about her, and yet she is so thoughtful, and they say, and I believe it, so brave. There is something else. She is intensely, essentially feminine. Asiatic women still guard the secret of what Western women show signs of losing. Men have always been selfish, but now an appalling danger confronts civilisation in the shape of the American selfish woman and her imitators in Europe.

In Japan the sphere of the sexes is still totally distinct; and although this may shock foreign feminine opinion, in practice it certainly seems to tend to the general happiness. Not only to the general happiness, but also to the general military efficiency. Women occupied in passing examinations, struggling through society, sport, plays, travel, with interludes of flirtation, can scarcely find the time the Japanese mother does to stir the young imaginations of her children with tales of derring-do.

In education, as I have just hinted, the Japanese are in advance of the English. Especially is this the case when the highest and lowest ranks in Japan compared with corresponding ranks in England, The chief reason seems to me to lie in the undeniable fact that neither boys nor youths in England are particularly anxious to learn, whereas Japanese of all ranks and ages seem to be consumed by an ardent desire to extend their knowledge and improve themselves. Scotch lads are the only specimens in the United Kingdom who show, as a class, a little natural hankering after knowledge, but they cannot compare for one moment with the

Japanese. If Japanese youths were to find themselves under professors who were desirous rather of teaching them athletics than learning, they would not need the assistance of their parents to make very short work of such an establishment. My very servant is always trying to get English lessons out of me on the cheap, and although I see through his artifice and am bored by his methods I secretly admire his ambition.

Chapter II – Some New Acquaintances

Tokio, April 16th, 1904.— One month to-day since I landed in Japan! I feel inclined sometimes to think my time has been absolutely wasted; but this is chiefly in pessimistic moods, when all these enforced entertainments seem to clash over violently with the mobilising of troops, and the fine bracing atmosphere of battles and adventures galore, in which I spiritually already live, move, and have my being. I am still the guest of my old Sandhurst comrade and friend, Sir Claude MacDonald, whose career, during our thirty years of separation, I had always watched with sympathetic interest, and who has always deserved right well his good luck in finding himself over and over again at the right place just in the very nick of time. May his shadow never grow less!

I have already seen a good deal of Japanese society. I have met Baron Komura, Minister of Foreign Affairs, very frequently, as well as the Prime Minister, Major-General Count Eatsura; the War Minister, Lieutenant-General Teraoutsi; the Naval Minister, Baron Yamamoto; the President of the Imperial Council of Defence, the Marquis Yamagata; the Marquis Ito; the Chief of the General Staff of the Army, Lieutenant-General the Marquis Oyama; the Vice-

Chief of the General Staff of the Army, Lieutenant-General Baron Kodama; and last, but to me not least, the Chief of the second section of the General Staff, Major-General Sir Y. Fukushima, K.C.B.

KODAMA   OYAMA   FUKUSHIMA

Baron Komura talks perfect English in a somewhat strident voice. He is very small even for a Japanese, but very clever also, even for a Japanese. He has sunken cheeks, and large, inquiring, not to say searching, eyes. He reminds me in manner and carriage of one of our own Secretaries of State. I ventured one day to tell him so, when he laughed and said he feared would not feel flattered if he were able to overhear me. I made the lame and obvious reply that I had never yet seen the person, mole or female, who was flattered by being thought to resemble any one else, however good-looking that other person might be.

I never had the good fortune to say more than a few words at a time to the Prime Minister. He talks excellent German, and is a rotund, contented, but intensely clever-looking little man. He gives the impression of being a man as well as a politician, which is a good impression to receive from a Prime Minister, especially in stormy times such as these. I should think he was at the same time firm and calm, though I would not pretend he was by any means remarkable by his appearance. In England, politicians still shy at the shadow of Oliver Cromwell, and suspect at least a Boulanger in every successful soldier. But in Japan there is no such timidity, and not only is the Prime Minister a Major-General, but Yamamoto the sailor is sometimes spoken of as being his possible successor. He, Yamamoto, is the best looking of all the Japanese Ojisans according to our Western standard, much resembling an English sea captain, with an open face and a short grey beard.

The War Minister, Teraoutsi, is cold and reserved in manner, and his face wears ordinarily a somewhat cynical expression. He is typically Japanese -looking, his eyes being obliquely set very high in his head. His right hand was wounded in the old wars, so he has to shake hands with his left. In character, all who know him are agreed he is one of the kindest of men, and I myself can already bear witness to his sympathy and goodness of heart. He is said to be very helpful to young officers, especially when the help can be rendered by stealth, and he spares himself no trouble in assisting a deserving case. Even when a youngster has got into a serious scrape for once in a way, owing to thoughtlessness or inexperience, Lieutenant-General Teraoutsi will go great lengths to put him on his legs again, but he is quite merciless to proved incapacity. In the words of an admirer who knows him well, "when once he has satisfied himself that an officer is idle and indifferent, he is capable of keeping him down for fifteen years!" As the present War Minister was once an officer of the Military Cadet School, his characteristics are well known, and he has certainly succeeded in establishing a very wholesome funk throughout all ranks of the army. Withal he is of a dear and simple disposition. The other day I had the honour of being present at a great banquet at which Teraoutsi was the host, when suddenly an awful pause — the worst and longest angel's visit I have ever experienced — palsied the tongues of the 150 guests. After enduring this for some seconds, Teraoutsi the Terrible could stand it no longer, and called out to the bandmaster in anguished tones, "Play some music— quick!" at which every one roared with laughter, and the music proved after all superfluous.

Marshal the Marquis Yamagata is the Lord Roberts of Japan, in so far as fame and popularity are concerned. He very rarely goes out into society, so I was fortunate in meeting him twice; once at a reception given at the Chinese Embassy in honour of a Chinese Royal Prince, and once at the home of the War Minister. He is a handsome old warrior, with clean, clear-cut features; a great deal of gold in his teeth, which flashes out whenever he smiles, and a determined aquiline type of countenance. He is one of the old school of Samurai, and has a great reputation for bravery in a country where all are brave. One of many stories told about him is, that when he was a young man he swam out alone to try and sink the foreign warships at Yokohama with his sword. To know this, and to see the same man, who had such a primitive notion of the relative powers of armament, now employing against a great European Power all the science embodied in a nation in arms against a country like Russia, is to comprehend a little the change which during his lifetime has swept over Japan. As President (in virtue of seniority) of the Council of Imperial Defence, he is said by insiders to be the most powerful man in the Kingdom. In fact, my authorities on this point are so good that I myself have no doubt they must be right. In precedence at the Imperial Court, which is an enormously important matter in Japan, he ranks third after the Imperial Princes, the order being, Marquis Ito, President of the Privy Council; Prince M. Kujo; Marquis Yamagata; Marquis Oyama; Count Katsura, the Premier, &c. &c. He combines great strength of character with a broad-mindedness and openness which hostile critics maintain is not so common as it might be in Japanese society. He is perfectly charming to meet, and spoke to me with all the keenness of a gunner major about the vexed question of mobility and Weight of metal for field guns. Every one is sorry to think he is probably too old now to able to go again on active service as Commander-in-Chief of the armies in the field.

The career of the Marquis Ito is known to all the world. I have had the good fortune to meet him several times. He is most agreeable; a clever conversationalist, and one of those men who, whilst he knows everything, is quite content to keep the bushel down over his light and to merge himself as far as possible amidst other ordinary guests. It is a restful feature of Japanese society generally that it contains fewer people who wish to shine and push and impress others than an equal number of Europeans or Americans would produce under similar circumstances. The Japanese are more natural, and even if nature only leads to much silent eating and drinking, what are the odds so long as every one is happy? The type of countenance of the Marquis Ito is distinctly Mongolian.

When first I met the Marquis Oyama some three weeks ago, I experienced a sensation of relief at having at last struck what seemed to be a point of resemblance between our own well-tried, no-damned-merit system and the method of filling the very highest appointments in Japan. I confess in fact that the great Marquis impressed me rather as *trés grand seigneur*[*] of the Satsuma clan, with many widespread connections in political power, than as one who would even for a moment pretend to be an exceptionally studious, scientific, professional soldier. Nor could I find that he had ever done anything very wonderful except in the exhibition of courage and coolness under all circumstances. Ho first served with much credit but no special brilliancy in the Satsuma rebellion; then similarly in the campaign against China; and so he just gradually rose, and rose, doing what he was told and committing no blunders, until at last his career has culminated in his present great appointment of Chief of the Staff. The reasons given me by his friends for his selection for this, the most important post in the army, were his honesty, his great personal popularity and the influence of the Satsuma clan. The Marquis is perhaps a shade above the average Japanese in height, and not handsome according to the European standard (which is quite different from the Japanese standard), his large round face and small features being somewhat pitted with smallpox. I heard a story about the Marquis and one of his old friends which rather amused me. Once upon a time the two men were staying together at a tea-house, and the friend came to the bath, where he found the Marquis sitting up to

---

[*] "Very great lord."

his neck in hot water. "Just shake the sponge, will you, a moment," he said, "and hold your head steady, so that I can see which is which." The next person to get into the hot water should have been the friend, but I have been assured that if this was the case it was in actuality only and not metaphorically, for the great Oyama has no small vanities.

Even if I am right in my surmise that Oyama is not an ideal Chief of the Staff, with all the energies, aptitude and experiences which should be implied by that high title, there is no sort of doubt that he does possess some of the very different but equally valuable qualifications for a command. Ordinarily, nothing puts him out of temper, but when he does get angry he frightens every one. This is just as it should be. Good humour carries the business along without friction, whilst the latent, but ever present, possibility of an explosion keeps subordinates up to the mark and renders superfluous those small fault-findings and irritabilities which are so apt to wear out the finer parts of the machine. In action. Marquis Oyama is singularly imperturbable even for a Japanese, so the Japanese asseverate, and I was told the following anecdote in proof thereof:

Ten years ago he was in command of the forces attacking Port Arthur. As is well known, the attack on this fortress and its capture by assault without regular approaches, and with a comparatively weak force, was as dangerous and critical an operation as it is militarily possible to conceive. The action was just at its hottest when a telegram came to hand from Kinchow, where two battalions had been left to protect the Japanese rear when they advanced on Port Arthur. The telegram had been sent by the officer commanding, and it told how his two battalions were being attacked by 5000 or 6000 Chinese, and that he was very hard pressed, and urgently required reinforcements. The staff were much agitated, and it was with difficulty they mustered up courage to inform Oyama. He, however, although he had only one battalion and one squadron in reserve, and although he was being very hard put to it himself at the moment, only laughed and made nothing of the appeal for assistance, saying he would telegraph his reply a little later on in the day. Meanwhile his eye had chanced to light upon the body of a Chinaman lying near a temple only 2500 yards from the lines of Port Arthur, and naturally well under the fire of its guns. By the side of the Chinaman was a little dog, which barked and growled most furiously if any one attempted to approach his master. Oyama became greatly interested in this scene, and, although shells from the big guns were exploding all about the temple, he walked quietly up along the ridge to where the Chinaman was lying, then, taking a part of his ration from his haversack, approached the unhappy creature and soon contrived to pacify it. By this means the staff surgeon was able to examine its master, who, although his body was still warm, proved to be quite dead. As soon as Oyama heard this he gave the order for his only reserve to leave him and to march back at once to relieve the garrison at Kinchow. Evidently he had made use of the episode of the Chinaman and his dog so as to gain time to think over the situation quietly.

Meanwhile, as is known to many, the colonel in command at Kinchow had left his fort and had drawn up his men outside its walls, preferring to fight in the open. He had armed some coolies with captured muskets and rifles, and had left them as garrison of the citadel, but he himself sallied forth and at once began to fight. He was very hard pressed, but held his ground manfully, sending to Oyama for assistance as already described. At last the enemy, who displayed that day considerable confidence and courage, succeeded in completely enveloping the Japanese left flank, and there seemed nothing left for it but to hold on to the last, which was coming very quickly.

Suddenly, just at this moment of their direst strait, guns boomed out from the rampart of the citadel, and the shells, pitching amongst the most forward of the Chinamen, turned the scales in favour of the Japanese and drove off their enemies. No one was more surprised at this providential intervention than the colonel commanding. It seems there were four guns in the citadel, which had been left there by the Chinese. In the hospital ward an artillery sergeant lay sick, but when the fight grew bitter he rose from his bed and showed some invalids belonging to the infantry how to load, aim, and fire at the enemy. According to Chinese custom the shells were filled with sand instead of expensive high explosives, but, nevertheless, on this occasion at least, they proved sufficient for their purpose. During this desperate little engagement Port Arthur had been carried by assault, so the reserve battalion and squadron, like D'Erlon's column, vacillating between Quatre Bras and Ligny, had no fighting to compensate them for all their marching.

To complete these indications of Oyama, it is worth noting that he planted a cherry-tree at Kinchow to commemorate the engagement, and ordered each of his staff to write a poem celebrating the occasion. The old idea of associating the poetic and military arts has not yet entirely departed from the army of Japan. With us, on the contrary, to say a man writes poetry is to damn him with praise so faint that it is indistinguishable from a mild sort of amused contempt. In the furthest East an opinion precisely contrary holds the field, an opinion which was given expression to quite naturally by Oyama on this occasion. The Marquis has a great taste for old china, and has the means, apparently, to gratify it. He is a fine old fighter, but he is ten years older than he was when he took Port Arthur. Nevertheless, the Japanese are probably right not to put him on the shelf As another Japanese officer said to me: "We have hundreds of more highly educated, more accomplished, and scientific officers we could put in Oyama's place, but they would not be Oyama! He has a great reputation, he is beloved by the people, and, moreover, we do not turn out old leaders as long as they wish to continue to serve us."

Lieutenant-General Baron Kodama is in outline of feature a Sir Michael Biddulph in miniature. Several British officers noticed this strong resemblance, so it is not a case of my own imagination only. Japanese is his only language, and he does not lead the brilliant society life which the Marquis Oyama affects, being very seldom seen at fashionable Tokio functions. Owing to some exceptional circumstances, however, I have had the high honour of dining in his private house, which, in Japan, is a very different and more rare form of entertainment than a formal banquet at the host's official residence. The banquets are frequent to properly accredited foreigners; too frequent, indeed, for the taste of quiet folk. They are exactly what in India we call *burra khanas*. Very fine but very formal. I fancy the food, drink, and music are provided by the State, and those invited are of course ranged, to a man or woman,

Some New Acquaintances   29

in the strictest of strict procedure. Naturally a guest at one of these shows has as little chance of making a new friendship, falling in love, or doing anything except eating, drinking, and smoking, as he would have at a function presided over by the Lord Mayor of London.

When the foreigner, whether resident or traveller, does have the good fortune to get beyond the official banquet or club dinner, his fortune is good indeed. The eating, dining, and smoking, to judge by my own experience, remains of the best; but in all other points the generously promiscuous hospitality of the official is not, in my opinion, to be compared with the charming kindness of the individual. On the occasion in question, and on every other occasion when I met Lieutenant-General the Baron Kodama, he struck me as possessing the keenest sense of humour, the quickest power of repartee, and the most infectious hearty laugh imaginable. At the same time I cannot ever divest myself of the feeling that, whilst I am speaking to and admiring a highly polished modem gentleman of immense vitality, force, and determination of character, I am face to face with an Oriental of the Orientals, an Asiatic of the Asiatics. I would not put this down even in my diary if I thought such an appreciation would be either resented or denied. I believe, myself, it would be received with an amused assent. Indeed, I may say here that the Japanese ideals, especially as regards looks, are so utterly different from those of the European and American, that just as it is no compliment to them to be admired by the foreigner, so also may the foreigner make his little personal criticism or description without any fear of giving pain, unless it is purposely venomous.

The Lieutenant-General is gifted with a marvellously ready tact, always very much at command. Despite his *bonhomie* and devil-may-care jokes and manner, he has always been so essentially careful and serious that there are no stories of any sort against him — a rare distinction for a great man in Japan, where the Press gives the lead even to American journalism in supplying the people with personalities and innuendoes a^ut all conspicuous individualities who lend themselves to this system of attack even in the smallest degree. His permanent appointment is that of Governor of Formosa, where he has chopped off the heads of innumerable bandits and savages, and established at last a equilibrium. In telling me all about it he seemed to enjoy the recollection of cutting off the heads even more than he did the prospect of the financial equilibrium. He belongs to the Chiosu clan, which always helps a little even in these comparatively democratic days.

I feel that these impressionist sketches of my new acquaintances would not be complete were I to omit the famous Major-General Sir Y. Fukushima, K.C.B., Chief of the Second Section of the General Staff. His career affords one more example of the value of a lucky start. When he was a simple Major and Military Attaché at Berlin eleven years ago, the conversation on some festive occasion turned upon the distance one horse could be ridden day after day at a certain rate of speed. Fukushima declared his own horse capable of carrying him right away from Berlin to Vladivostock. He was laughed at, and thereby became hardened in his determination to make the attempt. He started off, and eventually did reach Vladivostock, having ridden all the way, but not on the same horse. The remarkable part of the story was not the ride— which was simple enough for any one in good health, furnished with a passport and sustained by his banker — but the effect it had in Japan. People and Press (or rather, perhaps, Press and people) went mad on the subject. The ordinary man merely gets his light extinguished when he drops it into the Thames, but Fortune's favourite just happens to let his fall into a patch of petroleum which is drifting down the stream at that moment. Army headquarters bowed to the popular enthusiasm — not with very good grace, perhaps, but still it had to bow. Fukushima was promoted from Major to be Lieutenant-Colonel. A public reception was given him at Tokio, where the people assembled in their thousands; and the smart General Staff, including at least one jealous rival, went in their *aiguillettes* and stars to do homage to the Siberian hero, who appeared very effectively staged in his ragged travelling clothes, and carrying a riding-switch which his enemies said had been specially dilapidated for the occasion. Afterwards these clothes and the emblematic riding-switch were religiously enshrined in a museum, where they may be seen to this day, although I should not at all wonder if they were ousted by the mass of memorials which the coming campaign will most assuredly engender.

I have jotted down the story of Fukushima as it was given me by a Japanese officer, for I find it interesting to discuss the germ of future Mafeking hysterics in a people who are so justly proud that they out-English the English, meaning thereby the English of the good old days, in their reserve and imperturbability of temper. I have always thought that one of the best tests of a future conqueror, either in boy or youth, is to watch narrowly the effect of a first success. Whether Dame Fortune's smile comes in the form of an unexpected windfall or whether as the reward of well-directed work, the majority of prize-winners are apt to see in their victory a fitting opportunity for a little temporary slacking off, a rest, a holiday, a jolly, or whatever it may be. To those who are going to come to the front, however, even a chance stroke of luck is like a spur or crack of the whip. It does not relax them for a moment, but braces them up rather to go on ahead with redoubled energy. Major-General Sir Y. Fukushima belongs to this smaller category. Since the days of the famous ride he has redoubled his efforts to keep himself to the front, and, on the whole, he has succeeded.

Not infrequently, however, success flings its votary into such strange situations that, whilst all his contemporaries are envying him, he wishes himself anything else in the wide world, a monk, a priest, an obscure fisherman, or even a bird to sit on the boughs and sing, free from all care and worry. Some such feelings as these must now, I should imagine, have taken possession of Fukushima, whose entire duty is to baffle and thwart in every possible way all the foreigners who have dealings with him; whilst, to enable him the more effectively to execute his disagreeable duty, he is officially described as their mentor and assistant. He is actually, I more than suspect, to the military attachés and correspondents a veritable wolf in sheep's clothing, though I must confess he bleats to such purpose that many of them — almost all of them, in fact — still regard him as a sort of information bureau, and quite their best friend and stand-by in Tokio. Several of them have confided to me that they have received valuable intelligence from him — intelligence which had not been vouchsafed to any one else. When it is remembered that he has not told one single man one single fact worth one single halfpenny to any foreign government or journal, it will be admitted that Major-General Sir Y. has been pretty clever.

The worst of this sort of thing is — it cannot last. We all realise in our hearts that we are foreign nuisances waiting to know things, and see things, and visit things before they are ripe for our inspection, and a little present frankness on Fukushima's part would probably save some future rancour and leave his present position of popularity unassailed. Nothing makes Europeans, and perhaps especially Americans, more mad than to feel they have been cleverly played upon. Personally I have never much minded when my requests for particulars have been responded to by generalities and genialities and banalities, for I have found some of these fed herrings to have an excellent savour.

Fukushima has an exceptional knowledge of our Indian troops and of their Russian rivals. I find he considers the Cossack to be purely an historical personage. He has, so Fukushima says, lost all his former Boer attributes, except that of horsemanship, and is now simply a yokel who is living on the Napoleonic legend; sometimes he is brave, sometimes not brave, just like other yokels; but he is never disciplined, and is almost invariably badly officered and led. Fukushima has also a fairly useful knowledge of the fighting values of our various classes of Indian native troops, and made some shrewd remarks upon their British officers and the faculty they displayed for associating themselves closely with their men. The British officer, in India, he said, became more Sikh than the Sikh; more Gurkha than the Gurkha; more Madrassee than the Madrassee. In some ways he considered the trait most admirable, and so it must be, if it is borne in mind that it is to that trait that we owe the existence of the only actively loyal either in Egypt or India, namely, the old retired native officers and soldiers.

On the other hand, there is also certainly some truth in Fukushima's further contention that there is an aggressive blindness in their *esprit de corps*; that they altogether overdo it, in fact. As proof of this he naturally referred to days of the Mutiny, when officers not only perished themselves, but went near to wreck the Empire with them, sooner than permit evil to be spoken or suggested of their men. He even hinted that long service in India might sometimes tend to make officers narrow and self-sufficient, and apt to imagine their army was perfect, than which, as every one knows, there is no more dangerous frame of mind. He was too polite, naturally, to say this in so many words, but there is a peculiarly penetrating quality about the true thought of a speaker which sometimes, even with a Japanese, escapes through the wrapping of his phrases. The views which I imagine Fukushima holds correctly represent, I believe, the facts; and if he had included Indian civilians as well, he would equally have hit the mark. What an excellent form of discipline it would be for some of these latter merely to come and spend one furlough in Japan, where they would live under the patronising and decidedly firm surveillance of "the native police"! Their ideas of Asia would possibly be mildly modified, and if so hundreds of thousands of our fellow subjects would hereafter feel the benefit. A little less contempt means a little more sympathy. A little less superiority means a little more accessibility and politeness, and with accessibility and politeness it becomes even possible to dream of occasional friendships which, between Englishman and Indian, are now practically non-existent. How excellent, too, would it be for Anglo-Indian and Eurasian railway guards, station masters and ticket collectors if they could only see "Natives" travelling quite happily without any one there to push or hustle them, as if they were dangerous lunatics, into the first handy compartment whether empty or already overcrowded!

    Well, General Fukushima is a fascinating subject of study, but I had better leave him alone until I know him a little better, although I doubt whether that will ever be. He also gives me the same sensation of being an Asiatic *au bout des ongles** which Kodama does, only in a rather different and more familiar sense. Fukushima is a linguist of great fluency in several tongues, who knows his way well about London, Berlin and St. Petersburg. Kodama is a purely Japanese-speaking, Japan-bred man. Yet these are the two who, more than any of the other Japanese men or

---

* "At your fingertips."

women I have met, make me realise that East is East and West is West; as it was in the beginning, is now, and ever shall be, Amen!

Chapter III – Three Pleasing Traits

Tokio, April 25th, 1904. — Three small trifles in this country have special power to please me. I may crack jokes with the servants, and treat them generally as fellow creatures, without danger of destroying their moral equilibrium, or of drawing upon myself the disapproving surprise of the rest of the company. I may walk in the most crowded streets with my hat in my hand instead of on my head, and not a man, woman or child stops to stare at me as if I were a freak fresh escaped from Barnum's. I may go to dinners and banquets and eat nothing, and my host is just as pleased as if I had sampled every dish in the bill of fare.

To serious-minded people these may seem but trivial reasons for feeling untrammelled and free from care; but in this case as in many others, the trivialities are emblematic of the deeper principles towards which they stretch their roots. Now as to the servant question. The Japanese seem to be as genuinely casual and democratic in their social relations as they are autocratic both by tradition and sentiment when there is business to the fora Therefore the common people, as they used to be called, are distinctly more respectful than with us to those in positions of authority. But only so long as they are on duty. The moment that duty is accomplished there seems to be no hateful punctilio on either side to prevent employer and employed from swapping jests or cigarettes, or from acting in any or every way as if they were members of the same human family. No doubt this is a general characteristic of the Asiatic, but it is also a natural consequence of the overshadowing power and divinity of the Emperor which tends to obliterate all minor, merely worldly differences between subjects. The Emperor can take my interpreter of to-day and transform him to-morrow into the Japanese Ambassador to London, a post in which, I dare say, he would acquit himself with much credit. When, on the other hand, the light of the Imperial countenance is turned away for a moment from even the greatest in the land, he expires quite completely and gently, like an electric light which has been switched off by the master of the house; whereas, with us, when the time or the occasion has come to cast such a man down from high place, he fights against the impending doom desperately and step by step, until at last, flickering and struggling painfully like a dying candle, his eclipse fills the atmosphere with noxious vapours.

Naturally, with such wonderful possibilities hanging over every one's head, it is not so easy as with us for feelings of petty personal pride and superiority to attain unwholesome luxuriance. There is plenty of race pride, but that hits the foreigner and does not affect the social relations of one Japanese to another. In Japan the average citizen thinks, with the full acquiescence of his fellows, that under the Emperor he and all others are practically equal. In America, as is well known, each man regards himself as a bit better than his neighbour; and the lower down the social scale you go, the stronger is this feeling, until, when you reach the oar-conductor or hotel clerk, you find the most uncompromising type of despot the world has ever known. No French aristocrat, with red heels to his boots, ever, in ante-Revolution days, could have permitted himself to look at or speak to his serfs in quite the same way as the American car-conductors or hotel clerks look at and speak to the innocent but trembling traveller. If he had, the Revolution would, I am sure, have been ten times more bloody.

In England we have, socially speaking, no individuals. The

population is marked off into petrified social castes, amongst which the financier plays Brahmin — the private soldier. Pariah. We have race pride, but it is almost swallowed up in caste pride. On the whole, of these three attitudes towards mankind in general and mankind in particular, I think I prefer that of the Japanese. An autocratic government with a genuinely democratic society is better than a democratic government with a society divided into strata, each autocratic to its inferiors and servile to its superiors, as in England, or servile to its inferiors and autocratic to its superiors, as in America.

Similarly as regards my pleasing immunity from ill-bred curiosity when I walk without my hat. This is merely an outward and visible sign that the Japanese mind has emancipated itself from the intolerable narrowness which affects to regard itself as outraged when any individual fails to do and be and appear the same as the other members of his set. It is not that our allies are deficient in curiosity. Far from it. If any one will sit down by the roadside to sketch he will soon have reason to know that they possess that quality in very full measure. But they are not so stupid as to attach even a stare's worth of curiosity to such an indifferent matter as the clothes a man wears or the manner in which he puts them on. Indeed it would be strange if they did, seeing that every stage in the evolution of dross, from early Plantagenet days to those of the modern member of Parliament, are to be seen in the streets, sometimes on the person of the same individual.

As to the Japanese dinner, I freely confess that the irresponsible, go-as-you-please methods by which it is characterised more than compensate me for the strange and unsatisfying toys which are set forth upon the doll's-house tables at irregular intervals during the course of the entertainment. All is so delightfully unconventional and easy. It does not matter in the least if you are late — half an hour late — an hour late — it is of no consequence — the others sit down and go on, and it is easy to catch them up by denying yourself a sorap of seaweed, a fried fern leaf, a morsel of sugar-candy, or whatever the first two or three courses may have been. Successions of tiny dishes are brought by piquant little damsels, and when the lacquer stools which sei-ve for tables are full, these dishes are cleared away with them. To press a dish upon a reluctant appetite would no more occur to a host than it would enter his mind to ask his guests to help themselves sparingly. Altogether a very welcome modification of Western manners.

Then, again, no one is tied to his place. At every stage of the feast any one is welcome to get up, stroll about and smoke a cigarette or drink a health at the other end of the room, or even to sit down for a time elsewhere and enjoy a change of company. Heavens t this privilege alone would sometimes he worth £50 a night in London. Finally, and perhaps most important, amusement, conversation and enjoyment generally, are catered for by a company of pretty girls, who have contracted to drive dull care from the guests at so much per head for so much an hour. These are no awkward amateurs at their business, as are so many women of the world, but they have from their childhood been carefully prepared for their delicate and difficult task. In England everything depends upon the hostess. It is she and her satellite the cook who make or mar the dinner in all and every sense. A hostess who feels thoroughly well and in good form, and is moreover equipped with the necessary amount of experience and of brains, can make the greatest assemblage of bores momentarily talkative and gay. Her energy and will put forth in her own house are magnetic, and with them she can move mountains, even mountains of flesh. But there is a limit to everything, and eight people perhaps form the maximum she can actually thus illuminate by projection. In Japan there is a hostess to each guest. Geishas are— whatever else they may be — essentially young and beautiful hostesses, each as anxious to make the entertainment a success as if she herself were the donor. If any one appears to be dull and neglected, even if he is an ugly old undistinguished and uninteresting fellow, they take him on, one by one, until the right one succeeds in making his sluggish pulses quicken and turns him, to his own amazement, into a gay and kittenish young spark. I am told that all Geishas are not so exquisitely perceptive or so self-sacrificing; that some of them are spoilt, and get cross, or give themselves airs, and even go so far as to look bored. I can only say to this I have never met the wrong sort of Geisha myself. They are delightful company, I think; full of tact, and quite smart at repartee. Two nights ago I had a great flirtation during dinner with a young lady called Miss Flourishing Dragon. When I was saying good-night I confessed to her my deep admiration. She replied that the ideograph expressing her name also meant British Dominion, and that for all the future she would only use it in the latter sense. I had the curiosity afterwards to ask a great Japanese scholar if the ideograph would bear the double meaning, and I found that it would do so subject to a very small stretch of the pen.

At another dinner, given by one of the very greatest of the great men whose names I have taken liberties with, I was paralysed with horror by my host very gravely apologising to me for the absence among the attendant Geishas of O Suzame San, or the Honourable Miss Sparrow. I gasped out, "Where did your Excellency hear that story?" "Why," he replied, "I read it in the Japanese papers, of course; they are full of it." I was effectively frightened, and looked it; whereat my host was pleased to roar with laughter, and admit that he had only been getting a rise out of me. After all, there was not so very much in the story, and it only amused Tokio because the *dramatis personae* — myself excepted — were very well known to every one. The Honourable Miss Sparrow is one of the prettiest girls who has run about making mischief since Helen of Troy set towns blazing. She sat by me at dinner one happy night at a banquet, and we got on like one of the blazing towns. At last I wanted to pay her a compliment which went beyond her limited knowledge of English. I therefore begged a distinguished naval officer, who flattered himself on his fluency, to translate to her the following: "I wish, most Honourable Miss Sparrow, that I had a beautiful golden cage into which I might put you and carry you off home." My naval friend said, "Oh, yes, certainly, I can translate that easily." He accordingly said something to the little lady, when her face clouded over; she became very silent, and took the first opportunity she could of leaving me. Afterwards a Japanese general came up to me, and asked if I knew how my compliment had been translated. I said "No," and he then told me that the actual translation had been: "As you are a sparrow, I wish you would shut yourself up in a box." This is what comes of a soldier trusting a naval officer to be his intermediary with a lady!

Three Pleasing Traits

Tokio, April 30th 1904. — I received a copy to-day of a leading French newspaper, with an article in it by a well-known writer giving an interview with me. The date of the paper was March 13th, and the so-called interview must have taken place in the Mediterranean or on the Red Sea either just before or just after the commencement of hostilities. This shows how careful one should be, and how the "chiel amang us takin' notes" may assume the most perfect disguises. The good ship *Armand Béhic*, by which I was travelling, was full at the time of French officers and civil functionaries, and I should have thought it a fairly safe place for airing my opinions, so long as they did not in any way impugn the invincibility of their ally. Still, I seem to have had sufficient nerve to have just flirted with the idea, for here is the only paragraph in the article in which the reporter makes me deal with the impending war: *"Si nous étions encore au temps où l'on opposait des masses aux masses, je n'aurais pas hésité une seconde à diagnostiquer l'écrasement presque immédiat des Japonais. L'armée russe est une muraille de poitrines intrépides. Malheureusement pour elle, on ne fait plus la guerre— nous l'avons appris à nos dépens— en opposant au feu de l'ennemi un rampart de chair valeureuse. La resistance et la victoire sont du côté du tirailleur qui collabore aussi isolé que possible, avec intelligence et discipline, au plan d'ensemble. Les Boers avaient cette intelligence individuelle; ils manquaient de discipline. Je crois que les soldats Japonais ont l'une et l'autre. Us pourraient ménager des surprises à leurs courageux adversaires."**

---

* "If we were still in the days when masses were pitted against masses, I would not have hesitated for a second to diagnose the almost immediate crushing of the Japanese. The Russian army is a wall of fearless breasts. Unfortunately for the Russian army, war is no longer fought by opposing the enemy's fire with a rampart of valiant flesh. Resistance and victory are on the side of the skirmisher who works as independently as possible, with intelligence and discipline, on the overall plan. The Boers had this individual intelligence; they lacked discipline. I believe the Japanese soldiers have both. They could provide surprises to their brave opponents."

Chapter IV – From Tokio to the Yalu

S.S. Suminoye Maru, May 4th, 1904. — *Tout vient à bout à qui sait attendre.*[*] At last we are off, with a rush and a scramble at the end of a grand send-off by the *élite* and οἱ πολλοί[†] of Tokio society. We left the capital on April 30th, and arrived next afternoon at Shimonoseki. The whole of the railway journey was for us something not unlike the campaigning tour of a politician in England, in so far as crowded stations, deputations, and young ladies with bouquets, can make East resemble West.

Presumably, most of the officials who came to bid God-speed to the foreign officers, as well as the school boys and school girls in ranks all down the platforms, were there by order, but many outsiders also attended from courtesy or curiosity. The ladies of the Red Cross Society were very much to the fore, many of them the wives of officers serving at the front. There was an immense amount of repressed enthusiasm about the crowd, and whether they

---

[*] "All things come to those who wait."

[†] "The many,"

sang the war song, or danced or cheered, in every case it was that repression which struck me most. Not one specimen of the half-drunken 'Arry appeared — he who so fatally turns up in Europe on similar occasions, to strike sentiment quite dead with his loud horse-laugh.

We arrived as Shimonoseki on the 2nd, and left on the forenoon of the 3rd. Just before starting we got news of the battle of the Yalu, telegraphed from army head-quarters at Tokio Although we were mad at having missed the fight, this was a happy send-off for the English contingent, and I was specially pleased myself, as I got a wire from an old friend, saying, "And so the big guns did it after all...best congratulations." This was with reference to the argument about the value of big guns which I had had with another officer at General Kodama's dinner-table during my stay in Tokio. It is very amusing to think that whilst I was advocating the employment in war of something more powerful than an ordinary field gun, and even getting quite hot on the matter, several of the senior officers of the Japanese headquarters should have listened and spoken as if the question was purely academic, although they must all have known perfectly well that they were going to use heavy guns in the impending action. I suppose they are the 12-centimetre howitzers. We should hardly describe them as heavy guns, but the small horses of the Japanese force them to a lighter standard.

We are now comfortably stowed away on the *Suminoye Maru*, a military transport of 884 net tonnage. The captain seems a good chap, and served most of his youth in a sailing ship hailing from Glasgow. As a compliment to the alliance he flew a Union Jack, of imposing dimensions, at the fore. I have an idea that this is an honour reserved for the Lord Warden of the Cinque Ports, an Admiral of the Fleet, or some other very stupendous nautical swell; but in a Japanese military transport I cannot well lay down the law as to what honours they should or should not pay, and, anyway, the crews of the British ships in harbour have been fairly electrified, the men turning out in swarms and cheering us lustily.

At the mouth of the straits we passed within a few yards of the big German mail steamer on her way to Shimonoseki. The men on the bridge and the crew forrard evidently did not know what to make of us. The English passengers aboard were, however, in no manner of doubt that their flag was flying free at the fore of a Japanese military transport, and they sent us a rousing British cheer as a final send-off on our journey, than which it would have been impossible to wish a better omen.

Our party consists of Lieutenant-Colonel Hume, a gunner; Captain Jardine, 5th Lancers; and Captain Vincent, also a gunner, is expected to turn up at Chemulpho. There are two Americans; Colonel Crowder, from the United States Judge Advocate-General's Department; and Captain March, an artilleryman. Besides these there are eight Continental officers — two French, two Germans, one Swiss, one Austrian, one Italian, and one Swede. Our bear-leaders are Colonel Satow, a French-speaking officer of the Japanese artillery, and Captain the Marquis Saigo of the Imperial Guards, who speaks a little German. As these two officers generally take the ends of the table the conversation through politeness tends to be in French or German, and I foresee English will not have much of a look in during the journey, or, probably, hereafter.

The party has embarked as a service unit, all complete. We have with us on the ship our baggage, baggage carts and cart-horses, drivers, &c. &c. Also our riding horses and a fortnight's provisions. Wherever then the exigencies of the situation may compel us to land, we are sufficient unto ourselves and can march away without loss of time.

Suminoye Maru, May 6th. — Arrived yesterday at Chemulpho, and cast anchor close by the wrecks of the *Koreetz* and *Sungari*, having first passed the Varyag, whose glistening side just shows above the tide, like the flank of some huge dead sea monster. Put on my sword this morning and called on the British Consul, afterwards breakfasting at a small inn kept by a Frenchman and his Japanese wife. The Koreans seem very like Kashmiris. The same dirty white clothes; the same endurance under enormous loads; the same ox-like capacity for being driven and hustled about by beings of superior energy, of which we saw some evidence even during our stay of little more than an hour. Going back I was stupid enough to lose my footing trying to jump from the steam launch on to the companion ladder. I made a desperate hand clutch aa I went down, and the clutch met Colonel Satow'a firm hand-clasp instead of the proverbial straw. It was very clever of him, and saved me a wetting anyway.

Chinnampo Harbour, May 7th, 1904. — Sailing northwards over tranquil seas we made the estuary of the Pingyang river early this morning. At least, to be correct, at that hour we concluded we had got so far after consulting our maps and doing a little dead reckoning. Strange to be travelling thus like Christopher Columbus or stout Cortez, gazing upon each headland with a wild surmise; but so it is, for Japanese reticence ever refuses, charm we never so wisely, to inform us as to our next destination. Our suspicions were strengthened when we met a destroyer gliding ghost-like in her grey war-paint amongst the many islands. Swiftly she bore in on us, and then, satisfied with her scrutiny, bore away as quickly. *Asagiri*, or Morning Mist, was her name, and like a phantom she vanished again into the misty morning from which she had so suddenly emerged. On either bank of the broad river, green treeless mountains rose rank on rank, and far away ahead we saw and wondered at a great smudge of smoke, grimy and businesslike, hanging on the pale blue skirts of the morning. This might have been hanging over Nagasaki or Wei-hai-wei for anything we knew positively to the contrary; but it turned out to be Chinnampo, in whose harbour we shortly found ourselves, and the smoke was being produced by nineteen transports, some of them big ocean-going ships, all of them crammed with troops. The 1st Artillery Brigade was on board, of which the 15th Regiment was commanded by Colonel Shiba, who was a friend of mine — also a lot of infantry belonging to the Second Army. They were bound for Manchuria we were informed, but to what part of that country, which is as yet to me only a vague geographical expression, no Japanese would venture for a moment to presume to imagine. I hear we may not land; and so, whilst our cockle-shell lies steady for awhile on even keel, I recover a sufficiency of equilibrium to note some impressions.

Since leaving Chemulpho I have gleaned a little, a very little, about this shy and secluded land of Korea ftom Vincent, our latest joined recruit. He has spent over two months in the Hermit Kingdom, and has given me an account of his adventures in that quaint corner of the world; adventures in which the natives tend to become effaced from the recital, as I fancy they do in real life, before more virile and bustling types, such as Japanese generals, missionaries male and female, and American gold miners. I find that Vincent and I have already met, not only in South Africa, where we had the good fortune to work together in the last great drive of the war, from east to west of the Western Transvaal, but also last autumn at an hotel in Montreal, Canada, where I was receiving a deputation of beardless "veterans," and he was on his way to spend two years in Japan. Our British party is now complete, the three arms being represented, and I feel I am thrice blessed in having such good fellows to see me through whatever strange adventures we may be called upon to face. Vincent and Jardine are both language students and have already picked up enough to be in the position of the one-eyed amongst the blind compared with the rest of us. The idea of sending out young officers already possessing some knowledge of the East to be attached to the Japanese army and to learn their language is in every way an excellent one. The only pity is that it is not carried out on a scale ten times as great. There can be no better discipline for officers who will have much to do with Asiatics in the future than, for one brief period in their lives, to study the Asiatic character from a subordinate instead of a superior position; as un considered underlings, instead of awe-inspiring, unapproachable Sahibs. Few indeed are the men who devote much attention to the foibles, or even the feelings, of their inferiors, although all are ready to acknowledge how important such considerations become when it is the liking and esteem of a superior which they desire to secure. It is one thing to be a captain in a Sikh or Gurkha regiment where you are a personage very much to be conciliated, it is quite another thing to be attached to a Japanese regiment without any other claim to its consideration than what courtesy may grant freely to merit and good manners. In India British officers are always busy imposing their views on an Eastern race; in Japan they learn to seek for what the East has got to give to the West. From the military point of view also the professional advantage to young British officers of working with a fine army, strong just where their own is most weak, namely, in homogeneity and organisation, is not open to question. Moreover, their presence in some numbers in the Japanese army may tend to render its officers somewhat less *farouche** as regards the British, for I have already had time to take to heart the quite unexpected and decidedly unpleasant fact that the army is German perhaps, or French, in its tone and culture, but certainly not English. It is safe, indeed, to say that the military profession is less touched by English influence or sympathy than any other body of Japanese opinion; and unfortunately the army, although it remains a closed book as regards its ideals and feelings to the ordinary traveller or resident in Japan, happens to be second to no other section of the community in size, in consideration, and in importance.

To return to Vincent and his experiences in Korea. It seems he had found time since October to make two visits to Korea. He had crossed over to Fusan on the last day of 1903, and had spent three weeks there and at Chemulpho. Again in March 1904, travelling in the famous *Times* excursion boat the *Haimun*, he had made the crossing in company with what he described as "a heterogeneous conglomeration of miscellaneous nondescripts," and had got as far as Pingyang. I asked the ordinary hopeless questions which make the heart of the returned traveller sink into his boots, and got better answers than I deserved. Being called upon to give an opinion of Korea, he brushed aside the pistol presented at his head by pointing to a collier in harbour which, painted white and mounting a few antiquated guns, looked like the crow of ancient fable tricked out in the fine plumage of the peacock. He said, "Poor old Korea! that her navy should consist of this one ship, palmed off upon her by the Japanese as a man-of-war, is typical of the effete helplessness which characterises not only her government services but the whole of the nation from emperor to coolie man." Then, again, when I became inquisitive about Seoul, he said, If one quarter of

---

* "Fierce."

the labour which has been expended on the outer wall had been employed in building houses and streets, Seoul might have ranked as a respectable city." To my imagining this answer gives a much more satisfying description of the sort of place Seoul probably is in reality, than an elaborate description of poverty, mud huts, and open drains, jealously veiled by a magnificent overcoat or rind. The town, he said, was a hot-bed of intrigue and rumours. Long before the war began, gigantic men on equally gigantic steeds were reported to be pressing southwards over the frozen Yalu in ever increasing numbers, whilst thousands of yellow dwarfs with their faces set northwards were stealing into the treaty ports by each successive junk or peaceful trader, carrying with them in sacks their rifles and military equipment. Even Japanese generals of high renown were said to have cleverly disguised themselves as coolies and to be hauling and heaving in the docks until such time as the roar of the cannon should summon them to emerge fully armed at the head of their eager troops. One of these masquerading generals was supposed to be Kuroki, the headquarters of whose army is now the goal of our ambitions. Vincent has the advantage of most of us in having already made his acquaintance. Just about the time that Seoul fables represented his surreptitious landing in Korea, one of the general's sons, who was a friend of Vincent's, took him to call upon his father at his private house in Tokio. The whole Kuroki family were just being photographed in commemoration of the departure for the front which was then imminent. The general received Vincent most affably, and insisted upon opening a whisky bottle to celebrate the occasion. It was hard to realise, Vincent said, that this hospitable old gentleman, clad in homely kimono and slippers, was about to lead the flower of Japanese chivalry against the greatest, or at any rate the largest army in the world.

Amongst other interesting experiences Vincent had been so fortunate as to see the disembarkation of the Imperial Guards Division in this very harbour of Chinnampo on March 15, and succeeding days. At that time he was still one of the heterogeneous nondescripts on board the *Haimun*, who had pushed her way up the Pingyang inlet, ploughing a passage through masses of broken ice and frozen snow and charging the great blocks whenever she could not avoid them. The forces of nature were not, however, all that

THE LANDING-STAGES AT CHINNAMPO

had to be overcome. The gunboat *Tori No Umi*, or Bird of the Sea, and the destroyer *Hayn Tori*, or Speedy Bird, challenged their right to proceed. But a war correspondent will on occasion triumph over all obstacles, and eventually the inquisitive *Haimun* pushed her nose quite boldly in amongst a great fleet of warships and transports. She had, however, now come to the end of her tether. A launch was sent for Captain James, in which he was conveyed to the flagship, where the admiral told him he must be clear of the harbour by daylight next morning. Vincent meanwhile had thought it best to land before questions were asked, and had headed, as a Britisher always will when he has no flag of his own to follow, for the Stars and Stripes, which floated over a small but hospitable-looking edifice. Therein he was fortunate enough to find the agent of the Oriental Consolidated Mining Company, Captain Barstow, who at once proceeded to heap benefits upon him. Best of all, the garden of this agent closely overlooked the landing-stages, and from that sanctuary Vincent was able to watch the work of disembarkation going on without danger of interruption or arrest. This is the account he gave me.

Each transport, in addition to her ordinary equipment of boats, carried several large flat-bottomed sampans, such as are used in Japan for coasting purposes. These sampans, closely packed, carried about fifty men, or a corresponding amount of horses or war material. When filled they were rapidly towed by a fleet of steam launches up to four landing-stages about 150 yards long, to which they were attached by the skilful manoeuvres of two trained boatmen, who lived in the covered stern of each sampan. The piers connecting each stage "with the land consisted of a wooden plank gangway about 100 yards in length, supported on sampans which rested upon the mud at low water and floated when the tide came in. Thus the piers could be used continuously in spite of a twenty-feet rise and fall of tide. On the arrival of each sampan the men disembarked in an expeditious and orderly manner, and marched off at once to their quarters in the Korean town, all the houses of which had been appropriated for their accommodation. The cavalry led their horses ashore and picketed them amongst the fir-trees on the neighbouring hills, then returned for their saddles and the rest of their kit. The guns were landed very cleverly, and were at once dragged by hand out of the way of other disembarking troops. The pontoons were similarly treated. They arrived in three sections, and when put together fitted into trollies, which were each of them pulled by one horse. Under the excellent arrangements in force about twenty transports were enabled to land men and material simultaneously. Each vessel carried a number of little two-wheeled hand-carts, which were put together at once on landing, loaded up with sacks of rice, and wheeled off by three or four men to the depōts. By this means nothing was allowed to accumulate on or near the piers. In fact the most noticeable point of all about this disembarkation was the energy with which any troops, horses or stores were moved on the moment they set foot on land, so as not to block the gangways or exits even for a moment. The infantry came ashore in heavy marching order; very heavy indeed according to the British ideas. In addition to his ordinary blue cloth overcoat, each soldier wore a thick brown cloak with a sheepskin collar, and carried a red blanket, knapsack, haversack, water-bottle, entrenching tool, section of a *tente d'abris*,[*] spare boots, straw sandals, small rice-basket, cooking-pot, as well as, of course, his

---

[*] "Shelter tent."

rifle, belts, pouches and bayonet. The British soldier complains that he is being turned into a Christmas tree when half this equipment is given him to carry. It is the old story of the Pretorian Guards and their armour. The finest transport in the world will not compensate for want of carrying power on the part of the men, who cannot always fight with their luggage carts at their backs. On the other hand, it is possible to overdo things; and it is open to question whether the Japanese soldier, sturdy as he is, may not be too heavily weighted with all this paraphernalia.

THE TATONG RIVER AT PINGYANG

I should like to write the whole of Vincent's adventures; how he started off with some American miners escorting 30,000 silver yen in mule-carts; how the bullion convoy came into collision with a Japanese field battery, and how the money-bags had to give way to gun-metal. But this is a beastly little cabin, and I hope he may some day write his own story. He did eventually succeed in covering the forty-five miles between Chinnampo and Pingyang, passing on the road thousands of the two-wheeled carts he had just seen taken out of the ships. They were pulled by straining little men in the uniform of the Guards infantry. These were the military coolies, the rejections for height, and for height only, from the year's conscription. Every one stared at Vincent in his khaki and staff cap with a red band round it. It was difficult and sometimes impossible to pass the numerous bodies of troops who occupied the whole width of the narrow track by courtesy called a road. Often he had to cast round across country, getting involved thereby in deep and narrow dykes and other disagreeable obstacles. The newly purchased Chinese pony was not a Leicestershire hunter, and had no idea of playing the part even to please Vincent. Consequently, frequent grief and astonishment of the whole Japanese army at seeing a soldier in an unknown uniform skirmishing round their flanks in this intrepid style. The officers, too, looked askance, especially when he cantered past the headquarters staff, who were breakfasting in a small village. However, no one interfered, although he momentarily expected to be arrested. The fact of wearing a sword probably saved him, and eventually the path debouched upon the Pingyang flats. Looking thence he beheld the city, situated on an isolated ridge in the centre of a plain six miles wide, and with the Tatong river 400 yards broad, passing immediately to the east and south of it. The ridge is formed in the shape of a boat, with her bows pointing slightly east of north. The natives still cherish a legend that the original city was built in a boat, and that two large stone pillars in the plain towards the northern end are the posts to which once upon a time it was moored. Here, perhaps, we have the landing-place of Noah from the ark? Inside the city is a shrine built in honour of the rats who once saved the city by sallying forth at night and gnawing the bowstrings of the besieging Mongols. Arrived within the city walls, our tired adventurer was once more on his beam ends; and once more America came to the rescue in the shape of some fair missionaries, with tea and cake and biscuits, of which Vincent still spoke with watering mouth.

    Here his independent career had come to a close. He could not get permission to accompany the advancing army to Anju, and so he had to sit still and content himself with watching the Guards and Twelfth Division march past him. He seems to have been much struck with the discipline and orderly behaviour of all the troops. With the assistance of the missionaries he saw what he could of the Koreans, and came to the conclusion that they were hopelessly unable to stand alone. When young they seemed to be remarkably intelligent, but even this they seemed to lose when they grew older, whether from over smoking, or from being too much married, or from having no incentive to exercise their brains, he could not say. He found them entirely wanting in courage and cleanliness, but good-natured and fairly honest. They consider war to be a relic of barbarism, and prefer to be slaves rather than to go back from that comfortable conviction. After staying some time at Pingyang, Vincent got his orders to join me, and came on board at Chemulpho, just in time to see me fall overboard.

Rikwaho, near Chulsan, 9 a.m. May 9th, 1904. — The mystery resolves itself into Rikwaho, where we landed yesterday afternoon. Miles of muddy flats, with winding channels through them, ended in a pier like those seen by Vincent at Chinnampo. Close by we found a cosy little camp pitched on a round hill overlooking the bay, amidst a fine group of Scotch firs, which were the only big trees anywhere within sight. I wanted to see how Hume, Jardine and Vincent could walk, so I took them a breather up a high mountain, on which was established a signalling post, consisting of a corporal and three soldiers. The men looked a little strangely ut us at first, but Vincent and Jardine being able to speak Japanese and explain who we were, they soon became transformed from suspicious guardians of the mountain into courteous hosts, and ended by insisting on brewing us each a cup of tea, which turned out to be no tea at all, but merely hot water in which a few grains of barley had been boiled. The Japanese esteem tea so highly that they always speak of the honourable tea as we do of the daughter of a viscount. This stuff, however, was distinctly dishonourable, although we pretended to like it very much. On getting back to camp we received our dinner in the form of a "bento," which is a soldier's canteen or other small box containing a cooked meal. This first bento contained about a dessert-spoonful of cold pork cut into small pieces, and a large quantity of cold rice. I cleaned up the bento to the last grain of rice; felt for a few minutes as if I had over-eaten myself, and presently became rather hungrier and more empty than ever. Vincent tells me that the property of expansion followed by a sinking or melting away to nothing is peculiar to rice. It seems to me this is a bad outlook from the commissariat point of view. A European might as well devour snow-flakes for all the satisfaction he gets out of it. How much I regretted I had passed on to my servant a nice box of biscuits given me on landing by the Commandant of the port!

Antung, May 13th, 1904. — "Much have I travelled in the realms of gold" since my last entry, and half an hour must now positively be devoted to transcribing hasty jottings into my diary. The day after landing at Rikwaho, our gay cavalcade, representing all the uniforms of Europe, rode soberly away northwards along a corduroy road which the Japanese had made with infinite labour across rice-swamps for the passage of the howitzer regiment to the Yalu.

The country is a jumble of big green hills and broad valleys, a mixture of the Scottish border and Central Asia. The valleys are spacious, well watered, and fertile; the hills, dotted here and there with fir clumps, ought in ordinary years to furnish good grazing for cattle, but these, I fancy, have found their way into Cossack stomachs — at any rate, we saw no flocks or herds along the line of march. The pink plum and white pear blossom were lovely to behold. We slept that night in a Korean house, more dirty than any I have been in since I was driven by cold many years ago to take refuge in huts belonging to close relatives of these Koreans; their very doubles in appearance, manner — and, in so far as I can judge, character — the Baltis, to the north of Kashmir. For dinner (I see it sadly noted down) I had a filled-up plate of rice, with a little pork wherewith to give it savour. Bread, coffee, vegetables, tea, sugar and salt seemed dreams of the past, although hopes were held out that the last three items would be forthcoming next day. On this occasion we had to content ourselves with hot water, a beverage hitherto associated in my mind with dyspeptic ladies, or with steaming bowls of grog.

Next day we marched through the same sort of country without any adventure. It was on this date that we first began to notice that our bear-leaders, Lieut.-Colonel Satow and Captain the Marquis Saigo, were altogether too terribly afraid lest we should see something which we ought not to see. They were even suspected of having made a *détour* of a mile to prevent us passing by some wounded soldiers who were being carried back from the front on litters by Korean coolies. I hope and believe that when we meet officers of high rank, reticence will not be carried by them quite to these extremes! On the 11th our route led us through steeper and more wooded hills, including position after position, where a few Boers would very effectively have delayed and harassed an advancing army. Strange that the Cossacks have made nothing out of such opportunities! We encountered great numbers of the two-wheeled carts, with three little Japs pulling and shoving them along. Also thousands of Korean coolies carrying bags of rice.

ARTILLERY IN DIFFICULTIES AT PINGYANG

All the villages within a mile of either side of the road had been burnt by the retreating Cossacks, so as to deprive the advancing Japanese troops of shelter. I doubt if it is ever worth while to do this sort of thing, whether it be in Korea or in South Africa. Certainly these blackened ruins give the landscape a melancholy appearance, which is not lessened by seeing Koreans, who have had their stock of cattle lifted, harnessing themselves into ploughs, and endeavouring without much success to till the ground. One farmer was more fortunate, however, and he was doing great things in ridges and furrows with the aid of a cow and a donkey which he had managed to yoke together. As we drew nearer to the Yalu valley we crossed a succession of ridges covered with a very fine forest of Scotch firs. About four miles from Wiju we topped the last of these ridges, and looked northwards across the broad Yalu at the Manchurian mountains, which ran back, range on range, as far as the eye could reach. The beauty of the scene — the sight of that historic stream — wrought me to enthusiasm. I waved my cap in the air and shouted "Banzai" to the amusement of our Japanese escort, who, matter-of-fact as they are, also well appreciated the significance of the fair prospect which lay, like a map, unrolled at our feet.

From where we stood the Yalu seemed broken into several streams which flow through a level plain of white sand two or three miles wide. On the north of this plain, steep hills of grass and rock rise to a height of 500 to 600 feet. The position looks a formidable one to tackle. We rode on towards Wiju, and soon came across a first example of Japanese minor tactics. The road we were following was open to view from the Russian side of the river, and an officer posted there with good glasses could have made an accurate computation of what passed over into the Yalu valley during the day. To prevent this the Japanese had called on the forests to assist them; and Macbeth could not have been more astonished when he saw Birnam Wood marching on Dunsinane than the Russians when they observed a fine avenue of full-grown fir-trees standing one morning on each side of a road where no trees had ever stood before. The thing was done in style. No scrubby saplings or unsightly gaps, but a handsome closely planted avenue of forest trees, which would have lent itself profitably to the descriptive talents of an advertising house-agent. Our avenue led us to our destination for the night — Wiju, which is an extraordinarily dirty town, nestling amongst its accumulations of filth in a hollow by the left bank of the river. We were installed in the Korean theatre, and I observe that my chief memorandum on this important night is one in which I record my joy and gratitude at receiving a present of five eggs from the Governor of the town.

These, it is also noted, I ate with much relish at 11 p.m. After feeding for several days upon nothing but rice, five eggs made a landmark unequalled to the retrospective eye by anything short of a general engagement of the first magnitude. How little do most of the good folk in England who thoughtlessly mumble, "give us this day our daily bread," realise how much they are asking for, or how they would feel if for once in a way the bread was to make itself scarce! How grievously I myself have fallen short in soldierlike performance by already crying out for the fleshpots of Egypt, seeing I repeatedly boasted to the Tokio War Office about my readiness and eager desire to live on precisely the same fare as the private soldiers!

We left Wiju next morning early; yesterday, that is to say. The town was full of wounded, and Vincent and Jardine, who spoke to many of them, tell me they were all cheery; all as keen as possible to get back to their corps before another fight could take place. We marched to Antung, but as it was only a short distance we had time to examine the Russian trenches and the Japanese line of attack on our way. My first impressions about the strength of the position were more than confirmed. It is shaped on the lines of a natural fortress. The hills held by the Russians rise abruptly out of the smooth sand like a regular parapet, whilst the Aiho runs just where, in a redoubt on such a scale, the ditch would have been placed. Thence the most perfect glacis imaginable, of fiat ploughed land stretches away southward for some 2000 yards until it meets the Yalu, itself no mean obstacle for men advancing to a desperate attack to leave in their immediate rear. I have made many notes about the fight, but I shall not commit myself by writing any connected account of the operations until I get a chance of hearing what the principal actors on the winning side had to say on the subject. I have, however, to-day sent home a summary of my first impressions and a short cable,[*] as it seems important to note facts which may determine whether this first engagement by its result merely gives proof of a superiority of armament, generalship,

---

[*] By the irony of fate this hurried preliminary communication got into the Press, and went the round of the Press labelled as "General Hamilton's criticism on the battle."

numbers, morale, or some of those other more or less ephemeral and accidental factors which find their exemplification in a Bull's Run or in a Majuba; or whether it showed something infinitely more serious, namely, that the Russians, as a race, had found themselves overmatched on the battle-field.

We spent this forenoon in going over the Hamaton (Chinese, Frog Pond) battle-field. It looks as if the Russians here had been caught at a disadvantage; but although we were accompanied by an officer who had been present, there were many points I could not understand; and, as with the crossing of the Yalu, I will defer writing upon the subject till I can manage an interview with the men who actually commanded the Japanese troops on that occasion.

Chapter V – Fenghuangcheng

Fenghuangcheng, May 27th, 1904. — Here I am at the headquarters of this famous First Army, living in a small Chinese house as naturally as if I had been born a Mandarin. I have just come back from a delightful visit to Major-General Watanabe, the very man to whom I hoped to address myself in the concluding lines of my last entry. I have also had a three days' lecture on the battle of the Yalu, as well as several conversations with subordinate commanders, and I now feel competent to say something about it. First, however, I must write myself up to date as far as my memory will serve.

On the 14th we left the kind General Shibuya, Chief of the Line of Communications, who had been our hospitable host at Antung. Notwithstanding a dinner *à la Chinois* of literal puppy dogs' tails and snails, for which I had to return thanks in a French oration, I awoke as lively as a cricket on the morning of the 14th, when we started on our march to Tosanjo, seventeen miles on our road to Fenghuangcheng. Whilst resting half-way in a beautiful wood of oak-trees, carpeted with iris flowers and lilies of the valley, I found the bloody coat of a Russian with a bullet-hole in

Fenghuangcheng 59

front on the right side of the chest and another in the middle of the back. He had marched far, poor fellow, with such a dreadful wound. Probably he was buried a few yards off. An incident such as this makes me feel very sad; much more so than a battle-field covered with hundreds of corpses. When death occurs on so vast a scale as to remind mortals of the universal fate, they are instinctively reconciled to it as an incident inherent in mortality. But with the death of the individual it is different. The lot has fallen on him whilst his comrades have escaped, and men feel the full tragedy of what they can so easily imagine might have happened to themselves.

At night we put up at a farm-house, and all stretched out round the walls as close as we could pack. Next morning I saw several pheasants, and longed for a gun. We marched at 10 a.m., and our road led us through a real white man's country, as Americans or English would selfishly describe it. No wonder the Russians and Japanese are fighting for it. It is well worth a seven years' war. A Frenchman thought he saw some resemblance between its soil and that of Berri in *la belle France*. An American proclaimed the land to be more fertile than the great corn belt along the Mississippi. A Grerman declared that Manchuria reminded him of the Hartz mountains with all their valleys flattened out and quadrupled in size by some beneficent genius. I can bring no comparison from Great Britain. The sharp-pointed mountains stuck about the plain on no particular system are puzzling and unfamiliar. The pig-tailed farmers in blue cotton clothes, who have replaced the white-robed Koreans in topknots and chimney-pot hats, are not more different to my countrymen than their country is to our country. But it is evidently a land flowing with the Far Eastern equivalents of milk and honey. No more slipshod Korean farming; no more wretched mud hovels. Everywhere furrows, almost supernaturally parallel, contain tender sprouting blades of millet and Indian corn, sown, tended and weeded like a rich man's garden, amongst which rise substantial brick-built houses with cosy-looking roofs of tiles, and fruit-trees clustering round about them. At this time of year the climate is absolutely perfect, and everything looks green and beautiful. The sight of crystal-clear water running over pebbles or sand is always present to refresh the eye, and here neither man nor beast need suffer from the pangs of thirst.

At last we saw Fenghuangcheng looking like a picture transferred to nature from an old China teapot, very prettily situated in the centre of a cultivated plain, from which the young kaoliung was just beginning to raise its head modestly, as if it were an ordinary crop instead of a giant growth, capable, so they told us, of concealing brigades of cavalry. We rode through the streets of the outer town, which were simply thronged with soldiers of all arms, buying indescribable cakes and sweets from Chinese merchants. I doubt if any one in this world has ever had a better chance of studying the exact facial expression assumed by a profound astonishment than I had that afternoon. Many of the Japanese coming from remote country districts had never seen a European before, except a dead or wounded Russian, and the Chinese were equally amazed. This procession through the streets brought home to me very forcibly how isolated we were about to find ourselves amidst these thousands of Asiatics, with no door of communication open except the one to which the Press censor holds the key.

At 3 p.m. we filed in through the great arched gate of the citadel and went direct to headquarters. The General and his staff were out, and so we sat in the waiting-room and were served with tea and biscuits by the tallest soldier in the Japanese army, as he proudly told us in very good English. It seems his father was English. The breeds had mixed well in this instance, for he was tall even for a European, and handsome also in a heavy-looking style. After a little the Marshal Baron Kuroki came in with his A.D.C., Prince Kuni, and Major-General S. Fujii, chief of the staff. They walked through our anteroom into an inner room, to which I was presently summoned. Here I had a few minutes' conversation, as well as the advantage of a second helping of biscuits. Meanwhile the officers of the general staff had come into the outer room, and were talking to the other foreign officers there assembled. Eventually the attachés were brought into our room, one at a time, and presented to his Highness the Prince, the Marshal Kuroki not intervening in any way, effacing himself entirely in fact, and remaining, like myself, a spectator. Then Kuroki went, leaving me *tête-à-tête* with the Prince, and spoke a few words to each foreign officer individually. Finally, he came back to the inner room, and then the officers of the Japanese general staff entered one by one and were formally presented to me. Shortly afterwards I took my leave. The whole of this elaborate procedure had evidently been thought out carefully. Marshal Kuroki has a charming face, and a gentle sympathetic smile. He looks intelligent, and I would be prepared to hear of his being a scholar or an artist. But I see no trace of the blunt, determined, bulldog expression which some men of action seem to acquire in the course of struggles, or of the quick, alert, penetrating look, alternating with phases of reflection and even absence of mind, which characterises another and perhaps a higher type.

Major-General Fujii greatly impressed me. I should think he possessed good humour, wide knowledge, and energy to an unusual degree; and certainly a chief of the staff has need of all these qualities, and not least of the first. We talked about the *rôle* of heavy artillery in modern war, and about its effect in South Africa and on the Yalu. I told him how much I had admired the cleverness of the Japanese in planting a pine avenue down from the southern heights of the river valley towards Wiju. He said I ought to have seen the trees when they were green, not withered as they must be by now. I rejoined that the avenue was not withered in the least, and that I imagined that the trees must have taken root to commemorate the great victory, at which the great general staff were pleased to smile. I find, by the way, that the mildest joke suffices to make a Jap roar with laughter, provided always that there is nothing personal about it, nothing, in fact, of the nature of chaff, mild or otherwise. If there is, he shrivels up like a sensitive plant, and very likely you find out afterwards you have made an enemy.

From the date of our arrival until now not much of importance has happened; but this quiet time is valuable as it enables me to make the acquaintance of Japanese generals and other officers, and to get glimpses of useful points of military detail, drill, administration, &c. There are eight or nine newspaper correspondents here, most of them English. They are very good fellows, some of them old friends of the South African War time.

But they are quite beside themselves just now at the restrictions placed upon them, and at the impenetrable secretiveness of the Japanese. This secretiveness is an admirable military characteristic. It is true that subordinates carry it too far. They are in fact so terrified lest they should unwittingly say too much that they make all safe by saying nothing at all. For instance, out ruling this morning we met an officer who said "good morning" in such a specially forthcoming and friendly manner that he positively invited further conversation. Accordingly Vincent asked him where he was going, and he replied, "To the 12th Division." We inquired whether it was far, just for something to say, as of course we knew the distance well enough, and he answered, "I don't know." If you were to ask some of them who won the battle of the Yalu, they would say, "I don't know." This is desperately annoying, I admit, as it is a real damper on conversational effort to be suspected of fishing for important news when in reality you are merely endeavouring to utter a few commonplace banalities. Nevertheless, if secretiveness carried to such a pitch is a fault, it is a fault on the right side. Generals or high staff officers who are not afraid of being suspected of indiscretions, often permit themselves great freedom in the discussion of non-essential questions, but then they have confidence in themselves and in their power to discriminate between important and unimportant matters, which is just what the juniors lack. I can see perfectly well that when we stop to talk with any young officer in the streets he is on pins and needles all the time until he has escaped. He is in terror lest some officer of rank should come round the corner and see him, and that subsequently, if it transpired that we had acquired too much knowledge, the incident would be recalled, and he would be suspected of having let the cat out of the bag. If, on the other hand, we meet him at a party where it is an accepted feature of the entertainment that we should be spoken to, or else on a hillside or other secluded spot where there is no danger of his being seen, he becomes what might, by comparison, be considered quite talkative.

It is easy to understand that whilst this is unpleasant to us, it is gall and wormwood to war correspondents, spoilt as they are by the amazing want of reticence which characterises the British, who not only wash all their dirty linen in public, but implore all passers-by to take a hand in the process. I know of course that the criticisms of a free Press are supposed to be, like the east wind, very unpleasant, but salutary enough to those who are strong. We, however, carry the thing a bit too far. Upon my word, I believe it is healthier to live in a fool's paradise than to swim complacently on the surface of dirty water into which foul linen is constantly being flung in full view of all the other nations. I therefore sympathise with the newspaper men very sincerely as men, but as a soldier I sympathise a great deal more with the Japanese. One lot are fighting for their country, the others would be the first to admit that they are working for the gallery. Some of the correspondents also chafe a good deal at the idea that they are classed with the newspaper men of Japan, who are not respected as highly in their own country as journalists in America or England. I doubt this being the case. The Japanese we have to deal with are a pure military caste, and they are naturally bored by ' the presence of civilians at the front. As far as I can make out they regard the attachés as a necessary evil, the correspondents as an unnecessary evil, but I do not observe much difference in the treatment meted out to us respectively. There are bitter complaints because foreigners are not permitted to walk up and look at Japanese guns, magazines, store depôts, &c. Let one of them go, even in the piping times of peace, and set foot upon the gun park at, say, Meerut for instance, and he will speedily learn that the Japanese are not singular in taking a few elementary precautions. All this is very trivial, but trifles loom large when there is nothing of any importance happening to bring them down to their true perspective.

On the 24th I met Marshal Kuroki, who told me that a Cossack lieutenant and private had just been brought in as prisoners. The officer had lost his horse, which broke away from him, and the private had stuck to his superior. They were bivouacking in a wood when the Chinese gave them away to the nearest post on the line of communications. The only soldiers there were men of the military train who had no rifles; only side-arms. However, they determined to capture the Cossacks, and cutting themselves "shillelaghs" from trees, they surrounded the wood, and at a preconcerted signal rushed the two Russians before they could handle their firearms. The officer was a fine-looking young fellow.

He refused to give any information whatever, and only begged that he might be exchanged at the earliest possible date. General Kuroki laughed in telling me the story at the absurdity of world-renowned Cossacks being taken prisoners by two or three soldiers of the train, aided by coolie cart-drawers. It was clever and plucky of the Japanese certainly, but I do not quite see how the Russians could have effectively defended themselves against a swarm of these determined little fellows.

Chapter VI – The Position on the Yalu

I have now got all the information immediately available about the Yalu fight, and my last two visits were especially useful. One was to Major-General Inouye commanding the Twelfth Division, who told me interesting things about the musketry of the Russians and the adventures of the Fifth Company 24th Regiment. The other to Major-General Watanabe, commanding the Second Brigade of Guards, who was senior officer present at the Hamaton fight in the afternoon of May 1. He is a most charming person. He not only gave me a number of useful notes, but also an original sketch of the battle-field which had been drawn for his own use, with all the dispositions of the troops marked upon it. I think then I am now in a position to form a fairly correct idea of the course of the battle, and I shall try and put it down as clearly as I can without going too much into detail.

Towards the end of April 1904 General Kaschtalinsky with some 6000 men at his back had taken up a defensive position across the Pekin road where it passes through the village of Chiuliencheng on the Yalu. Just over the water at Wiju stood Kuroki, busily engaged in bestowing the last touches to the First

Army of Japan, that living key which the great general staff at Tokio had so long been fashioning to fit the Manchurian lock.

With the possible exception of a final engagement, a first serious encounter is generally the most crucial. However insignificant the forces on either side may be, and however paltry the mere material losses and gains, the result must always profoundly influence the course of a war, not only by the effects produced on the morale of the fighting men, and on the prestige of their respective countries, but still more by offering the initiative to the victorious general. Indeed, when it is considered that the impending conflict was in this case to be between European and Asiatic types who had never before joined battle, it must be admitted that it would be difficult to over-estimate its importance.

The Russian army is the largest on earth, as the hosts of the twentieth century are reckoned; that of Japan is of moderate dimensions. The mere peace effectives of the Czar largely outnumber the mobilised war strength of the Mikado's troops. Yet, for this imminent battle of the Yalu — the first in the history of the world, consciously watched by the whole of Asia — the representative of the smaller army had brought with him to the point of contact a force seven times greater than that of his immediate opponent. Doubtless the Japanese commander was very much nearer his base, but still such an explanation does not cover all the ground, and I do not think any European or American would have ventured to predict, a few weeks previously, that the Russians would fight their first fight on Manchurian soil with a force only half the size of the army which that pariah of Government departments, the execrated British War Office, was able to concentrate in one quarter of the time to take part in the battle of mournful Monday before Ladysmith.

Before embarking upon an account of the fight I think some consideration should be given to the following points:

First: How did the Japanese realise the weakness of the Russians in Manchuria so much better than any European or American observers?

Secondly: Why did Kuropatkin send any troops to the Yalu at all if he was not able to concentrate there in sufficient force?

Taking these points seriatim, it is instructive to contrast the attitudes of Great Britain and Japan towards the numerous recently published fairy-tales on the subject of Russia, and her destiny in the furthest East. How often have we in England been assured by those who spoke with authority, that Russia had come to Manchuria to stay; that Manchuria was already Russia; that Fate and the Czar had so ordained, and that mere Anglo-Saxons could only bow down before the accomplished fact?

We believed it. So often was the tale told, so respectable were the witnesses, that although a rebellious spirit may here and there have protested, yet, for the most part, it was accepted as incontestable, and one more trick was placed with a sigh to the credit of our chief rival in Asia. But Japan! Thoughtfully, attentively, Japan had weighed the evidence, and had come to a precisely contrary conclusion. If the full reasons for this divergence of opinion could be known, it would probably be found to lie, not so much in the superiority of her diplomatic and military sources of information, as in a fundamental difference in the attitude of the two allied nations towards those sources. The Japanese accept what their experts tell them. On the other hand, the average Anglo-Saxon revolts at the very word expert, which is in itself an assumption that some one knows something better than he does. The one fortunate exception to this general rule is the navy. A trip to Margate on a breezy day has sufficed to convince the great "man in the street," by methods before which even his omniscience must bow, that he is out of his depth in matters nautical. He leaves them accordingly severely alone, and approves of his parliamentary representative following his example, thus giving all ranks a chance of escaping those periodic reorganisations which are to the spirit of the army what transplantation is to the vitality of a tree. Hence the efficiency of the British navy.

Be this as it may, Japan had weighed the power of Russia, and had quite made up her mind about her own immediate future in the Far East — a determination in which the future not only of Czardom, but even perhaps of Christendom, was also to be involved. The momentous decision was not signalised by bluster or fuss; on the contrary, as the fatal moment drew near she acknowledged the tension only by an accentuation of her customary suavity, till it reached a point which, to the occidental perception, was indistinguishable from humility. Now, unless I very much misread the character of our allies, humility is a frame of mind which was, and always will be, very &r from their hearts in dealing with any Western nation. Is it to be wondered at that Russia failed to realise how, under this depreciatory attitude, there lurked a fixed and desperate purpose to extract every single concession considered necessary to the future of Japan, or, at the given moment, to cry havoc and let loose the dogs of war? The Japanese method only seems new because it is so very very old. Machiavelian Italy knew all about it, and it is unquestionably more gentlemanly and effective as a procedure than the bark-without-preparing-to-bite system of drifting towards war which prevails in England and America.

Just as Europe misunderstood the diplomatic attitude of Japan, so also she accepted without question exaggerations concerning the military strength of the Russians in the Far East. How easily did Russia obtain a full endorsement of all the statements of her agents from the Press and public of Western civilisation! With what amused contempt did the Japanese listen both to the statements and their endorsements! I believe myself they served her purpose. At any rate, to the best of my belief she never had the smallest idea of publishing the truth of the matter, even to the extent of taking her friends into her confidence. I had been a few weeks at Tokio when I was specially privileged at an interview, lasting several hours, to hear from the lips of a very great man what purported to be an exact account of the strength of the Russian forces. This account, technically called a distribution statement, gave the station and actual strength of every Russian unit east of Lake Baikal. It was for the month of October 1903, and there was also a supplementary document showing in detail the number of additional men, guns and horses which had arrived on the scene of operations between that period and the end of January 1904. I was surprised, not only at the masses of professedly precise figures which had been got together, but at the formidable strength of the Russians. There were supposed to be 180 full battalions of infantry, and with cavalry, artillery and engineers, the total of the Russian forces in Manchuria came approximately to 200,000 men. I asked if I might communicate this long statement, and was told that I might do so as a very special mark of favour and of trust. Home went the statement, but, unfortunately, since I have come here I have ascertained that it was entirely misleading. I now know that at the very time I fondly imagined I was being taken into the intimate confidence of the highest authorities, the Japanese in the field knew well that the whole mobile field army at the command of the Russian Generalissimo would barely amount to 80,000 men by the 1st of May. All is fair in love and war, and it is something even to have gained the experience that the Japanese trust nobody.

Not only did our allies know the numbers at Kuropatkin's disposal, but they had also made up their minds that it would be impossible for him to place a large proportion of these troops on the Yalu, because, first, they were satisfied that it would take some 3000 Chinese carts to maintain 30,000 Russians so far away from their regular communications, and these carts had not yet been collected; secondly, because they had too much belief in Kuropatkin's generalship and ability. Once the ports were free of ice it was incredible to them that he would venture to launch too large a proportion of his small field force upon distant adventures amongst the Manchurian mountains. A study of the map of Korea and Manchuria, even in an ordinary atlas, will make the position clear. Chiuliencheng lies at the extreme left flank of Kuropatkin's sea-exposed frontier of 400 miles, a frontier which had very bad lateral communications. Had he committed the bulk of his small field army to the task of guarding the Yalu, then either an army from Japan or the first army re-embarking suddenly at Chulsan might have sailed for Newchwang and forestalled him at Kaiping, cutting the force on the Yalu from their communications as well as from the garrison of Fort Arthur. Until the ice had broken up, Kuropatkin's communications to the Yalu, or even to Anju, Pingyang, and the whole of the north of Korea, were perfectly safe. After that date he was bound to keep the main body of his comparatively small force in a central position.

To the strategist, indeed, the difficulty of grasping the scope of Kuropatkin's scheme lies, not so much in accounting for his having sent so few men to the Yalu, as in satisfactorily comprehending why he sent so many. No doubt it was highly desirable, from the Russian military point of view, to deny Manchuria's soil for as long as possible to the Japanese, not only on account of prestige but also because every day gained meant the advent of increased munitions and reinforcements by the Trans-Siberian railway. But a retarding force of Cossacks, mounted infantry and horse artillery, such as ought to have been operating in Northern Korea during the months of March and April, might have done this without running too much risk, whilst infantry and field guns usually mean serious fighting, and if their numbers are insufficient they are very likely to get caught.

This brings me to my second point: Why did Kuropatkin send Sassulitch to Fenghuangcheng with a force too small to fight effectively, too big and too immobile to extricate itself creditably, when once it had come into contact with the enemy's superior forces?

If in private life a sober quiet individual upsets all previous estimates of his character by marrying hb cook, it is not necessary to say *cherchez la femme*, because she stands there as large as life. Where a gross and palpable blunder in elementary strategy is made by a general of repute it should be equally unnecessary nowadays to seek for the statesman, who is usually quite apparent. It is difficult, no doubt, for a ruler of any sort to restrain himself from interference with his instruments. Thus, in the old days, theologians having the power, used it for the purpose of routing the ungodly, as at Dunbar and many other places, where the result was good for the ungodly. Still, the Church could at least sometimes inspire the soldiery with individual fanaticism which might compensate for much bad direction. Per contra, the statesman has nothing in his gift but disaster so soon as he leaves his own business of creating or obviating wars, and endeavours to conduct them. The American War, for instance, was a war where the feebly timorous civilian strategy of the Federals was a perpetual and never-failing standby to its weaker adversary; whilst the greatest victory the North ever scored was when Jefferson Davis took a leaf out of Lincoln's book, and had the ineptitude to replace that competent, sagacious, careful commander Joseph E. Johnston by a mere thrusting divisional general, infinitely his inferior in all the higher attributes of generalship.

South Africa yields another and a more recent example. The

The Position on the Yalu　　　　　　　　　　　　71

detachment of a force of all arms to Dundee in 1899 was exactly parallel to the detachment of a force of all, arms to the Yalu in 1904; and there is little reason to doubt that these two examples of civilian strategy were urged upon responsible commanders for similar reasons, which probably seemed unimpeachable to those who put them forward. Civil authority in Natal declared that if Dundee was evacuated, British prestige would be lowered amongst the Dutch; the Kaffirs would become restive, and Durban would be cut off from some useful coal mines. Substitute Manchus and Chinese for Dutch and Kaffirs, and timber concessions for coal mines, and the reasons given to Sir George White are identical the those which were given, so say the Japanese, by the Viceroy of Manchuria to General Kuropatkin. Excellent reasons in their way, but in each case the soldier's opinion was right, although for political purposes it had to give way to the judgment of a Governor or Viceroy. The fact is, that a big soldier must be potentially if not actually a statesman. Who now questions which was the more far-seeing statesman, Montcalm or Vaudreuil? The idea that a soldier should be a mere bulldog, to attack unreflectingly at the moment and manner decreed by the politician, will find no warrant in common sense or in history. More than one soldier has failed from not realising this truth, and I believe that statesmen also have even more frequently failed to realise that when once they have enunciated the policy they must leave the soldier a free hand to carry out that policy. To borrow another example from the American Civil War, Lincoln was entirely within his rights as a statesman in insisting upon the importance of safeguarding Washington. He realised that if it fell into the hands of the Confederates, England and France might take steps to break the blockade, and to pour arms, supplies, and, perhaps, even volunteers into the South. Where Lincoln was mistaken was in attempting to dictate to McClellan and other Generals how Washington was to be defended. The Japanese are quite clear and decided in their theories on this interesting subject, ami applying them to the situation on the Yalu seem to take it for granted that it was entirely the pressure brought to bear by Alexieff which forced Kuropatkin to detach a considerable and yet insufficient part of his force to the Korean northern frontier.

Returning to the Yalu, and accepting the Japanese estimates, it seems that in the latter part of April 1904, Lieut.-General Sassulitch with 15,000 infantry, 5000 cavalry, and 60 guns as his total available force in the triangle, Fenghuangcheng, Antung, Changsong, had deputed Kaschtalinsky with 6000 men and 30 guns to entrench himself on the north bank of the river in the neighbourhood of its junction with the Aiho. There it had been decreed by fate that it would be his duty, alone and practically unsupported, to give the much-needed fillip to Russian prestige by disputing the passage of those rivers with a Japanese army of over 40,000 men, having at its back twenty howitzers in addition to its own full complement of artillery. Not that supports were altogether out of reach. As far as the Japanese know, the balance of the 20,000 men under Sassulitch was distributed as shown on Map II.,[*] and as the bulk of them were within twelve miles of Chiuliencheng, it seemed that a concentration to oppose a crossing at that place would be easy. Easy or not, it was absolutely essential to the Russians to effect it, seeing that even with the most complete concentration the force was still too weak for the task which had been assigned to it.

On the 4th April reconnoitring patrols of Japanese cavalry had visited Wiju and Yongampho, and were followed by the advance guard of the army under Major-General Asada, which commenced its entrance into Wiju on the 8th. This advance guard had started as a full brigade, but insuperable difficulties of supply and transport had left headquarters no option but to reduce its strength considerably. Part of the brigade was accordingly halted at Kasan, five days' march from the Talu; and the actual strength of the advance guard, which commenced coming into Wiju by driblets on the 8th and was not concentrated there till the 13th, was only two batteries of artillery, one regiment of cavalry, and one regiment of infantry. These facts are sufficiently surprising. No one dares do these things at manoeuvres, and yet when empires are at stake they are not only done but they succeed. For some days after the

---

[*] Publisher's note: A copy of this map is found on the pages before the Table of Contents..

concentration of this feeble detachment at Wiju there were no other Japanese troops within supporting distance. General Kuroki was well aware of the serious danger he was running. When the Japanese headquarters were at Pingyang the question of this advance had been earnestly debated. It was known the Russians had boats on the Yalu; but the anxious question was, whether they had a sufficient number of them to build a bridge when the ice broke up, which it did just as the advance guard reached Easan. It was during this debate at Pingyang that the lines of communications staff announced that the full brigade must be reduced if the force was to go further, and it seemed to several of the junior staff officers to be tempting fate to push a weak detachment into the very jaws of the Russians if those jaws were capable of dosing upon it. Eventually the headquarters decided to toke the risk, although they have confessed to me that the evidence before them lather tended to show that the Russians had the means of crossing if they were anxious to do so. The fact was that, unless the point of the advance guard pushed on, the Japanese must have delayed almost indefinitely the carrying out of a general scheme, whose details down to its very dates had already been worked out at Tokio. For the main body of the army was not able to get on at all until Chulsan could be made good as a port for the disembarkation of stores, provisions, heavy guns, &c., and to cover Chulsan it was essential that the Asada detachment should be thrust out well to the front, though whether quite as far as Wiju seems very much open to question. When I have questioned the Japanese on this point they have usually ended by admitting that their only valid excuse for taking such a risk lay in their estimate of the inertia of the enemy.

On the north bank of the river, actually within cannon shot of this unsupported Japanese detachment of 2000 infantry, 600 cavalry and 12 guns, were 6000 Russian infantry, 1000 cavalry and 30 guns. The Russians had been long in the neighbourhood, and should have had perfect channels of information. They had drawn all the native boats to their own bank, and the Yalu offered no serious obstacle to an offensive movement against a weak detachment. If they thought their force insufficient, they could within twenty-four hours have doubled their infantry and guns and trebled their cavalry. Here was a chance for the lieutenants of Kuropatkin! Fortune was in a mood to be wooed, and he who worships at her shrine dares never let his anxious gaze wander for one moment from those opportunities which are the fugitive smiles of the goddess.

It was not to be. Not until April 12 — four days, that is to say, after the Japanese advance guard had begun to come in to Wiju — did the Russians make even a semblance of an attempt to grasp the initiative, which was slipping hourly away through their fingers. When the attempt was made, the scale upon which it was conducted proved that they had hardly risen to the situation. A party of some fifty of their men came close up to the town and tried to cross by boat. One company of Japanese infantry drove them off easily, killing an officer and a private soldier. The officer was Lieutenant Demidrovitch, of the 12th Regiment, and on him was found a written order telling him to pass through the Japanese outpost line and reconnoitre south of Wiju. My Japanese friends tell me that every one felt sorry for the poor young fellow, ordered to undertake with 50 men a duty which his General had hesitated to carry out with 6000.

This episode of the advance guard of the First Army is one which possesses an exceptional interest of its own. Is it not, after all, as easy to see the distinguishing marks of national character in a skirmish as in a battle, and even sometimes in an abstention as much as in an action? The loss of such a chance by the Russian commander will bring home to officers and men who have served in South Africa more forcibly than any lengthy treatise the gulf which separates the Muscovite from the Boer. It is quite certain that if Delarey, Botha, DeWet, Smuts, or many less distinguished Boer leaders, had been in command on the north bank of the Yalu, the small Japanese detachment marching from Kasan would either have been attacked on its way to Wyu, or, having been permitted to arrive, would have had to fight for its life against every enemy within a radius of thirty miles long before any troops of its main army could have got within supporting distance.

I confess then that the hesitation of the Russians to take advantage of such an opening is to me more convincing augury of the ultimate success of the Japanese than any showy crossing of the

The Position on the Yalu 75

Yalu river to the thundering accompaniment of a vastly superior artillery. Looking at the matter purely from the point of view of autumn manoeuvres, a minor Russian success at this stage would have made the subsequent situation much less of a foregone conclusion and infinitely more interesting. As a soldier, therefore, I must own to a sentiment of professional regret that Kaschtalinsky did not enrich military history by leading his force, whilst yet there was time, to deliver a blow at this isolated advance guard of Asada's.

On 20th April the whole of the First Army had completed its concentration in the neighbourhood of Wiju without any hindrance or difficulties beyond those provided, somewhat bountifully it must he admitted, by nature. The enemy, having been passive when a great reward lay well within the grasp of their initiative, was not likely to give trouble now that the superiority of force had passed very definitely from the northern to the southern bank of the river. Still, although all danger of a Russian attack had now disappeared, it was very desirable to prevent Sassulitch from concentrating opposite Wiju to oppose the crossing. He could do this in twelve hours, or less, and the careful Japanese wanted a full ten days to complete all arrangements before delivering their blow. Nothing was to be left to chance. Fords were to be sounded, mountain paths explored, redoubts built against the possibility of a counter attack; timber, nails, cables, anchors were to be collected for bridges, and, in fact, every little detail was to be gone into and rehearsed 60 that, when the curtain rang up, the actors should be in their places and word-perfect at least.

Whilst all this was in progress Sassulitch must remain spread out over twenty-five miles of front, uncertain where the crossing would take place. It seemed a difficult thing to manage, but it was done. The detachment under Major-General Sasaki at Changsong, thirty miles up the river, helped to cause uneasiness regarding the extreme Russian left, and on the other flank the navy was called in to make demonstrations at Antung. The depth of the channel would not permit even light-draught aimed launches or torpedo-boats to ascend the river beyond that part, but the appearance of a certain naval activity seems to have had its effect, and the Russians remained dispersed in face of the concentrated Japanese. In an early entry I wrote about the improvised avenues of trees by which the Japanese concealed the movement of troops and supplies along their lines of communications; and with the same end in view, strict orders were issued that neither officer nor man of the First Army was on any account to show himself on the high ground which ran along the southern bank of the Yalu. Very different ideas prevailed on the north side of the river, where the natural keenness of the soldiers to see something of their enemies was not in any way controlled. Consequently, the crests of the hills above the Russian position were habitually lined with spectators staring across the river, in the hope of being able to satisfy their curiosity. So little did the Russians trouble themselves about concealment, that they even permitted their men to water the horses in the Aiho between 2 and 4 p.m., and to exercise them on the sandy flats which extend between the north bank of that river and the Russian position at the base of the hills. All this was highly tantalising to the Japanese artillery, who lay under cover watching their enemies play about within range of their guns, like a fox-terrier forbidden to bark at the rabbits lest it should prematurely frighten the careless gambolling creatures before all the nets are in position.

The plan of battle was arranged long before the army left Japan. It was even settled that the Twelfth Division on the right should advance through the mountainous triangle between the Yalu and the Aiho and turn the enemy's left; although the sweep of this turning movement, and whether it should keep touch with the rest of the army or work clear of it down the Kuantienchen road, was left to be decided on the spot. No doubt the Japanese had alternative plans; hut their main plan, the plan most carefully studied and relied upon, was brought with them from Japan and put into execution without essential modification on 1st May. The rearguard action of Hamaton was of course unforeseen, and is therefore the more interesting military operation of the two, as extempore effort makes demands upon qualities of a very different order from those which are employed in elaborate and studious preparations.

The position which the Russians had prepared in order to oppose the crossing of the Yalu was about twenty-four miles in length, having its right three or four miles to the west of Antung, its centre at Chiuliencheng, and its left thrown back along the Aiho to a point a mile or two north of Sheechong. The defending force for these latter two sections of Sassulitch's line had its right resting on Chiuliencheng, whence the troops were fairly equally distributed to the top of the hill just north of Ishiko. Thence to Sheechong there were only small detached posts, as the country was so bad that it was not thought likely the Japanese would choose such a spot for a crossing. At Sheechong the right bank of the Aiho was again strongly held to guard against a Japanese turning movement on Hamaton down the Kuantienchen road. These exact dispositions only became known to the Japanese after the battle. To understand such a position and the movements which took place, it is absolutely necessary to study II., whereon are placed the works, bridges, and dispositions of the troops according to the information I have received. This saves hard writing and harder reading. Especially is this the case in the description of a battle fought on the Korean frontier; for here, on the border, Chinese, Koreans, Japanese, and Russians have each made it a point of honour to inflict their own special nomenclature on the innocent *riverain* hamlets, and in so doing have seemed to take a special delight in removing their renderings, as far as consonants and vowels can go, from those which have been adopted by their rivals.

To return to the position. The plain or valley which forms a bed for the Yalu and Aiho, with their main and subsidiary channels, averages about four miles across. It consists of smooth white sand, or sandy plough, and except where some trees and brushwood grow on Osekito and Kinteito islands, it gives no cover of any description, excepting what may be obtained here and there from the hank of one of the channels. In other words, the Russians had an exceptional field of fire; indeed it would be impossible to find a better. Their shelter trenches ran along the base of the spurs just where they began their rise out of the sandy river bed on the right or northern bank of the Aiho, and had a command of some twenty or thirty feet over the level plain. These spurs ran down towards the river from higher hills further north, and they ended for the most part in an under feature or knoll from 100 to 300 feet in height, which sloped steeply down to the sand. The hills were,

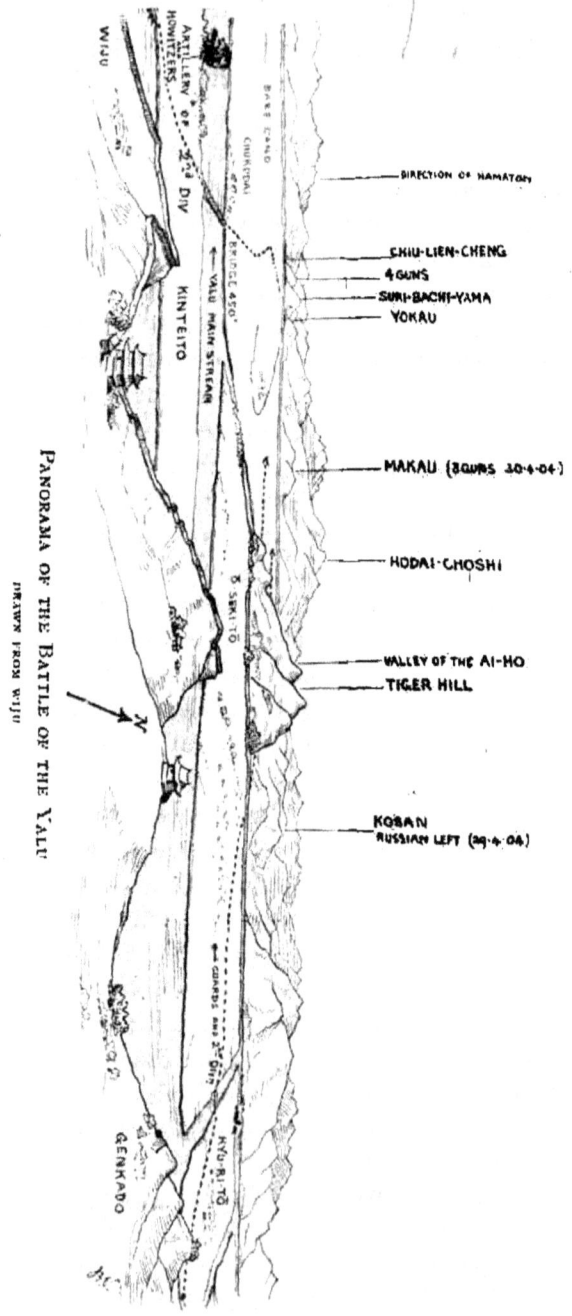

Panorama of the Battle of the Yalu
drawn from Wiju

generally speaking, bare and rocky, although here and there a little low scrub or a few trees gave natural cover. Artificial cover in the shape of rifle pits and short lengths of concealed trench might very easily have been worked in amongst the broken ground and hollows along the face of the hills, and defences of this description would have been very difficult to detect even at a distance of a few hundred yards. The Russians had not chosen to make this use of the ground, and had preferred to construct long straight sections of simple and extremely conspicuous breastwork riveted with boughs. Thereby they threw away the advantage given them by the broken rocky ground. Such conspicuous simple entrenchments might equally well, or perhaps better, have been made a little way out on the smooth bed of the river, where both shrapnel and high explosive shell would have lost much of their effect in the soft sand.

A portion of the Russian artillery was prepared to come into action in the open, but epaulements had been constructed for twelve guns just above Chiuliencheng on the top of a low hill. The Russian engineer or artilleryman who designed this target must have taken his idea from his grandfather's text-book. The gims were in three lines one behind the other, an antique device for getting a very heavy fire on a very restricted front, but one which, in modern war, ensures that shells long fused for the first row will surely catch either the second or the third.* There was a flimsy parapet, just enough to attract attention, not enough to give cover, there was no trench or place of refuge for the *personnel*. Nothing could have been worse, for the great essential nowadays in any such prepared positions is sunken, shell-proof cover fur the men, and after that, cover from sight, and, as much as possible, from shot, for the guns. But let no British officer cast a stone or be sarcastic on this score. For our own ideas were precisely similar until the South African War came to make us more cunning.

The chief strength of the position as it was used by the Russians lay, first, in its excellent field of fire; secondly, in the

---

* Later experience has taught me that I was here doing the Russians an injustice. The positions prepared in rear were probably merely alternative positions.

Aiho, which ensured the delay of the attacking force just where the fire of the defenders should have begun to be deadly. This river, 100 yards wide and four to five feet deep, runs at a distance of from 300 to 800 yards from the Russian position along its whole length. It served to the Chiuliencheng position much the same purpose as the Tugela did to the Colenso position, and indeed the general resemblance between these two defensive lines has impressed itself strongly upon every one who has seen both battle-fields. In either case there was the same open field of fire from which the steep hills rose abruptly, the same difficult river to cross within easy, sometimes point-blank range from the riflemen in the trenches at the base of the hills, and, most curious resemblance of all, the same commanding hill on the left flank of the position, which was on the wrong side of the river from the point of view of the defence. Tiger Hill was to the Russians exactly what Hlangwane was to tho Boers. It should not have token two minutes to see that, especially from the Russian point of view, Tiger Hill was the key to the position; but it is not easy for the British, who took two months to recognise similar properties in Hlangwane, to make any criticism.

The Yalu is much more important, geographically and commercially, than the Aiho, the southern stream being 250 yards, and the main stream nearly 400 yards in breadth, both being unfordable. In regard to this battle, however, the larger river played a subordinate part, although it lent its name to the conflict. By daylight on 30th April it had ceased to interpose between the Russian left wing and the Japanese Twelfth Division, and it was crossed without fighting during the night of 30th April-lst May by the Guards and Second Division. So long as the Russian defence remained passive, the Yalu, lying beyond rifle shot from their trenches, was bound to subside into an obstacle merely physical, once the artillery on the northern bank was silenced.

I think I have now given as complete a description of the position as is necessary to complement the excellent ; but it is worth while, perhaps, to explain that its northern section, which became the actual battlefield, possessed two very obvious outposts, on which good entrenchments and vigorous active defenders might have caused the Japanese a great deal of embarrassment in all their

The Position on the Yalu 81

preliminary arrangements. The first of these was Chukodai village, on the Yalu, between that river and the Aiho. It completely commanded the main road between Wiju and Chiuliencheng, and, as it turned out, its garrison must have been expelled before the Japanese could have established their artillery on Kinteito island during the night of 30th April The second, Tiger Hill, was a rocky tongue or promontory, the extreme point of the triangle of mountains which divided the Aiho and the Yalu. It was supposed by the Koreans to resemble a crouching tiger looking down the river, and stood full 250 feet above their beds at the point where they united.

As I have already suggested, this rocky hill was more than an outpost; it was actually the key to the position. As long as the Russians held it they could sweep the valley of the Yalu with their artillery for 6000 yards below Wiju, and render a daylight crossing practically impossible. In the hands, of the Japanese it could be used as a pivot from which to operate against either flank or the centre of the Russian position. It was safeguarded against a *coup de main* by the unfordable Yalu, and if it had been crowned with semipermanent defensive works, the whole of the Japanese scheme of operations must, in my opinion, have been recast. The Russians do appear to have appreciated the peculiar tactical value of Tiger Hill under the stress of an impending attack, when they, too late, endeavoured to dig a few trenches. But it is strange indeed that the Russians, during their six weeks' occupation, should have neglected to fortify it strongly. Had they done so the Japanese must have experienced much delay, difficulty and loss in taking it, and must also have plainly shown their hand, whereby the eyes of Sassulitch might have been opened, and the balance of his force moved up in time to dispute the crossing of the Aiho. For, as it is the aim of the commander of the attack to throw a great superiority of force suddenly upon some vital point, or key, in his enemy's position, so the aim of the commander of the defence is to thwart this intention by transferring a correspondingly powerful force (according to his means) from points merely threatened to the decisive spot. The *rôle* of the defender is, to my mind, the hardest to accomplish brilliantly. He needs both imagination and iron determination. Imagination to divine the full intention of his enemy from his preliminary movements; determination to change his dispositions forthwith, regardless of the long faces of his disapproving staff, and despite the outcry of the subordinates who lose a portion of their troops. For it may be taken as an axiom that all local commanders are firmly convinced, always, that it is upon them that the brunt of the fighting is destined to fall.

The key to a position is a portion of the line of defence, the possession of which enables the defender to hold his ground, but which, once taken by the attacker, forces the defence to abandon the whole position and retreat. The village of Froschwiller, at the battle of Woerth, is a. well-known example. Tactically such a "key" may be a ridge from which guns can render all other positions within five miles untenable; or it may be a point from which the enemy's communications can be threatened, or which gives access to supplies, or enables a hand to be held out to friends; or it may possess any other important recommendations, material or moral, which may easily be imagined. One advantage of being on the offensive is that occasionally a commander has the privilege of declaring what suit is to be trumps — i.e., he declares a certain part of the enemy's position to be the key merely by attacking it. This is notably the case where the line of defence is a river running through fiat country, as the assailant then fights for a decisive point wherever he attempts to cross it. When the real line of defence is broken aground beyond the river, to which the river only forms a protective shield, this theory, of course, only holds good to a more limited extent.

The .front of the Russian position along the Yalu was twenty-four miles in length, but the Japanese attacked only its left section, extending from Chiuliencheng to the extreme Russian left near Sheechong on the Aiho, a distance of six or seven miles. The presence of eight battalions, twenty-four guns, and several thousand Russian cavalry in the neighbourhood of Antung did not help the seven battalions and thirty guns on the Chiuliencheng-Sheechong line in their defence of the passage of the river between those points. The Russians, in short, were trying to hold too long a line for their force; and unless their Intelligence Department and the prescience of their General warranted the fullest confidence that they would be able to concentrate so as to forestall the

Japanese attempt to cross with their whole force, they would have done better to content themselves from the first with holding Antung and Hamaton, and with merely watching the upper reaches of the river with a line of outposts. The Russians, in short, might with great advantage have copied Lee's dispositions for guarding the river before the battle of Fredericksburg, namely, a series of strong detachments so placed os to be able to concentrate rapidly, and anticipate the enemy at any threatened point, while the whole length of the river line was patrolled with cavalry. If my memory serves me right, the length of river to be watched — namely, twenty-four miles — was much the same in either instance.

I feel I have been dabbling too long on the brink of the Yalu, and that I must pull myself together and dash in. First though, for just about as much time as it would take me to pull off my boots and stockings, I pause to summarise the Russian military situation on the eve of this, the first land engagement of the war.

1. The strength of Kuropatkin's field army was less than half of what it was supposed to he hy the outside world.

2. He was unable to send as much as one-third of this field army to the Yalu.

3. Less than one-half of the Russian troops actually on the Yalu were, thus far, concentrated opposite the concentrated Japanese army to dispute the passage of the river.

4. The handful of men who were actually on the ground prepared to fight what may well turn out to have been one of the decisive battles of the world, were not generally considered Russia's best troops, or a fair representative sample of her army, although certainly in the actual event they tried most gallantly to do their duty.

Chapter VII – The Battle of the Yalu

Kuboki's army having concentrated on April 20th opposite the position at which it meant to cross, it might have been expected that the Japanese would endeavour to strike whilst the iron was hot and before the enemy could modify his dispositions unfavourably to their intentions. Our allies are, however, a very careful people, who like to test the strength of the last stitch in the last gaiter button, and in the Russians they believed they had an enemy prepared to indulge them to the top of their bent by sitting as still as a family group before the photographer's camera till all was fully prepared. It was desirable in the interests of this leave-nothing-to-chance policy to sound the stretches of the Aiho between its known fords, and to construct an ample number of bridges over the Yalu. Neither of these enterprises were practicable until the islands of Kyurito, Osekito and Kinteito had been captured, and on the night of the 25th-26th they were all successfully occupied. Only in the case of Kyurito island did the Russians give any trouble. The let Battalion of the Imperial Guards bad been detailed for the attack, and the story of it was given me a day or two ago by a young officer who was present. At the selected point of crossing, the stream was 100 yards broad, with a depth of two and a half yards and a current of one and a quarter yards per second. Two boats were available, and supports were extended along the left bank of the stream in older to assist the crossing with their fire should there be any opposition. At 4 a.m. on the morning of the 26th the crossing began. It was dark, and land troops may be excused if they experience some nervous tension on a strange element, approaching for the first time a strange and formidable foe. All was very still except the plash of the oars, which sounded with intolerable loudness in the ears of the little party. Suddenly a long tongue of yellow flame darted upwards out of the opposite bank, reflecting itself in the black water and lighting up the boats packed tight with soldiers of the Guard. Then from the darkness behind the flame rattled out a succession of volleys. The bullets came whizzing past and into the Japanese, killing or wounding some thirty men in the crowded boats, and lashing the water into foam all about them. There is nothing more apt to demoralise the soldier than to have the darkness under which he creeps to his secret mission suddenly dispelled, leaving him exposed, whilst his enemy, whom he means to surprise, quite reverses that process. The Japanese stood the test. The Russian aim was bad, and the rowers never faltered or hung back till they touched laud on the bank of the island, when the Guardsmen quickly leaped on shore without further opposition from the enemy, who, well satisfied with their exploit, fell back under cover of the night. It was then found that the sentry on the river bank had been provided with a bundle of dried grass which was fixed to the end of a pole and set by him at the water's edge. This he had lit on hearing some suspicious sound, and retiring back himself into the shadow had been joined there by the picquet, who opened fire in comparative safety. If this incident reveals the Russians in an aspect of enterprise and cleverness, it shows the Japanese in what I hope may prove to be an unusual condition of miscalculation and want of thorough preparation. The troops who had been extended along the left bank to support the crossing of their comrades had been posted a few yards below the point whence the boats started. Naturally these drifted; and thus, at the critical moment, masked the fire of the supports, who could not use their rifles, and only served to catch a few of the spare Russian bullets.

Now that the Japanese had gained possession of the islands upon terms so easy, they were able to reconnoitre and to make a bridge to Kinteito, which latter proceeding drew the first shells of the land campaign from the Russians, and the first defiant answering "Banzai" from the Japanese, who were engaged upon the work. This Kinteito bridge was built on trestles, and measured 260 yards in length; it was constructed entirely of local materials, and owing to the delay caused by the shelling it took 45 hours in the making. The interesting point about it is, however, neither the materials of which it was built nor the time occupied in its construction, but in the fact that it was never meant to be anything more than a blind, to draw the artillery fire of the Russians, disclose the position of their guns, and obtain an advance sample of the skill of the gunners and the power of their weapon. The remaining bridges are shown upon II. In all there were ten of them, of an aggregate length of 1660 yards, or 100 yards less than a mile, one-third of which was of regular pontoon construction, the remaining two-thirds, an improvisation. In making the latter it was found that small-sized Chinese junks served as an admirable substitute for a pontoon, and that the ploughs of the unfortunate Koreans made the best anchors imaginable. Thus did the Japanese plough the waves of the Yalu in sober fact and not by poetical licence. It is as well to say hero that the Japanese are extremely proud of their bridging feats, and, I think, with justice. They are not quite so well pleased with their pontoon. The boats are well enough, they say, but the scantling and wooden platforms are too slight and fragile to stand the knocking about inseparable from service conditions.

It was about time now to issue orders for the attack. A reconnaissance had been made of the mountainous triangle of country through which the Twelfth Division was to manoeuvre so as to turn the Russians out of Tiger Hill and then operate against their left, and a definite and important decision had been come to regarding its proposed line of advance. The original idea of detaching this division to make a very wide sweep round so as to come down on the left rear of the Russians by the comparatively easy Kuantienchen road, was at the last moment definitely

The Battle of the Yalu 87

abandoned. Not without regret; but after a minute study of the conditions under which such a movement must be carried out, it was decided that the plan was too adventurous, and had not sufficiently taken into account either the known obstacles, or the unknown dangers, of following such a route. It would have been almost impracticable, so the Japanese say, to arrange for supply and transport for the three or four days during which the division must depend upon its own resources, and no positive intelligence could be obtained as to the strength of the Russian troops at Kuantienchen and Aiyanmen, who, if in any force, would be in a position to fall on the flank of such a wide sweeping line of advance. The division therefore received orders to adopt the alternative scheme, whereby, making a much closer circuit, their left should get into touch with the light of the Imperial Guards on the day of the battle. The route actually followed under these orders is clearly shown upon II.

The chief original objection to this scheme had been that the enemy's cavalry might have come down behind the Twelfth Division from Aiyanmen; crossed the Yalu, and cut the Japanese communications with Pingyang or Chinnampo. Now that the whole army was concentrated at Wiju, covering the short, new, safe line of communications to Chulsan, there was no cause to fear any such enterprise. The other objection was on account of the extremely broken and difficult country which the division would have to traverse. The triangle of country between the Aiho and the Yalu was not, however, found to be as impracticable as it had presented itself to the memories of the veterans of the Chinese War, who had traversed it with a similar purpose ten years previously. From this it would appear that old soldiers in Japan are like old soldiers elsewhere, and that their exploits are in no danger of diminishing or dwindling away in importance by lapse of time! Once the Twelfth Division succeeded in crossing the Aiho, however, it would find itself confronted by a great and rugged mountain 1000 feet high. It was called Hodaichoshi, and as it was impossible to reconnoitre across the Aiho, it was also impossible to foretell in what way it would be best to surmount or circumvent it.

The only other objection to the movement now ordered was one which applied with two-fold force to the first idea, which had been abandoned. It was the objection to almost all turning movements, namely, that the force which has to be detached for the purpose must run the risks which are always involved in a temporary isolation. According to the instructions issued, the Twelfth Division would have to cross the river Yalu at Suikaochin one clear day in advance of the other two divisions. One-third of the army would thus be divided from the remainder by a broad river, and would risk being overwhelmed by the Russians before assistance could come to it.

1 mention this theoretical objection as its existence has always been carefully impressed on me by the Japanese, with a view, I think, of lending a dash of adventure to their strategy, which erred, they instinctively recognise, on the side of too much deliberation and slowness. I do not myself believe that the Twelfth Division ever ran the slightest danger of any such counter-stroke from the Russians. Was it likely that General Sassulitch, who had, until now, shown but little enterprise, would risk having his army cut in two by thrusting a large portion of it eastwards across the Aiho, leaving two Japanese divisions a free opening to cut in and sever its line of communications and retreat on Fenghuangcheng? I think not. I go further. I believe history will consider that the First Army commander was over-cautious. Considering the operations from the point of view of the arm-chair, it seems dear that he should have hardened his heart and sent the Twelfth Division right round by Changsong and thence by the Kuantienchen road, as first suggested. He had a magnificent chance of doing something great — he preferred the certainty of doing something good.

The plan being settled and preparations being complete, demonstrations were made by gunboats on the 25th and 26th at Yongampho, and some junks laden with timber in the estuary of the Yalu were manoeuvred so as to help to confirm Sassulitch in his impression that a disembarkation or crossing might take place at Antung. The actual attack orders were issued at 10 a.m. on April 28th. Under these orders the Twelfth Division had to cross the Yalu at Suikaochin at 3 a.m. on the 30th, and move as shown on the map. Their special duty was to cover the passage of the main army over the river. A detachment of this division, consisting of one battalion and one squadron, was to make a very pronounced

The Battle of the Yalu

turning movement by Kyokaku and to threaten the enemy's left rear, but so weak a column could not be expected to produce any serious effect. By the evening of the 30th the division was to take up a line as shown on the map (for the orders were carried out to the letter), and, continuing to march the next day, it was to form up on the right of the Imperial Guards on the east bank of the Aiho before dawn on May 1st. The Second Division, starting at midnight, was to march *viâ* bridges "c," "d," "e," and "f," and deploy for attack on Chukodai island before dawn on May 1st.

The Imperial Guards were to follow the Second Division over the same bridges, and deploy between that Division and the Twelfth Division.

The artillery and the reserves were to take post as shown on the map.

Although these orders were issued three days in advance, nothing, occurred in the interval to cause any modifications, which is, in itself, significant of the quiescence of the Russians. There was, however, one small outburst of activity on their part which at least threatened to disturb the cut and dried monotony of the programme. When, on the 26th, the Russians had evacuated Kyurito island they had also thought fit to clear out of Tiger Hill, exactly as the Boers evacuated Hlangwane, its Natal prototype, on the first approach of Buller. Just as in the South African instance Louis Botha, recognising the predominating tactical value of the place, took heart of grace and reoccupied it at the very last moment, so also Kaschtalinsky with his mountain; and there the parallel ends. Tiger Hill, it may be remembered, is the rock which composes the apex of the angle whose two sides are form^ by the Yalu and Aiho rivers. It was held by one company of Guards, who were covering reconnoitring parties engaged in fixing the routes to be taken by their respective divisions when marching by night to take up their positions for the battle. At 4 p.m. on the 29th a battalion of Russian infantry crossed the Aiho with four guns, near Ishiko, and attacked this company. It fell back without much loss, and the Russians occupied Tiger Hill. The map shows even more clearly than my previous argument that these Russians had come to quite the wrong place from the point of view of Kuroki. Their force was so weak, however (so was Botha's), in comparison with the weighty masses of troops which were about to march over and in the rear of Tiger Hill, that the Japanese determined they could afford to leave them to be dealt with by the Twelfth Division, especially as their tardy efforts to entrench themselves were easily frustrated by the artillery of the Guards.

The morning of the 30th arrived, and with it the moment for the Twelfth Division to make a difficult, and, to some extent, a hazardous advance. Some Japanese officers of my acquaintance say that it was to assist this advance that it was determined to force on the artillery fight; others, that it was to place their own superiority beyond question, and, if possible, crush the enemy's guns definitely in an artillery duel the day before the battle; others again, that it was a combination of these reasons. Curiously enough, I, a foreign if allied officer, have been placed, by the kindness of a powerful friend, in possession of the exact truth concerning this interesting point, a knowledge which is not, I believe, shared by many others.

The question as to whether the bombardment should begin on the 30th, or be deferred until the 1st, was very keenly, and even hotly, debated at the headquarters of the First Army. By one side it was urged that it was most desirable to make the enemy show his hand, as the only certain information about his artillery was the position of the twelve guns north of Chiuliencheng. By the other, it was strongly insisted that it was not worth the while of the Japanese to gain this certitude at the cost of prematurely divulging the howitzers. There was a real danger, it was argued, that, on learning the full strength of the Japanese artillery, the Russians might withdraw their own guns northwards out of range of the howitzers. If the Yalu bed had been an ordinary valley this would not have mattered vary much, but as the river was there, it would be impossible to advance the howitzers next day, to follow up the enemy. Thus the battle would have to be delayed or fought without the howitzers. So evenly divided were opinions, that it was actually decided to leave the matter to chance. Those who best know the Japanese are the very people who will find it most difficult to credit this statement. Nevertheless, I cannot be mistaken, for my information on this point is absolutely authentic.

Until midday the sun was at the backs of the howitzers. After

The Battle of the Yalu

that it would be in their eyes. The artillery were given orders to mass on Kinteito island during the night of the 29th-30th. They were to open fire at the first good opportunity given them by the Russian guns. If the Russian guns gave them no opening they were not to fire at all.

It was further the secret intention of the small group who control the destinies of the First Army, that if their guns had not opened fire by noon, an order should be sent down to them forbidding them to fire on that day under any circumstances. By daybreak on the 30th the whole of the artillery of the Second Division, together with the five batteries of twelve centimetre howitzers, in all seventy-two field guns and twenty howitzers, were admirably entrenched on the soft, sandy soil of Kinteito, which lent itself well to the purpose. Every advantage was taken of the natural lie of the ground, and much artifice was employed to conceal the position from the Russian gunners on the north bank of the river. Trees were transplanted a short distance in front of the batteries to hide the telltale flash of discharge, and were carefully chosen from amongst those which were growing either directly in front or directly behind the entrenchment which was to be concealed. Thus next morning the landscape appeared unchanged from the Russian side of the river, as the fact that a tree of a particular shape had advanced or retired 200 or 300 yards during the night, was naturally imperceptible. Poles were stuck into the sand and connected by a string on which branches were expended. The earth dug out of the deep gun-pits was most carefully, and with great labour, scattered broadcast, so as not to disclose any irregularity of terrain. The howitzer pits and epaulements were connected by trenches, and numbers of covered ways leading down to the river bank showed the trouble that had been taken to ensure a plentiful supply of water for laying the dust, which is otherwise so apt to rise with the shock of discharge and give away the position.

When all had been done that could be done to ensure concealment, then all was done that could be done in the time to ensure safety if concealment should chance to fail. Bomb-proof shelters were made for the men, and were dug so deep and so strongly roofed over with heavy baulks of timber and earth, that they would have resisted heavy siege artillery, let alone the field guns, which were all that they had to fear. Telephone stations, depots for reserve ammunition, &c., were all strongly fortified with earthworks and heavy timber baulks, so arranged as to be invisible from the other side of the river, whence we, when we rode over after inspecting them, were unable to locate them, although, of course, we knew their approximate position. Thus, screened from observation and protected against fire, every possible precaution had been taken towards minimising the effect of the enemy's guns. It now only remained to perfect the arrangements for offensive action. With this object, two observation stations (marked on the map) were established on the high ground some 3000 or 4000 yards in rear of the batteries, from whence a good view could be obtained of the Russian camp behind Chiuliencheng, and of the lateral communications, such as they were, which ran in rear of the Russian entrenchments. These observation stations were connected with the howitzer batteries by telephone, and both batteries and observation stations having duplicate maps of the enemy's position marked out in small squares, the observers on the southern heights were able, by merely telephoning down the number of a square, to switch the whole fire effect of the masked batteries on to any spot where they from their elevation could see a suitable mark present itself. Platforms were also erected in trees on the flanks of the batteries, from whence officers would be able to make local observations of the effect of their fire. All this was accomplished in one night, and, although the soil was light and easy to dig, yet, when I saw those deep trenches, the platforms, and the enormous baulks of timber, and recognised that the very trees had been shifted about as unconcernedly as a gardener transplants a rose-bush I confess I was fairly surprised.

 By daybreak all was in order. The old Hanoverian Colonel who taught me what little I know, used always to insist that "Ordnung und Punktlichtkeit"[*] were the only secure foundations for military genius; and here, if anywhere, were Ordnung and Punktlichtkeit in the highest degree. The artillery, as I have already explained, had merely been told they were free to open if the enemy's guns took

---

[*] "Order and punctuality."

the initiative, but that otherwise they must remain silent. They had of course not the vestige of an idea that even this qualified permission would be withdrawn at midday. Indeed, they do not know this now, and they probably never will know it.

Still they were burning with eagerness to begin, and lay there anxiously awaiting the challenge of the Russian cannon. On the previous mornings these guns had commenced firing at the bridges at seven o'clock precisely, but as luck would have it they left them alone on this fateful day. The language used in the batteries would have rivalled that of our army in Flanders if the Japanese possessed any stock of bad words, which, by the way, they do not. Minutes dragged themselves out into hours, and up to 10 a.m. no one had made an attempt to tread on the tail of the Japanese coat. It had become necessary therefore to trail it a little more ostentatiously and defiantly.

I find it impossible to believe that the two boatloads of Japanese engineers who chose that hour to paddle up and down the main channel of the Yalu opposite Chukodai were engaged in a *bonâ fide* attempt to survey the river, as I have been officially informed. I prefer to remember the traditional *camaraderie* between gunners and sappers, and to assume that some sporting artilleryman persuaded some equally sporting engineer to take a step which must set the cannon balls rolling. For no guns in the world could resist a couple of large pontoon boats full of men rowing quietly about on a broad river within very easy range of their muzzles. Therefore inevitably the Russians opened on the boats, and instantly seventy-two guns and twenty howitzers were at them. The Russians never had a chance, but just for the first ten minutes the *rafale*[*] of their quick-firing artillery enabled them to look dangerous to the anxious headquarters staff and infantry looking on at a distance. After that, not only the overwhelming superiority of the Japanese in batteries and in weight of metal, but also all their careful preparations told with crushing effect. The Japanese were invisible and comparatively invulnerable, the Russians were conspicuous and everywhere most vulnerable. In

---

[*] "Gust."

thirty minutes the Russian guns were silenced. At 11 a.m. they brought up a fresh battery on to the knoll east of Makau and opened fire, but these guns were also silenced in a couple of minutes by two or three batteries of Guards artillery, which bad that morning advanced on to Kyurito island. Thus, in an easy triumph ended the anxiously anticipated artillery duel, probably the last of its sort that will ever take place. Why, why did the Russian great general staff disdain to take a lesson from the Boers, who had so recently repeated for the benefit of the British, and for that of all the world as well if it chose to take heed, the lesson of how an inferior artillery should be worked?

During the artillery fight, the Twelfth Division had taken up the position assigned to it without any contretemps, and by their presence there forced the Russian battalion on Tiger Hill to fall back hastily with its four guns, so as to avoid being cut off from the main body. The hill was reoccupied by a battalion of Guards as a garrison, as well as by a second battalion who were employed in preparing a road across the islands for the guns. Simultaneously with the evacuation of Tiger Hill by the Russians, *i.e.*, at noon, the bridging of the main stream was put in hand by the Japanese, as shown on the map at "e" and "g," as well as the bridging of the lesser branch at "f" just under Tiger Hill. These bridges were all completed soon after dark. During the day arrangements had to be made to get the Second Division artillery across the main stream of the Yalu to support the infantry attack more vigorously than would be possible if it contented itself with doing so from the position it had fought from during the artillery duel. The river was 500 yards wide at this spot, and a bridge was out of the question, so it was decided that the guns should be ferried across during the night. In the darkness this proved a very slow and awkward business, so much so that by daybreak on May 1st, only three batteries and the escorting battalion of infantry had got across and entrenched themselves near Chukodai village, although by that time all three infantry divisions had reached their allotted positions. These positions are clearly shown on the map, likewise that of the artillery belonging to the several divisions. In frontage, extension, depth, brigade reserves, divisional reserves and army reserves, the arrangements were exactly those of a German army corps attacking a skeleton enemy.

It was 7 a.m. when the infantry began to move forward, drawing no sign from the enemy, for neither from Suribachiyama[*] nor from the hill to the north of it was a shot fired. The formidable Russian position became yet more impressively formidable from its silence. A Japanese officer, speaking to me of this advance, said, "When the enemy fires very heavily, it is unpleasant; but when he does not fire at all, it is terrible." The chief of the staff also said to me, "No one knew whether it was the intention of the Russians to tempt us to come closer in before beginning, or whether they had altogether retreated, but the majority held to the former opinion"; he added, "the silence was very trying."

Then, at last, six guns of the Russian battery near Makau appeared in action and fired a few rounds. At this the whole of the attacking force breathed more freely and stepped forward with gay alacrity. The artillery of the Guards was upon the battery like a cat springing on a mouse, and in two or three minutes had reduced it to silence. The Russians then tried to withdraw, and were smashed and ruined in so doing, a high explosive shell by an extraordinarily lucky fluke hitting the leading limber and halting the battery under fire, as it was coming down a path so narrow that the rear teams could not pass the disabled limber. It took about eight minutes to destroy this battery completely.

It was not until the Japanese reached the Aiho that the Russian infantry joined in, and then they opened with volleys. The river should have been filled with dead and wounded. The defenders had the precise range, and it was only 300 to 800 yards from their trenches. Actually, however, no very serious damage was done.

The Russian soldier is the worst shot existing in any great army in Europe. This came within my cognisance whilst I was Commandant of the Musketry School at Hythe. He gets but few rounds for practice, and these are fired mostly in volleys. A volley is the negation of marksmanship as far as the individual is concerned, for he never knows, and never can know, whether his

---

[*] The hill was called Suribachiyama by the Japanese soldiers owing to its resemblance to an inverted bowl of a description used in Japan for pounding beans for soup.

bullet was one of those that missed, or one of those that hit, the target. Moreover, the volley method is incompatible with the attainment of the maximum rapidity of fire possible with the modern magazine rifle, for each man has to wait until the slowest soldier is ready before he can come to the present, and even then cannot fire as soon as he has drawn a bead on his object, but must pull the trigger when his commander thinks he has done so, which is a very different matter. The volley is not only the negation of accuracy, but also the negation oi individualism and wide extensions. Occasionally it has its use as a reassertion of discipline on rallied troops; for very deliberate very long range fire at a large, slowly moving, or stationary object, and for both offence and defence in night attacks, but for the general purposes of war it is dead as the dodo.

Altogether, I take it then, the Japanese were in luck to have had volley-firing Russians behind the parapets, instead of a few hundred Boer sharpshooters. The Russian trenches were similarly placed to those from which the old Boer warned his little nephew firing at his side not to hurry, and to continue still to take careful aim; "for," said he, "notwithstanding the Rooineks are now only 400 paces from us, and are coming on bravely enough, not a man of them can ever reach you here if you hit one with every three cartridges, as you were taught to do with the springbok under pain of a whipping." The Boers, it must be allowed, would have been invisible, whereas the Russians were plainly to be seen, not only by the infantry of the attack, but also by its artillery, which makes a considerable difference. There can be no doubt that showers of shrapnel and ceaseless hairbreadth escapes from bullets tend to make the aim of even the best soldier considerably less accurate than when he is well concealed and firing through a good loophole, whereas the indifferent soldier is only too apt to stick his head down and fire at random, if he fires at all.

Bad as the Russian marksmanship is acknowledged on all hands to have been, still the ground was so open and showed up so well the dark uniforms of the Japanese in their close formations that they suffered some loss, especially when crossing the Aiho. Not very much, but enough to make them halt and, in some instances, fall back. The Japanese of pre-Yalu days were not the same as the Japanese who are going to march some day soon — I hope very soon — on Liaoyang. At least, their own officers tell me that all ranks have now doubled in self-confidence and assurance of eventual victory. They fell back, but quietly and not very far. The idea had been to hold off from the assault and to continue the fight at indecisive range until the turning movement of the Twelfth Division should make itself felt. Just as with the Gordon Highlanders at Doornkop, however, it was quickly realised by regimental officers and men that the fire was too hot to admit of a prolonged duel between troops in the open and troops under cover, and that the only alternative to going back was to go forward. Instinctively the whole line endeavoured to press on, the Guards without success, until the Second Division on the left, which is by the way quite the finest body of troops with the First Army, carried Chiuliencheng and the west side of Suribachiyama. The troops in front of the Guards had then to beat a hurried retreat, and at the same time the Russian left at Sekijo began to fall back south on Hamaton, and south-west to the Pekin road.

In such accounts of this battle as have so far come to hand in Japanese newspapers, it appears to be believed that the Russians quitted the field because of their left being turned by the Twelfth Division. On the contrary, it was the assault and capture of the position held by the Russian right which forced on the general retirement.

When the Twelfth Division advanced to cross the Aiho they at first experienced very little opposition. They were not even fired at during their passage of the river except by the guns from Sekijo, which were very speedily silenced. The weak Russian outposts along the right bank of this section of the river had already fallen back, partly, no doubt, because they had nothing with which to reply to the Japanese thirty-six mountain guns, partly, perhaps, because they may have already got some inkling that the advance of the Japanese centre and left might cut them off from the Pekin road. The Russian forces afterwards encountered by the Twelfth Division were not opposite their point of crossing, but were posted near Sekijo, facing north, and awaiting an advance of the Japanese by the route they had originally intended to follow, viz., from Changsong by the Kuantienchen road. Had the Sekijo troops been judiciously posted on the lower slopes of Hodaichoshi opposite Shiroshiko, the Twelfth Division could hardly, I think, have got across without much loss and considerable delay, as the Aiho was much deeper here than further downstream, and it was all the men could do to ford it, even though practically unopposed.

The famous Russian position on the Yalu was fairly in Japanese hands by 9 a.m., at the surprisingly small cost of some 300 casualties. I repeat that if the Russians had been marksmen, and had so posted themselves as to offer a less perfect target for the Japanese artillery, they should have accounted for, at the very least, five times as many of their opponents. Their general line of defence had several faults, but it did possess that merit which compensates for many faults — an unrivalled field of fire, which could not have been filled in with a more desirable mark than the German formations and dark blue uniforms of the Japanese infantry. Or, to take another supposition, had the remnants of the Russian artillery fallen back during the night out of range of the Japanese howitzers and field guns, hut within range of the Aiho, they might, and would, by indirect fire, have made their enemy pay much more heavily for their crossing. But the God of War does not seem to have been suggesting many brilliant ideas to the defenders on the north bank of the river.

It was now 9 a.m., and lest the Japanese staff be too much crammed down the throat of the unfortunate always-weighed-in-civilian-balances-and-found-wanting British subaltern, I should like to tell him that, although all the world has heard of the eagerness of the victors to get their guns over the Yalu, they were, I will not say more eager, but certainly more successful with their champagne, which arrived in the Kussiun trenches at that hour. Thus, hardly had the stern and deadly rattle of musketry receded into the mountains than it was joyously replaced by the slight and frivolous pop which salutes the arrival on the scene of

> "The subtle alchemist that in a trice
> Life's leaden metal into gold transmutes."

The battle was won but the harvest was not reaped, and "What scoundrel cried 'Halt'? Now is no time for halting!" as the bolting

The Battle of the Yalu

Madrassee cavalrymen called out to the unfortunate officer who was trying to rally their squadron. Whether the Japanese will ever give the exact particulars of what passed between 9 a.m. and 2 p.m. that day I do not know. At present any staff officer speaking on the subject slurs over the whole period with the somewhat unconvincing explanation that the Guards and the Second Division were very tired and hungry and needed rest and refreshment. If this is to be taken literally, as meaning that these troops were so exhausted that they could not march a mile or two further to keep at close grip with the enemy, then the statement is nothing less than a libel on the sturdy Japanese infantry; but if it means that the minds and energies of the funerals and Staff were fairly used up, then, I believe, we have here the secret not only of this, but of many another, strangely inconclusive ending to a very decisive initial success.

It is perhaps necessary to have been a responsible commander during an attack to realise the immense reaction of relief when success is attained, a reaction coincident with an intense longing to tempt fate no further. "You have won your battle," a voice seems to whisper in your ear; "the enemy are going; for God's sake let them go; what right have you to order still more men to lose their lives this day"

However this may be, I believe I have by constant inquiries and by the special kindness of one of the most accomplished and charming of the Japanese officers, whose name I need not give, gained possession now of a fairly clear and true account of what actually did happen at, and previous to, the Hamaton fight. It is very slight, but I suspect it contains certain points of interest which may never reach the world in any official version issued by the Japanese general staff after the war. Such as it is, here it is: The reserves had been ordered at 8 a.m. to march with all speed on Suribachiyama, and at 9 a.m. a bridge was thrown across the Aiho to enable two batteries to cross over and co-operate with these reserves. The Russians had for the most part slipped out of their trenches in good time, and had not, therefore, suffered very heavy loss in getting dear. Two battalions of their reserves had come up from the north-west of Antung, and with three Maxims had taken up a position on a hill some 3000 yards west of Chiuliencheng, from which they were covering the retirement of their defeated comrades. As previously stated, the Japanese scheme of operations had contemplated a containing action in front hy the Guards and Second Division, whilst the Twelfth Division turned the enemy's left. By crossing the Aiho, however, the containing part of the line had come within decisive range and had to go on, go back, or perish. They went on, and carried the breastworks without waiting for the Twelfth Division to make itself felt.

Now that the Russians had taken up another position not very far back, there was on opportunity of reverting to the original idea by giving time for the Twelfth Division to envelop the left flank of the Russian second line of defence. Unfortunately, this division had not been able to make a wide enough sweep to clear the enemy's left, and the presence of a Russian force at Sekijo had transformed their turning movement into another frontal attack. The resistance of the enemy was, indeed, so strong at Sekijo, on the right of the Twelfth Division, that it had the result of causing their commander to bring up his left in a northerly direction with a view to enveloping the Russians, who were holding his right in check and cutting them off from the Pekin road. Instead, therefore, of having wheeled somewhat to the left so as to face west towards Hamaton, the Twelfth Division at 10 a.m. had wheeled somewhat to the right, and were facing and moving in a northerly direction. Orders were sent telling them to march on Hamaton, and beyond this nothing much was done until about 11.30 a.m. At that hour Kuroki ordered the Second Division to advance Antung by the road which runs along the Yalu. It was to be preceded by the 2nd Cavalry Regiment. The four reserve battalions, consisting of two battalions of the Imperial Guards and two of the 30th Regiment, were ordered to pursue down the Pekin road, preceded by the Guards' cavalry. It will be seen from Map II. that the effect of this order would be to direct the reserves and Guards' cavalry straight upon the left of the enemy's rear-guard.

At midday Major-General Baron Nishi, the commander of the Second Division, rode up to Suribachiyama, where the army headquarters commander and staff were assembled, and reported that he hesitated to carry out his orders without further reference, as he felt bound to point out that they could only be obeyed at a

The Battle of the Yalu 101

cost of life which might, for all he knew, be disproportionate to the advantage to be gained by forcing his way past. The Russian rearguard, he said, commanded the only practicable road to Antung so completely that, if he was to march to that place, the only method of doing so would be to first make a frontal attack on the Russians and drive them out of their position. He added that he would have done this without reference were it not that he had no guns to help him. The howitzers could not come up for a long time yet, and the ground was so broken that there was no position from which the Second Division Field Artillery could be brought into action against the enemy.

CHIULIENCHENG

There are not many commanders who have resolution enough at the end of a terribly anxious night and morning to reject a series of plausible arguments for leaving well alone. I have heard Lord Kitchener remark under similar circumstances: "Your reasons for not doing what you were told to do are the best I ever heard; now go and do it!" Kuroki, however, determined that, as the main position had been carried, it was not desirable that further heavy sacrifices should be imposed upon the troops by a direct attack upon the rear-guard, and he authorised Major-General Nishi to stand by and do nothing pending further orders. It was a pity, but no doubt it is a very exceptional man who is able to detach his mind from the terribly impressive now of a hard-fought field into the *then* of the far future. Yet this is necessary to a full comprehension that what may seem heavy further sacrifices at such a moment may he literally trifling compared to the ultimate sacrifices which may have to be paid for an incomplete victory — for a thrust only half driven home.

To return from general principles to their application. On May 1st Nishi stood fast, and the four battalions of the reserve also made no progress. Whether, like the Second Division, they were restrained with the acquiescence or under the orders of superior authority, or whether they found the task too difficult, they merely skirmished with the enemy, and up to 2 p.m. had not advanced more than a few hundred yards from Suribachiyama. Meanwhile the Twelfth Division was advancing but slowly, owing to the constant resistance of the enemy and the extreme fatigue of the men. The fact that the Twelfth were able to move on is proof that the Guards and Second could have done so also, and disposes of the official theory that they were too exhausted. For a reference to the map will show that neither of them had done so much marching over valleys and mountains as their comrades on the right.

At last the advance troops of the Twelfth reached a point whence they threatened to cut off the two battalions of the Russian rear-guard from their line of retreat by the Pekin road to Fenghuangcheng. By this time (2 p.m.) the bulk of the defeat^ Russians, with their baggage, had got clear away under cover of the rear-guard, and were marching, safe from anything but cavalry, on Fenghuangcheng. It was full time then for these Russian battalions to begin to fall back. Unfortunately for them, two batteries of artillery, with their escort, were still blocked on the bad mountain track leading just behind the position to Hamaton. I have asked many officers to give me their ideas as to why these guns were so belated. It might have been well worth while to lose the two batteries for the sake of the effect of even five minutes of their fire on the Japanese troops struggling through the Aiho. Or, if the rearguard had been employing them to keep the Japanese at a distance, and to cause them loss during their occupation of Chiuliencheng, then also they might have been sacrificed with a clear conscience. Seeing, however, that they did not fire a shot during all this period it seems strange that measures had not been taken to remove them altogether from the danger-zone of the battle-field. The most plausible explanation I have heard is, that the Russians did mean to employ them with the rear-guard, but that, owing to bad ground and losses amongst the teams, they were at the last moment unable to bring them into position on such bad ground. Waggons, travelling soup-kitchens, and such like impedimenta, rendered the track to their front almost impassable. The Twelfth Division advance troops were getting uncomfortably close to Hamaton on the only line of retreat. The moment had come when the commander of the rear-guard had to fall back and leave the guns to their fate, or else make up his mind to lose both rear-guard and batteries. He decided to try and extricate his infantry, and shortly after 2 p.m. the evacuation of the hill 8000 yards west of Chiuliencheng was begun. Directly he saw this movement, orders were issued by Kuroki to the whole of his army to advance and pursue.

Reference should now be made to the map of the Hamaton fight (No. III., see pages 106-107), which not only shows what happened more clearly than any description, but is in itself a most interesting document, being a facsimile of the original map given me by Major-General Watanabe, who commanded the Japanese troops at the engagement in this part of the field. It was drawn during, and immediately after, the battle for his own use; and when it is remembered that the days are not very long in early May, it is proof of quick draughtsmanship on the part of his staff. The first troops to get to close touch with the enemy were the 2nd and 3rd battalions of the 4th Guards, and the 1st battalion 30th Regiment. This was about 2.45 p.m., and simultaneously the leading troops of the Twelfth Division began to appear on the scene. At first — and, indeed, for a considerable time — the Division was only represented by one company, since become famous in the First Army, the 5th company of the 24th Regiment. Had the Twelfth Division been turning the Russian left by the ordinary wheel inwards, this company, being on the extreme left of the left battalion of the line, must have been the last of the whole force to find itself in a position to out off the enemy's retreat. As already explained, however, the Division had been forced by the conditions prevailing in its own section of the battle-field to bring up its left shoulders and move for some distance northwards. When pursuit was ordered, then the left ' of the line was just about level and east of Hamaton, and thus the left company got a bit of a start in the race for that point — a start of which they made the very best use.

The map is eloquent concerning the vital and urgent necessity to the Russians of driving off this company. It will be observed that it directly menaced their line of retreat, as it was already nearer to Hamaton than they were, on a rise commanding, at short rifle range, the road up which the artillery were now retiring. Accordingly a strong effort was made by the Russians to shake off the 5th company, in the course of which the main part of their force took up the following position to resist the troops directly pressing upon their rear. Their left was then holding the point which is marked 11/3 on the map, and their line at this stage of the conflict stood upon the same ground as that on which the Japanese are shown, as far as the point marked 11/4, which is where their right appears to have rested.

At 3 p.m. General Watanabe appeared on the scene with the 1st battalion of the 4th Regiment of the Guards, and took command of the Japanese forces. A few minutes before 4 p.m. he ordered the 30th Regiment to attack the enemy's front vigorously, whilst the 10th company, 4th Guards, was directed to turn the Russian right flank. This turning movement was successful, and the Russian right retired across the narrow valley and toiled painfully up on to the long, bare, razorbacked hill to the position in which it is shown in the sketch. I say "painfully" advisedly, for I have climbed the hill, and it is very nearly a hands and knees business, even for an unencumbered man, the slope being 45 degrees, and covered with loose pebbles and disintegrated rock, giving but poor foothold.

It was now too late for the Russian artillery to hope to escape, yet still there was time for the infantry to get clear were it not that the heroic self-devotion of the 5th company of the 24th Regiment interposed a fatal obstacle. On its left the Russians, in greatly superior force, were within 300 yards on its front, *i.e.*, a little north of the road they were within 200 yards. The captain of the company was shot, and the subaltern who succeeded him in

The Battle of the Yalu

command very shortly met with the same fate. Half the company were killed or wounded, and their ammunition was running short; still they held on, and in doing so held the Russians in check. At 4.30 p.m. the position of affairs was like this: The Russian left and centre were still in their old position, from 11/3 to I on the road. A party had been detached from the extreme left at 11/3, und had reached the vicinity of 9/3, where they were attacking the left of the 5th company, 24th Regiment. The Russian right had been driven from 30/i and 11/4 back to where it is shown on the summit of the long razor-backed hill. The 10th and 12th companies had climbed the hill after them where they are shown on the map by the figures 10/4 and 12/4. From thence these two companies were able to shoot across the narrow valley into the backs of the Russian left at, and about, the point marked 11/4. The Russians stood this punishment for a few minutes, and then, being at the same time vigorously pressed in front, they gave way all along the eastern hill and ran down into the valley between it and the razor-backed hill. The attacking Japanese immediately pressed into the ridge they had evacuated, and the local situation was then exactly as shown on the map. I say "local situation" because just at that moment, 4.40 p.m., the remainder of the 24th Regiment and some of the mountain guns and men of the Twelfth Division were coming on to the held in support of their 5th company in time, and barely in time, to wipe out 300 Russians who were in the act of making a bayonet attack upon its shattered remnants.

Barely in modern war have troops found themselves in so utterly hopeless a plight as did the unfortunate Russians at 4.45 p.m. Even with the aid of General Watanabe's excellent map it is difficult to convey a full conception of this hopelessness to one who has not seen the ground. The western or razor-backed hill was, as I have said, exceedingly steep, with a slope of 45 degrees. It was absolutely bare of any sort of cover, and rose about 450 feet above the valley through which the road ran. The valley was dead-level plough, also without cover to hide as much as a mouse. The eastern hill, off which the Russians had just been driven, was 550 feet in height, and also very steep. There was no cover. The shattered but undaunted wreck of the 5th company of the 24th Regiment still barred the exit from the trap, and it was now being reinforced

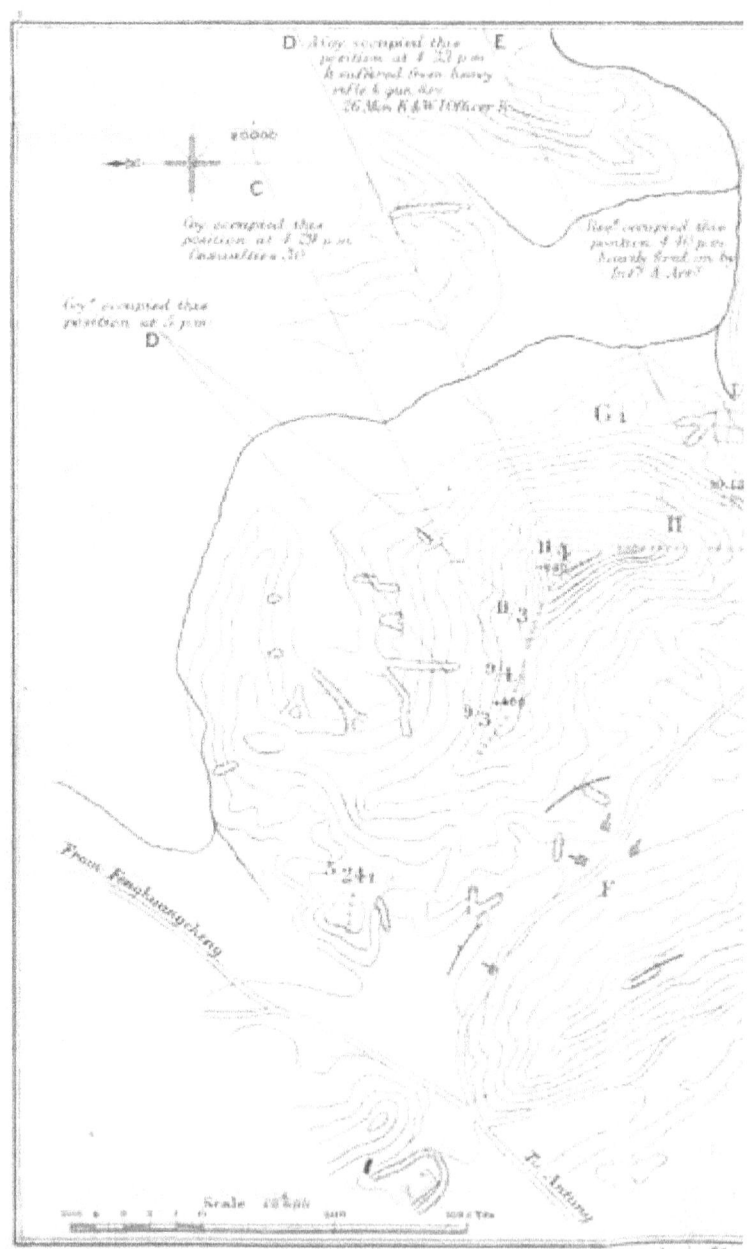

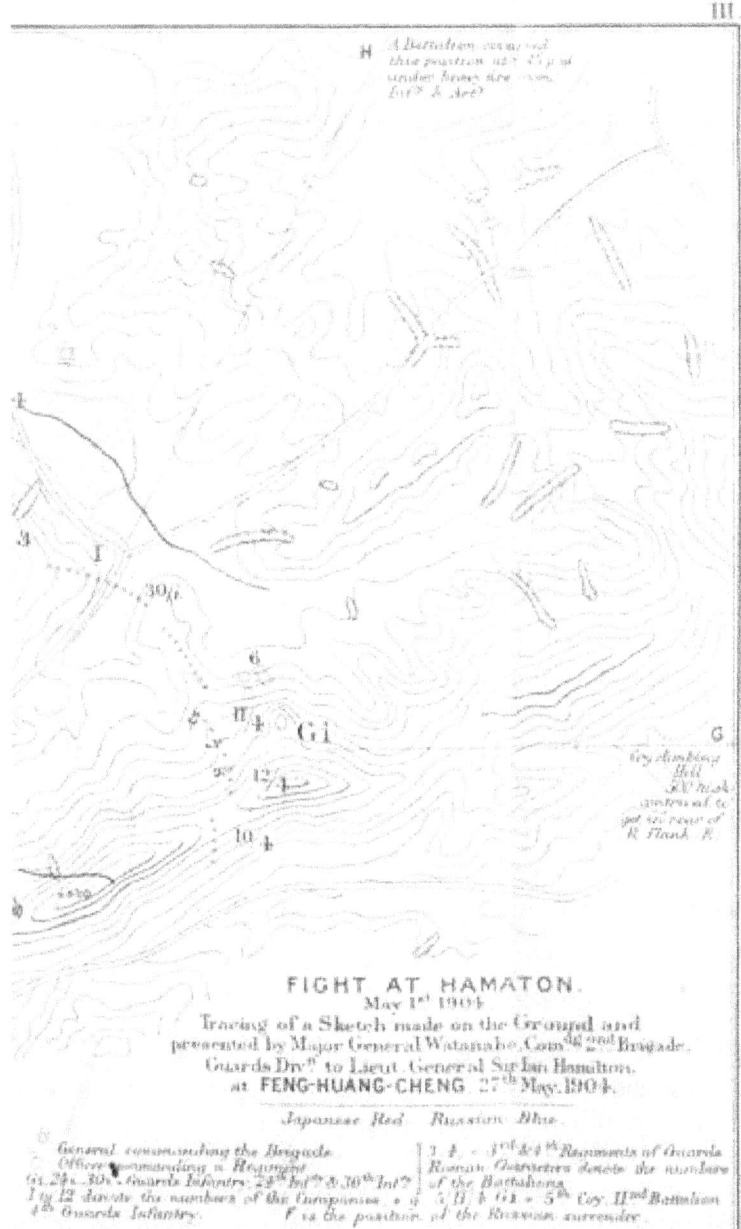

every moment by guns and infantry from the Twelfth Division. Once the Russians had been forced down into this pit they seemed so completely finished that Major-General Watanabe and his staff thought the fighting was over.

The greatest breadth of the valley was only some 800 yards. The guns, waggons and infantry, with which it was filled, were all in the most inextricable confusion, and commanded by the Japanese as people in the stalls of a theatre are commanded by the people in the gallery. Nevertheless (to their everlasting credit be it said), the Russians refused to give in, and whilst some dug to try and get cover, others fired, and some, again, tried to escape over the northern spur of the razor-back. These last were all killed. A Japanese officer told me that he hated seeing the poor fellows bowled over. They could only walk very, very slowly up the steep incline, and there were hundreds of rifles on them from the top of the big hill east of the road. Every good sportsman would disdain to kill game under such conditions; and yet, where fellow creatures are concerned, there is no alternative but to take prisoners or to kill. How many lives, both British and Dutch, may not the squeamishness of our guns after the storming of Talana Hill have cost us? The Russian guns were pointed in every direction and gallantly kept up their fire for a time, but the discharges were becoming less and less frequent as the layers were shot down. The rifle fire also slackened down, but the digging still went on, and it was time to make an end. General Watanabe therefore ordered the 10th company of the 4th Guards to charge with the bayonet. At that moment up went the white flag!

I wonder if I have written out this story so as to render comment superfluous? There is not, as a matter of fact, very much scope for it. The certainty that seventy-two guns, some of them 12 centimetres, would silence the sixteen field guns north of Chiuliencheng and Suribachiyama detracts from the interest of the contest and tends to obscure rather than illuminate the archaic artillery tactics of the Russians. None the less, it is impossible to refrain from considering what might have happened had they withdraw their artillery positions in the first instance to points in the higher hills in rear, where they would have been themselves out of shot of the Japanese guns, whilst, with their longer ranging weapons, they could still have covered the Yalu river and the Aiho, as well as the intervening islands, with a sufficiency of shrapnel. It would not then have even been necessary for them to conceal their positions or use indirect fire. By a combination of indirect fire, and long-range direct fire enfilading the line of the Aiho, the Russian guns might, I believe, have done great work for their country on May 1st, notwithstanding their numerical inferiority. Especially would this have been the case if the guns had been not only concealed but also dispersed by divisions. After all, the first essential of hitting an enemy is to see him, and a captain of one of the Japanese howitzer batteries told me that throughout the artillery action of April 30th the Russians never had a notion of his whereabouts. Not one single missile of any description came within 300 yards of the Japanese howitzers, whose shooting was carried out, therefore, as calmly as if they had been at practice camp. It was equally good too. On one spot, 15 yards by 14 yards, where a Russian battery had been, I counted eight craters made by their high explosive shells.

Again, accepting the Russian artillery positions as they actually were on April 30th, it is, I believe, fair criticism to say that if the St. Petersburg general staff had made careful study of the tactics to be adopted by an inferior artillery in face of a greatly superior number of the enemy's guns, as exemplified by the Boer gunners in the course of the South African War, their batteries might have come better out of the ordeal to which they were subjected. One of the very first lessons impressed upon us in South Africa was that guns which are palpably overmatched in the preliminary artillery duel, should be prompt to recognise the fact, and withdraw from the unequal combat before they can be put definitely *hors de combat*.* If the guns cannot be withdrawn, then, at least, the *personnel* can be drawn back under cover until the storm has passed. It is an exceptional thing for a gun in action to he struck by a shell so as to be put out of action, and a battery may be left exposed to the fiercest bombardment even with high explosive shells, and be not a pennyworth the worse after half an hour of it.

---

*" Out of action."

There is, I admit, a certain danger in training men to take cover, and leave their guns on any plea whatsoever; for subordinates, in the stress of action, are not the best judges of when the occasion is fitting, and, if the principle were once admitted, they might take the wrong one. But after all, it ought not to be difficult to impress upon them that it is not to save his own miserable carcass that any brave soldier takes cover: it is to preserve himself until he can lay down his life to the best advantage. The duty of artillery is to support their infantry in its attack, and to defend it when it is attacked. It is their duty then to see that no mere regimental vainglory tempts them to persevere so long in an artillery contest as seriously to impair their power of afterwards interposing with effect, at all and any risk to themselves, in the infantry fight. The Americans, who in some respects left off, at the end of their civil war, at a point hardly reached on the Continent even yet, gave the world a good instance of this at Gettysburg, in the attack on Cemetery Hill, where, on July 2nd, 1863, Hunt, the commander of the Federal artillery, withdrew his guns when be judged they were overmatched. The Confederates thought he was crushed, and launched the fresh and famous Pickett's Virginian Brigade at the Hill. The guns were run forward again, careless, now that the supreme moment had arrived, of loss or danger, and the brigade was destroyed.

I give this instance because it just happens to come into my head; but there is nothing new under the sun, and perhaps an even better example of how an inferior artillery should decline the artillery duel and reserve itself for the advance of the enemy's in&ntry would be furnished by a study of the manner in which Lee fought his guns on the defence at the battle of Fredericksburg. Not so long after the American civil war came the Franco-Prussian war» and the neglect of the French artillery to observe the true rtle of an inferior artillery on the defence (which they might so easily have learnt from the example of Fredericksburg) was a contributing factor in their defeat at Woerth. The British army was just as bad or worse. In 1898 and 1899 it was apparently accepted as an axiom by our artillery at their training and at manoeuvres, that concealment was futile, and that when the batteries of the attack attempted to pave the way for their infantry advance, the defending guns, even if inferior, must necessarily exhaust themselves in an unequal duel. When the Boers acted as Lee did, soldiers were surprised. The moral of all this would appear to be, that it is not only the Russian army but all European armies who are incapable of profiting by the experiences of others, be the writing never so dear on the pages of history. Had the Russian gunners in this instance, viz., on April 30th, recognised, after ten minutes, that the contest was hopeless, they might have thwarted the Japanese plan of so destroying their batteries as to incapacitate them from taking part in the battle next day. They would have had the advantage of seeing the hand of the Japanese, and during the night they could either have taken up new positions to the rear to punish the troops crossing the Aiho and to cover the retreat, or else they could have retired altogether out of reach of pursuit. But to remain on the battle-field without coming into action was indeed a most unfortunate compromise!

The infantry combat, like that of the artillery, was too one-sided to yield much of a harvest to military criticism. The fact that 40,000 men forced a passage in the face of 6000 tends to divert attention from the faults of the weaker side, by the mere fact that the success of the Japanese was practically inevitable, however wise the dispositions and tactics of the defenders might have been. The glaringly conspicuous nature of the Russian infantry trenches was perhaps the worst of these faults. No artillery could have desired a better mark. Only one thing could have compensated for the entire lack of concealment, namely, that complete protection which a plain breastwork does not give to the most vital and the most sensitive part of a man's frame, his head. There was no attempt made anywhere to provide head cover. But it is not possible to blame the Russians for this omission, for nowhere on the Continent are soldiers taught the value of loopholes as a supplement to field entrenchments.

From Majuba time onwards I have always held the opinion that loopholes double the value of any cover, and all I have seen since has tended to confirm me in this view. Even during an attack the soldier can usually find cover for his body, and, if not, he can rapidly extemporise it with stones or spade work. Under such conditions he is at least on an equal footing with an adversary who has to show his head over the straight line of a conspicuous breastwork before he can fire. Indeed, he is far less visible, and thus less vulnerable to distant artillery fire. To give to a defender that indisputable advantage which is necessary to counteract the depression of having to wait whilst the enemy is advancing, he should be provided with a loophole, or head cover of some sort. Then, and only then, will the average soldier retain confidence enough to use cool, deliberate, aimed fire amidst the showers of shrapnel and rifle bullets which whistle and sing past his ears. Otherwise he fires hastily and fires high, the instinct of self-preservation impelling him to "loose off" as quickly as possible, and get his head those twelve inches lower which will give him, at least momentarily, immunity from deadly danger. I am quite aware that the soldier creations of the novelist and war correspondent never duck their heads; but how often in actual fighting, behind rocks or in an entrenchment without loopholes, have I not heard an officer or n.c.o. call out, "Heads up! Hold up your heads, men!" But I fear I am entering into interminable detail.

As for the cavalry, Russian and Japanese, they did nothing, which seemed very much to surprise some of my friends. To one who holds, as I do, that the day has passed when cavalry of Frederick the Great type can hope to produce any effect on the field of battle, this was not surprising, but quite natural and just exactly what was to be expected. Cavalry trained to act as good solid infantry when dismounted might have done much, either on the Russian or Japanese side, at the battle of the Yalu, and afterwards; but even the warmest advocate of shook tactics and swords must allow, when he follows the course of events on this occasion over the actual ground, that there was no place or opportunity where the horse could possibly have been of any value except to bring a rifleman rapidly up to the right spot.

Speaking now more generally, the Russian position was length without depth. The lateral communications were naturally bad, and were also under view from the Japanese observation stations on the hills on the left bank of the river, and under Are from the Japanese guns in the river bed. So soon as the line was pierced at any point, the whole force had with difficulty to make good its retreat by one single road. These defects apply not only to the position taken up by Sassulitch, but also to the portion of that position under Kaschtalinsky which was actually attacked. I presume Sassulitch will be blamed for not having foreseen the intention of the Japanese to cross where they did, and for not having concentrated accordingly. It is obvious that if he had done so he would have at least doubled the actual slender Russian chance of scoring a success. Certainly it would seem that when the six bridges were constructed he should have got more than an inkling of where the enemy was going to make his effort. The Russians must, at any rate, have known of the existence of the three bridges they fired at. But if there was still room for doubt, then surely, by midday on April 30, when twenty howitzers had sent their very unmistakable salutations across the river, it should have been possible to come to a definite conclusion that Chiuliencheng and its neighbourhood was to be the battle-field. For 12-centimetre howitzers are not to be whisked here and there for mere demonstrations. They themselves may not be appreciably heavier than field guns, but their ammunition is much heavier; they require suitable platforms, and generally do not lend themselves to feints and ruses. Besides, the Twelfth Division had actually crossed the Yalu at dawn on that day, and was obviously and unmistakably quite committed to an attempt to join hands with the rest of its army somewhere near the junction of the two rivers.

It seems to me certainly that Sassulitch would have been justified in concentrating the bulk of his force in immediate close support of Kaschtalinsky during the night of the 30th. Still, on the other hand, it is fair to remember that even up to the last there was cause to be anxious about a landing at Antung. This is a typical instance of the influence of sea command upon land strategy. It was at least conceivable that the whole of the First Army might be making a demonstration, and that as soon as a Russian concentration had taken place at Chiuliencheng an independent Japanese expeditionary force would come steaming up to Antung from Chinnampo and cut the line of communication to Fenghuangcheng. "A fellow feeling makes us wondrous kind," and let those who think they would have done better do the rest of the criticism. One thing is certain. The results of this battle are not to be measured by the forces engaged, by the territory dominated, by the guns and captives taken, or by any other mere material criterion.

When war was declared the Japanese were formidable enough in all conscience. They were brave, disciplined, enthusiastic, efficiently officered, honestly administered. They believed that the Russians were weak in several of these essentials. At the back of their minds, however, there existed a certain vague apprehension lest in some undefined, inexplicable way the European might after all prove the better man when they met him on the battle-field. That feeling is now gone, and gone never to return. Certain philosophers have advanced the fatalistic theory that wars and victories and defeats are all pre-ordained; that innumerable trifling acts, feelings, thoughts, of hundreds of thousands of unknown people, inevitably result in triumphs or catastrophes for their countries; and that so-called great commanders are merely the labels employed by history to record these great phenomena.

Such theorists are in my opinion very dangerous guides. I admit that the brilliant, good or bad General, like the good or bad Jew, may be vouchsafed to a nation according to its deserts. But the great General is no mere label of an event; he makes history. So far he has not appeared on the Manchurian stage. Civilians may be dazzled by the brilliance of Kuroki's achievement, but soldiers must be more critical. On April 25th the Japanese stood, and knew the}'^ stood, in overwhelming force, only separated by two rivers from their enemy. Nothing, however, would induce them to make the plunge until they had completed their most minute preparations. Let the Germans admire this if they will; it is not the principle by which Marlborough, Napoleon, or Lee won their reputations. On the day they meet a first-class General this passion for making all things absolutely safe may be the min of our careful little friends.

I have had an unexpected windfall in the shape of a conversation with Lieutenant-Colonel Kurita, who gave me an account of an attempt the Russian cavalry had made to cut the lines of communications in KoreaHe is the staff officer who, at headquarters, is in charge of those communications, and the story

The Battle of the Yalu   115

comes in very well as a supplement to the battle of the Yalu.

There was a certain Russian Lieutenant-Colonel Matoriroff, who was very well known by reputation to the Japanese Intelligence Bureau, owing to his having travelled a great deal in Northern Korea for the purpose of spying out the land before the outbreak of the war.

On May 10th, when the headquarters of the First Army were still at Antung, a report came in to say that the town of Anju was surrounded by the enemy. At this very period the line of communication of the First Army was in the act of being shifted from Korea, the intention being that it should have its base at Antung, whilst the old line would be handed over to the special troops which had been sent out to form an army of occupation for Korea. Thus at that particular moment the headquarters of the First Army had no idea of the amount of garrison left at Anju, and General Kuroki felt extremely worried and anxious; for although the order to shift the line of communication had been definitely issued, nevertheless it was practically certain that many things of value bad not yet been removed from the old line of communication posts. The report of the appearance of the Russians at Anju was sent by the Post-Commander at Kasan, but in his first message nothing was stated beyond the bare fact.

It turned out afterwards that the garrison of Anju consisted at that moment of seventy infantry reservists under the command of a captain; in addition, one noncommissioned officer and eight men of the Supply Department were lying sick in the town; one intendant with a non-commissioned officer and interpreter were engaged there in cleaning rice; five trained soldiers and two gendarmes were in charge of coolies, and there were five postmen and nine telegraphists, besides a doctor, an apothecary, and fifty enlisted coolies. The rifles of the men killed at the battle of the Yalu had been sent back as far as Anju, and out of the foregoing heterogeneous crew no less than thirty were found who claimed to have some idea of using a firearm. Thus, in extremity, the potential garrison might be reckoned to be 100 rifles of sorts! It would be difficult to find a stronger argument in favour of some kind of universal training, or to realise more acutely what a falling off the British show in this respect since the days of their famous ancestors who fought at Agincourt and Crecy. Out of seventy-five Japanese, men of all trades, thirty could handle a rifle. It would be interesting to know what proportion of Britishers out of a similar mixed crowd would know the difference between the butt and muzzle of a rifle. On a rough calculation I should say one in five.

On the evening of the 9th news was brought in to the post that there were Russian troops in the vicinity; but no confirmation of this could be obtained. Many similar rumours had gained currency, and had proved to be unfounded, so not much importance was attached to the statement. Afterwards it transpired that Matoriroff had led 500 Cossacks down from Manchuria, and by his special knowledge of the country had been enabled to keep off the roads, and to avoid all contact with the Japanese.

The town of Anju is surrounded by a castellated rampart, somewhat resembling that which surrounds Fenghuangcheng. In each case the walls ore about thirty feet high, forming an oblong about 300 yards by 200 yards, and there is a ramp inside, so that men are covered up to their shoulders when they stand on the wall to shoot. At Anju there are seven large gates.

Shortly after dawn the enemy appeared, riding towards the eastern gate. The sentry fired at them, and they seemed to hesitate, thus giving the captain time to collect his hundred riflemen, and to distribute them to the various gateways. At 7 a.m. the number of the enemy increased, and 200 of them appeared on the hill immediately east of Anju. Opposed to these 200 were thirty Japanese, scattered at intervals along that portion of the enceinte. A few minutes after seven, fifty mounted Russians charged the eastern gate at a gallop. The roadway along which they charged was sunken in parts, and only the five or six Japanese actually on the gateway had a clear field of vision. These men opened magazine fire, and most fortunately chanced to kill the officer who was leading the charge, as well as four or five of his following. On this the enemy fell back, the nearest of their men having got to within about fifty yards of the gate. Almost simultaneously another party of Russians appeared from the north, and tried to bum the bridge across the Chongohun river. There was a provision store 800 yards outside the castle walls to the west, where all supplies were stocked in the first instance after they had been landed from the river. Eight men had been told off as a detached post to guard this important, but dangerously isolated, depôt. Three of these men now advanced from the shelter of the provision store, and, under an extremely hot fire, extinguished the flames, which were just beginning to catch hold of the bridge. Strange to say, they were not touched, and got safely back to their detachment. Each of them afterwards received the kanjo, or "writing of honour," from the General Officer commanding.

A party of the enemy now appeared from the east, and, dismounting, began to close in on the town; another party came up from the south, and from the north yet another party came in support of the men who had tried to set fire to the bridge. By ten o'clock the castle of Anju was surrounded on all sides. Every gate was closed, and the small garrison defended itself to the best of its ability, but without much hope of ultimate success. At 3 p.m. the enemy worked close up to the provision store, and the eight men guarding it had a very hard struggle. Luckily, just in the very nick of time, a Japanese reinforcement of an officer and seventy non-commissioned officers and men appeared on the scene of action. This little party had halted the previous night on its way from Pingyang, and knew nothing of the attack until they got within a mile of Anju and heard the firing. They were merely marching in the ordinary course of relief.

The officer in command of the detachment, however, quickly realised the situation, and advanced briskly in fighting formation, taking the enemy to the south of the town in the rear. This was too much for the Russians in that section of the attack, and they rapidly retreated to the east, whilst the party who were pressing the defenders of the provision store so hard that in a few minutes more it must have been captured, ell back to the westward. A clear road was thus opened to the castle of Anju, and the reinforcement entered, receiving a very hearty welcome. The great moral encouragement received by the garrison was perhaps of even more value than the additional seventy rifles, sorely as these were needed.

After a brief consultation the two officers came to the conclusion that they should now take the offensive. Accordingly, they sallied forth with about half their force from the south-east

LANDING-PLACE AT RIKWAHO—WOUNDED FROM THE YALU

gate, and after exchanging a few shots at close quarters with the enemy, made a bayonet charge, causing their adversaries to fall back before them to the higher ground about 400 yards distant, where they remained until it became dark. The Japanese hung on to the ground they had won, and planned an attack, to be carried out at daybreak next morning. When it became light, however, it was found that during the night the enemy had withdrawn his forces. The Japanese losses were three men killed and seven wounded. The enemy had consisted of three squadrons of Cossacks under the personal leadership of Lieutenant-Colonel Matoriroff, which were stiffened by one company of mounted infantry from the 1st Regiment of Siberian Sharpshooters and one company of mounted infantry from the 15th Regiment of Siberian Sharpshooters. The total strength of the Russians amounted to 500 men. Their losses were two officers and fourteen non-commissioned officers and men killed, thirty-five wounded, and one non-commissioned officer and one man captured.

The Japanese Post Commander was an old non-commissioned officer who had been promoted to the rank of officer at the time of the late Chinese war. When the time came for him to be promoted captain he had sent in a petition earnestly submitting to higher authority his own respectful opinion that he was not good enough to command a company of infantry. He proved good enough, however, not only to command a company of infantry, but to obtain a "writing of honour" whilst fighting in that capacity.

Chapter VIII – The Attachés Are Entertained

Fenghuangcheng, May 19th, 1904. — I have been anxious for some time past to ascertain whether the experiences of the Yalu have caused the Japanese to modify in any way their attack formations, but it was only this morning that I got the chance for which I have been waiting. Had I asked officially, the authorities would have got up some cut-and-dried affair for all the attachés, which was not in the least what I wanted. However, at 7 a.m. on this May morning I was out for a solitary ride, when I came upon a company crouching in a depression of the ground, evidently prepared for business. Part of the hollow in which I made this lucky find had been used as a grave-yard by the Manchus, and its large earthen mounds lent the men good cover both from observation and from fire. I determined to die at my post sooner than miss such a chance of seeing something, and so I drew rein and waited at a respectful distance to watch events. The captain came up at once, as I thought he would, ostensibly to say "good morning," really to find out who I was and what I wanted. This is the sort of occasion it is some good being a General. Anything less would, I am persuaded, have been politely requested to withdraw;

but luckily my man spoke German, and I was able to impress him with the fact that I was rather senior to be thus summarily dealt with, and that I was withal merely an innocent seeker after knowedge. Thence forward, he became exceedingly courteous, and explained to me without reserve the instruction he was about to impart. First he told me about his company. It had taken an active part in the attack on Chiuliencheng, and from its position with the reserve had been able to observe all that passed at Hamaton. The captain was well satisfied with the German system of extensions. They might be a little wasteful of life, but for as long at any rate as the Russians used even closer formations, he was not in favour of any great modification in the direction of taking up a wider frontage.

All the other company officers and one-third of the men were to-day on garrison duty. He proposed, therefore, to make use of the morning's exercise to instruct the non-commissioned officers. With this object he intended to fall out at an early stage and let them conduct the proceedings to their conclusion. The idea upon which the company was going to work was that they were the left unit of an attacking Japanese army, and that the enemy opposed to them occupied the extreme right of a Russian defensive position. About 1500 yards to the north of the graveyard, where the company now lay crouched in concealment, rose a wooded hill some 100 feet in height. On this the Russian right company was supposed to be entrenched. For the first 200 yards between the Japanese and their objective the ground was undulating, and offered a fair amount of cover. Thence onwards, up to the foot of the enemy's position on the hill, the country was one dead level of freshly ploughed land, heavy to traverse, and quite devoid of cover. It was, in fact, just as ugly a bit of terrain as any soldier could desire not to have to cross under fire.

On a sharp word of command and the flourish of the captain's sword, a section, or one-third of his company, darted out of the hollow, made a forward rush of about 100 to 150 yards, then flung themselves down and opened fire. I jumped on my horse and cantered along with the section. The men ran with a rapidity which was positively startling. Each private soldier was going his very level best, with that tense concentrated look on his face which it takes at least a cricket-ball, football, or polo-ball to call up to the countenance of the average Anglo-Saxon.

The intervals between men were about one yard, but as the attack progressed these intervals tended to decrease until, here and there, they were actually shoulder to shoulder. Very little time was spent in firing, and in less than a minute another rush carried the section to within 1200 yards of the position. The first section was reinforced from the rear during its next advance by the second section, which came up at a great pace and prolonged the line to the left. To my surprise, this reinforcing section covered the whole distance of about 400 yards in one tremendous spurt. Our men could not do this, nor could the men of any Continental, Asiatic, or American army I have seen. The advance then continued by 100 yards rushes of alternate sections, only one minute at the most being allowed for shooting at each halt. At about 800 yards from the enemy's position the line was reinforced by the remaining section of the company, which had meanwhile worked its way independently, and without any firing, to the cover of a farm-house which stood just to the right of the general line of advance. This last reinforcement prolonged the line to the right, and thenceforth the rushes were made by alternate half companies until the final, stage, which was reached at 350 yards from the supposed Russian position. Here the bugles sounded; the men fixed bayonets and charged in with a loud shout of "Wa-a-a!" dashing over and through the deep plough with marvellous swiftness, and not subsiding into a walk until they had got two-thirds of the way up the hill.

It was explained to me that the Russians were supposed to have been seen quitting the position; thence the short time spent in rifle fire at the latter stages and the unreal acceleration of the exercise generally. I doubt whether the whole thing took more than a quarter of an hour. Certainly it did not last twenty minutes, although, having stupidly forgotten my watch, I could not time it exactly. It was clear that less attention was paid to the correctness of the drill and to the precision of intervals than to the amount of energy and intelligence brought to bear upon the exercise. Altogether I must say this attack gives one furiously to think. It is the Dervish charge made by men with modern rifles in their hands, and supported by an artillery which seems to be almost ns good as ours in personnel and better in material.

In congratulating the captain, I asked him if he did not think that the employment of so dense a formation from the outset must entail useless loss of life? He gave me the stock German answer, "You cannot have success without loss of life," and I did not argue the point. Undoubtedly, the formation was far too dense. If the same front had been taken up by one quarter the number of men from the 1500 yards point at which the section started until the 1000 or 800 yards stage was reached, then the enemy's attention would have equally been absorbed by the more extended firing line, and the bulk of the company might have joined in at 700 yards without having lost a man. I am not overlooking the theory that it is essential to cram rifles into the firing line as early as possible, so as to dominate the defender's fire from the outset, but my experience has taught me that with an enemy under cover the losses incurred by such a method are certain, whilst the gains are more than problematical. Moreover, the theory falls to the ground absolutely as applied to the attack I have just witnessed, for I don't believe the men fired ten rounds a rifle during the whole affair. It comes to this, then, that the Japanese expose four of their soldiers to fire at the long range, where one would suffice. If, of course, the men need the touch of a comrade's elbow to carry them on, that is argument I can understand; but I do not believe this of the brave Japanese, and to get the ranks half emptied by rifle bullets and shrapnel at long ranges is not the best way to conserve weight for the bayonet work at the end. The advance, as I have seen it practised to-day, is a formidable modification of its original German model, and the element of speed which has been introduced might prove exceedingly demoralising to second-rate troops, especially if they had not great confidence in their own marksmanship at the short ranges. I believe, nevertheless, that such a system of attack must fail against such marksmen as the British infantry have now become. If the Russians shoot as badly as they are said to do, then, of course, all is possible.

The one disturbing and novel factor in the problem is the truly astounding rapidity with which these little men covered the ground. It is impossible to ignore the point that if they exposed four times as many men to fire as seemed to be necessary, on the other hand these men ran so fast that they were only exposed to fire for a quarter of the time any other troops would be exposed. This combination of infantry tactics with cavalry speed of movement, which might, as I have said, demoralise second-rate troops, might also considerably disconcert even the very best of gunners and marksmen. Given, however, a handy short rifle, and men accustomed to snap-shooting, I do not see how the Japanese could hope to sprint across the last 300 yards, those fatal 300 yards, in the slapdash style I have just witnessed, unless, of course, their artillery had completely got the upper hand. However, with luck I shall live to see. I've no doubt they'll manage it somehow; for if ever I saw the combination of moral and physical qualities which go to make the true warrior, here they are. Perhaps my perceptions are dulled by two years of England spent under Capuan conditions and amongst people in whose eyes money and the luxuries it can command bulk somewhat largely; but, after all, I have lived the best part of my life in camps, and I feel as if I could still recognise the true metal.

May 29th, 1904. — I had a great time yesterday, and I must hasten to jot down the impressions left on my mind before time blurs the sharp edges. All the military attachés were invited by Kuroki to meet the Divisional Generals and Brigadiers of the First Army at a grand luncheon party. Attired in my blue serge, kept for important occasions, I led the representatives of Europe and America into a long anteroom in the headquarters block of buildings, where we found the Generals, each accompanied by his chief staff officer and an adjutant. They were standing by the wall, all in a line, very stiff, and awaiting presentation. The three Divisional Generals were, of course, the big guns of the occasion, and I must try if I cannot describe them. It is a relief to feel that even if these remarks should ever come to their notice, there is no fear at all of hurting any one's feelings. The Japanese standard of looks is entirely different to ours. The gay, gracious apple-cheeked damsels admired by the foreigner are vulgar and common to their own fellow countrymen, who prefer a girl with a dead pale face and a thin aquiline nose. A few days ago I told a Japanese friend that I thought a certain staff officer "looked rather like a weasel," and the remark was considered a compliment and repeated to him. Under such conditions it is evidently possible to speak not only the truth, but the whole truth.

The first of the Generals was Hasegawa, commanding the Imperial Guards. He has a determined martial type of figure and countenance — handsome, too, in a *vainqueur*,[*] almost swaggering style, but spoilt by his eyes being set too close together. His Brigadiers are Watanabe and Asada. Watanabe does not convey at first sight an impression of much energy or force. He looks very intelligent, but not strong either in physique or in character. When he speaks he discloses a pleasing personality, and one of the most human from the foreign standpoint that I have, so far, met in the army. He is popular with every one, and I am told he actually does possess his full share of energy and decision. Asada is a soldier-like man, a little bigger in figure and feature than the average Japanese officer. He is shy with foreigners, and escapes as soon as politeness permits from any contact with these uncanny creatures.

The second Lieutenant-General was Nishi,[†] commanding the Second Division. He is very lean and yellow, and his skull reveals itself clearly under the tightly drawn skin. He looks, in fact, thoroughly dyspeptic. He is all smiles, but their effect is lessened for Europeans by the fact that he never seems to be able to look any one in the face. With him were his Brigadiers, Okasaki, of the 15th, and Matsunaga, of the 3rd Brigade. The former struck me as being every inch a soldier. He is a well-built man of forty-eight or fifty, with an open, round, small-featured face, and very frank, agreeable and downright manners. He gives me the feeling that he must be kind and good, and it is only necessary to talk to him for a few minutes to see that he is sensible. The latter — Matsunaga — is more of the sailor type. Immensely powerful and broad in the beam, bluff, hearty and jovial.

---

[*] "Winner."

[†] Promoted after the battle of the Yalu.

The last of the Lieutenant-Generals was Inouye,* the Commander of the Twelfth Division. He is a quiet old man of a reserved disposition, who prefers his own company to that of any one else, and regards a social function as an affliction of the worst description. Sasaki and Kigoshi, his Brigadiers, were not present. As I have seen them within the past few days, I may as well describe them here. Sasaki, of the 12th Brigade, is not altogether unlike Okasaki. To their friends they are probably quite different, but I am, of course, only giving here the most impressionist impressions conceivable. The Japanese, and one or two of the attachés who know him, say he is open and exceptionally kind and courteous. I may remark that the highest praise a military attaché can give to any one is to say he is open. Kigoshi, who commands the 23rd Brigade, is a small man, whose proportionately still smaller face and features have a sharp, inquiring, almost fox-like expression. His looks, they say, do not belie him, and he is remarkably clever, cultivated and smart; withal exceptionally accessible, kind and hospitable.

In addition to these great men from outside, the whole of the staff of the First Army headquarters was, of course, present. The most notable of these are Colonel Matsuishi, Assistant Chief of Staff, a very good-looking man, and Major Fukuda, head of the Operations Section, not so good-looking. Both have been made in Germany, and bear all the insignia. Another European-trained officer is Colonel Hagino, chief of the Intelligence Section, who has lived seven years in Russia to prepare himself for his present duties; a middle-aged heavy-looking man, with a greyish beard and regular features. I have already come in contact with him several times. He is a most conscientious, hardworking, considerate personage; a trifle overcareful, ponderous, and precise from the military attaché point of view, but obviously upright and reliable in every sense. He tells me he likes the Russians very much, as he never received anything but kindness at their hands all the time he was in their country. Lieutenant-Colonel Kurita, head of the section which deals with transport and supply, is another German

---

* Promoted after the battle of the Yalu.

product. Hard-featured, dry, rather repellent in manner, he is nevertheless, I think, a very sensible and well-intentioned official, although, so far, I have not succeeded in getting him to commit himself to anything at all outside strict business lines. Major Watanabe, the Camp Commandant, has made his studies in France. He is vivacious, extra polite, talkative, and quite a typical Frenchman, imperial and all, on the outside; whether there is an inside I cannot yet conjecture. Major-General Kodama, the Commanding Engineer of the army, speaks only Japanese. He is very popular, and is also, I believe, a talented individual. He seems to be always in good humour, and appreciates and makes jokes which are sometimes good and oftener bad. Colonel Matsumoto, commanding the artillery of the army, is not a wildly exciting personality. He has nothing to do, so it is whispered in my ear, beyond arranging for the supply of ammunition from Japan. Judged by foreign standards, he would hardly seem likely to achieve any very startling combinations or evolve any very brilliant ideas. Why, I wonder, does a senior artilleryman sometimes tend to ripen into heaviness, whereas the artillery major commanding a battery is the pride of the whole profession of arms? This is one of the insoluble mysteries of the Service, only equalled by the failure of so large a proportion of the splendid squadron leaders of the Bengal cavalry to blossom out into dashing Brigadiers. Each generation sorrowfully admits the men at the top of the tree are effete, bat proudly points to the rows of coming men; yet ever the succeeding years continue to tell the same sad tale.

The last of these high officers I can remember is Taneguchi, the principal medical officer. He ranks with a Major-General and is German by training, as are all the medicos with the army. Even if they have not been to Germany, they must speak a little German, as all the Japanese medical scientific terms are borrowed from that country. The Japanese invariably adopt the German method instead of the British method whenever there is a difference. There are various little divergencies as to washing wounds before the first dressing; the number and depth of stitches for abdominal wounds, whether one for the muscle and one for the skin or only one to do double duty, &c. Indeed, I am told that an expert can tell at a glance by merely seeing the way a Japanese doctor cleans his hands after operating that he is German trained and that he thinks in German on medical subjects. In fact, in all these points they are German, and not British. I freely confess that, to me, this is a depressing discovery. Whatever the cause may be, the fact is indisputable that, despite all their wealth and titles and British prestige, our doctors have been handsomely worsted in that open world-competition of the nations where Japan crowns the victor with sincerest flattery. The Island Empire offers us a mirror, if we would only have the courage to look into it, where we may all see ourselves. Any people who are copied by the Japanese in any department of life may feel fairly secure of being momentarily near the top of the tree in that particular. But let them beware of too hastily concluding on this account that they are necessarily as good as their crafty little pupils. On the contrary, as a young Japanese officer slyly said to me when we were discussing their navy, "It is only in the dose and eager application of copying that we light upon the shortcomings of our models."

Even as I write it occurs to me that a certain amount of explanation for this preference for German military doctors may be found in the fret that just when Japan was casting about to modernise her army the Germans were fresh from the experiences of 1866 and 1870. There is certainly something in this, bat still if the British were equally good I think there would be at least one or two English-speaking doctors with the army. As for Surgeon-General Taneguchi, who led to this digression, he is gaunt and thin; he looks very wise, and as he never commits himself to anything more explicit than a grunt in a German accent, followed by precipitate flight, I will leave him the benefit of the doubt.

Although I already knew the headquarters staff pretty well and had exchanged calls with most of the Generals, the introductions were solemn and slow. After I had made the four or five obligatory bows and salutes to the first on the rank, I observed with some dismay that there were still at least a dozen of them standing in one long line as stiff as a row of pokers. Fortunately, a humorous incident came to relax the painful solemnity of the function. The next General to advance to my encounter was T. Kodama, the Commanding Engineer, and as he came forward he happened awkwardly to kick over a big earthenware bowl, making an alarming smash and commotion in the silence wherein these introductory ceremonies were being so religiously conducted. Now in Japan these bowls are used to grind up beans for soup. They are called *suribachi* or rice mortar, and the soldiers at the battle of the Yalu had christened the similarly shaped conical hill on which the Russians had a battery by the name of Suribachiyama or rice mortar mountain. So I said to the Commanding Engineer, who was as upset as the bowl itself by the clatter he had made, "Having knocked Suribachiyama on the Yalu to pieces, you have got into the habit and must now upset and kick Simbachiyaraa wherever you meet it." At this mild jest all the stiff row unbent, and the rest of the proceedings was robbed of some of its terrors.

Whilst we were waiting for luncheon the three Divisional Generals and myself were ushered into the small room in which I had first met General Kuroki. There we smoked cigarettes and chatted to the Lieutenant-General and to the Princes Kitashirakawa and Kuni. Luncheon was then announced, and having got into this small room there was the very devil to pay before we could get out. First, the two Princes had a bowing and protesting match, and it took at least two minutes until, moved by one impulse, they made a simultaneous bolt for the door and got through after a scuffle, Kitashirakawa leading by a short head. Next, Kuroki wanted me to go out before him, which I absolutely refused to do, and eventually he yielded and moved on. At his heels went Nishi. Every one knows these hesitations. They occur in a small way even in London. Nine times out of ten, every one is grateful to the man who, whatever his precedence, takes the lead. Eventually Hasegawa, Inouye and I managed, notwithstanding unlimited modesty, backing, shying and refusals, to find ourselves somehow on the right side of the door, and then we went to lunch without more ado.

It was pouring cats and dogs, or, as the Japanese put it, "spears and arrows," as we squelched through ankle-deep mud to a big flat-roofed marquee, bravely walled in with Japanese flags. Across the top of the tent, inside, were the Bising Sun and the Union Jack intertwined, the patterns suiting admirably, so much so that I could not help imagining how we might make a very handsome combination for general use over the Asiatic Continent by entering the fully risen sun in the centre of the Jack. The table was decorated with the flags of all the nations of the world save one. Not on the flags though, beautiful and significant as they doubtless were, did our eyes eagerly fix themselves. Absence, they say, makes the heart grow fonder, and lines of glorious already unfamiliar dishes invited an attack which I longed to lead *in propriâ personâ*.*

A European might as well fill his stomach by a dream of dinner as by a dinner of rice. He may go through the motions of eating and feel for the moment as replete as an alderman, but, alas I only for the moment, for before half an hour has passed he has to begin to tighten his belt. Here, however, was something that promised solid and, as such things go, enduring satisfaction. There was chicken, ham, cold pork, pink jelly and sponge cakes. Wines, labelled Sauterne, Château Lafitte and Pomery, circulated freely, and were equally freely absorbed. Although our feet were steadily sinking deeper into the slush and mud, our spirits rose steadily upwards until they touched boiling or speech-making point. Then General Kuroki rapped on the table, that familiar sound making my blood run cold with all its detestable associations. He said he welcomed the foreign attachés — he had meant to give them a nice treat, and was very sorry and disappointed that the rain should have spoilt his trifling entertainment. It was evident that I should have to answer, as every one's eyes were fixed on me in an uneasy questioning manner.

In all that assembly of eighty persons there was not one besides my own officers who could speak English, so I had to choose between German and French I felt like a tailor who is offered the choice of sword or pistol to fight a duel; that is to say, both were equally bad weapons in my hands for such an alarming purpose. I took French, and went at it slap-dash, telling them that in England the best protection against bad weather is considered to be a skinful of the champagne with which his Excellency had been pleased to make us so completely water-tight. I added some jokes, which seemed exceedingly funny at the time, but which in cold

---

* "In my own person."

black ink are merely silly, and wound up by saying we should do our best to repay his hospitality, if ever we had the chance, in Europe or America, as the case might be. It is a terribly difficult thing to speak on behalf of a cosmopolitan crowd. The only chance is to be purely personal and trivial. On impersonal and important subjects the aspirations and ideas of our party are naturally as far asunder as the poles.

After this oratorical display every one walked round the enclosure, in which the luncheon tent was pitched, to admire and marvel at the elaborate decorations which had been carried out by the soldiers in honour of the occasion. Here, indeed, was a striking contrast to anything that could be done by the fighting forces of other countries. The courtyard, which was about fifty yards square, was divided into sections, upon each of which men of the military train had been working busily for the past two or three days, with the result that they had succeeded in producing something between a Japanese Madame Tussaud's and a natural history museum. One group of exhibits consisted' of a gigantic frog, a snail and a snake. They were several thousand times larger than life, and quite alarmingly realistic. The frog was entirely constructed of sacking and Wellington boots; the snake was pieced together with many hundred Russian horse-shoes to represent the scales; and the snail was compounded of saddlery and cooking-pots. The conjunction of these three creatures conveyed some familiar fairy-tale to the Japanese mind. I was told what they were at the time, but I fear I have already forgotten the legends.

In another section of the enclosure was a truly remarkable representation of Chiuliencheng and the battle of the Yalu. The Manchurian hills were quite recognisable, being delineated by blankets sewn together and moulded over packing-cases and boughs. In front of the mountains real running water had been brought in to represent the Yalu and Aiho rivers, which were crossed by the pontoon and trestle bridges, complete and on a scale strictly in proportion to the general landscape. All details were given, even replicas of the notices on the bridges which had been put up at the time of the battle, saying that artillery and military trains were not to use them, but must go round by the fords. Next to this battle-field in miniature, with its rivers and mountains all complete, was a similar subject on a larger scale. It was a cardboard presentment of the preliminary formation for attack on the left bank of the Aiho. The guns were shown by cigars on paper wheels, and the infantry and cavalry were drawn to that scale on cardboard, and then cut out and ranged in battle array. I found this toy really instructive, as it gave a capital idea of the dispositions adopted. Japanese soldiers are certainly very clever. Our men could never do such things. Our allies are thoroughly artistic, and in their work they manage to show a deal of fancy as well as a keen sense of humour. It is always fair to remember, however, that this is a conscription army, containing all classes of men. Just outside the gates is the grave of a dentist who had been conscripted as a military coolie, and who, poor fellow, was, I suppose, less equal to drawing carts than back grinders.

No doubt there are artists, poets, merchants, lawyers, doctors, and all sorts and conditions of men who have found themselves on the outbreak of war suddenly turned into hewers of wood and drawers of water and food for the army. It must certainly be pretty hard for a prosperous shopkeeper, for instance, who has been accustomed to treat himself to a "hurl" in a rickshaw whenever he felt tired, to find himself dragging a similar conveyance; but it is not more hard than it is for the men of even higher standard who drew the fatal number, and then qualified themselves for the reserve of officers. These reserve officers, many of them, have been in America or China, and have worked up flourishing businesses. Now war breaks out, and they have to follow the flag. This conscription is certainly a hard tax. Fancy if one-fourth, the best fourth, of our adolescent manhood were earmarked for the army, and then, whether they were taken or not, or wherever they went or whatever position they attained, were liable for service and lived with the sword, so to say, hanging over them! Those who imagine that the casual Briton will accept such a system one day before he is forced to do so by some terrible catastrophe either know singularly little about their fellow countrymen, or, what is more probable, nothing at all about conscription.

In the evening we went to see some Japanese acting and Chinese juggling, got up specially for the military attachés. It was astonishingly good. I had the honour of sitting next Prince Kuni, and I never saw any one enjoy himself more thoroughly. It was explained to me afterwards that in Tokio it would be impossible for so high a personage to see anything so rude and unrefined, and that probably it was the first time in his life he had heard vulgar jokes and seen a vulgar dance. Not that they seemed vulgar to us; quite the contrary. The entertainment struck me as in many ways resembling the sort of thing got up by our own men in the intervals of a war. I remember something strangely similar at Bloemfontein, in South Africa. Here, at Fenghuangcheng, the theme was almost always martial. Arms and the hero had it all their own way.

One play, however, was less elementary than the others, and had an allegorical, political plot. An old woman (excellently well played) had a beautiful daughter, who was a Geisha. The Geisha was Korea, the old woman was China. A young man impersonating Japan came to woo the Honourable Miss Korea. Old Mrs. China, however, wanted more money than he was willing to give. She was opposed, therefore, to any formal engagement, although the girl was more than willing to reciprocate Eventually young Master Japan loses his temper, and after a very lively altercation with old Mrs. China he gives her a severe beating. It appears for a moment as if these highhanded methods were going to succeed. Mrs. China adopts a whining tone, and the girl sits on his knee. Meanwhile another young man, Russia to wit, comes a-wooing, cuts out Japan with both the fair ladies, and gets him chucked neck and crop out of the house. There he stays for some time, a most disconsolate object, listening to all the love-talk through the thin paper walls of the house. At length the poor rejected lover is stung by the sound of these endearments into consulting his friend, old man England, who is reputed to be fabulously rich. He begs him to give him the money which is necessary if he is to compete for the possession of the girl, and tries to persuade him that it will be to his interest to grant him such assistance. The Honourable Mr. England buttons up his pocket pretty tight at this appeal, but he takes the opportunity of making him a very fine speech full of noble sentiments. He tells him not to sit weeping there any longer listening to the love-making of his rivals but to remember he is the descendant of warriors, and that steel will do his business just as well as gold. The house applauds, and young Japan is transformed by this advice from a whining suppliant into a creature filled with fire and resolution. He also makes a speech, then gets his dagger, and apparently despatches them all except Mr. England. It turns out, however, that he had only pretended to wound the girl, and she only makes believe with a piece of red cloth that she is covered with blood until she is quite sure that her mother and late *fiancé* have both ceased to breathe.

I could not exactly follow the feelings of old Mr. England at this part of the business, but he appeared to be well pleased. The acting was first-rate. The actors were simple military coolies, but, as I have already noted, these coolies are drawn from all classes of the population, so very likely they are regular actors by profession. Certainly, to judge by the plot, they know something about the alliance regarding which their officers are careful to assume ignorance.

During the play our Sergeant-Major Ishido slipped quietly away, and peeping through a window saw the last Russian officer prisoner taking his dinner. It seems the unfortunate boy only arrived in the Far East from European Russia on May 1st. He is calmly confident that Russia must win in the long run, which is rather touching; and all he asks is that he may be exchanged for one of the numerous Japanese officers who have, according to him, already been captured. The Japanese tell me this is all nonsense, that no Japanese officers have been captured and that none will be captured, as it is infinitely easier for them to die than to suffer such an indignity. I hope our gallant allies are going to raise our standards a good many degrees in regard to all such questions. Ishido said the young Cossack appeared to be having a splendid dinner, and that there were two bottles of beer on the table. When he was made prisoner he had twenty roubles on him, and the Japanese have allowed him to spend this in buying food and tobacco to supplement his rations. I suppose this must be the young fellow Kuroki told me about the other day.

After the entertainment had come to an end, I walked home with two young Guardsmen, who chatted about the surprise of the Russian wounded when they found they got food and drink from the Japanese instead of the mutilation and torture they seemed to •expect. They also dilated on the wickedness of the Cossacks, who, when they were in Korea, killed the splendid bulls used in that country for draught and Ate them half raw, instead of satisfying themselves with the porkers produced by the trembling inhabitants. I must say I could not regard this conduct as very heinous, for the Korean pig is indeed a ghastly brute and the bulls would be hard to beat even in Leicestershire. However, I regret to say, our allies have very little sympathy with flesh eating in any shape or form, and that, I suppose, is one of the reasons I had to punch a fresh hole in my belt the other day.

Chapter IX – The Chinese General Pays a Visit

June 1st, 1904.— Not much doing. General Fujii came and told me as a secret for myself that Kuropatkin was marching down troops to try and relieve Port Arthur, and that General Oku, of the Second Army, was marching north to meet them, so that there would soon be another battle.

Had a visit from Colonel K——, who expressed much surprise at Alexieff's flight from Port Arthur. "It would have been," he said, "a good place for him to die in." The Japanese hate Alexieff very cordially, but, as far as I can make out, they seem rather to like Kuropatkin.

There has been some practice shooting here with the captured Russian guns. The targets were white screens at 5000 yards, with ten live pigs tied in front of them. The pigs which escaped the shrapnel had their throats cut afterwards and were eaten by the gunners. I am not supposed to know anything about this, but my friend who gave me the information tells me further that the Japanese are highly pleased with the guns in everything except their weight. They have captured a few Russian horses, and they have some Canadian horses bought at Tientsin at the time of the Boxer troubles. These they will eke out with some stout Chinese ponies, and they hope to he able to get along until they capture their next lot of guns, when they will have to send over to Australia, unless they are lucky in getting a good number of Russian horses at the same time.

June 8th, 1904. — Not much has happened during the past week. I have a lovely ride every morning before breakfast, and now I shall be able to indulge in excursions of some length, as our bounds which confined us within a radius of one mile from the city walls have been considerably extended.

This indulgence, like most others, only makes us long for more. We gaze at the woods, mountains, valleys and streams beyond our demesne much as Mrs. Bluebeard must have regarded the closed door of the forbidden chamber; but I am personally persuaded we shall see everything in due course if only we have patience, plenty of patience. This is a sermon I am perpetually preaching, but the text is not very popular at present. Apart from professional curiosity the country is in itself beautiful enough co tempt the lover of nature to explore its further recesses. At the present time the uncultivated hills and glades are carpeted thick with English grasses, daisies, dandelions, and buttercups, and the woods are bright with may-blossom standing out in masses amidst clumps of dark fir-trees and very light green oaks. There are but few birds and apparently hardly any game. A half-tame wolf lives in the outskirts of a village near here. The only birds we have noticed up to date are the great grey shrike, some golden orioles with a beautiful mellow note, cuckoos, goldfinches, magpies, mynahs, hawks, kingfishers, woodpeckers, grey wagtails, as well as the ubiquitous sparrow. I got this information from Vincent, who is a fanatic on the subject. He will run miles through the forest to get a closer view of anything he thinks may be an ornithological curio.

On the 4th we had a visit from General Tangei, Commander of "the Chinese Eastern Flying Column of Mounted and Dismounted Troops," as was printed in bold black ideographs on his pink visiting card, an inch broad and a foot long. Tangei is a fine-looking man of about fifty, dressed in a most becoming costume.

He wears a round white hat, from which hung down behind two long plumes of red horsehair. I think there was a peacock feather somewhere too, but I can't exactly remember. His clothes were of purple and khaki silk, and at his side he carried a French sword fixed into a Russian gold lace sling belt. He said he had bought this from a Chinese General at Mukden; but he looked uneasy when I asked him about it, and I expect it was given him by the Russians. He used to command 4500 men, but has now only 200, as the Russians fixed that number as the maximum. I got on very well with him and quite enjoyed my talk. Certainly the Chinese are much "easier" socially than our friends the Japanese.

I paid my return visit this morning, and as I had given warning I was coming I got a grand reception. We walked up the main street of the city, then went down a narrow lane to the left. Directly we turned into the lane our ears were assailed by loud and barbarous sounds, as if Mr. Wood's orchestra at the Queen's Hall had mutinied and each musician was not only playing his own tune but endeavouring to smother all the others. On entering a courtyard we saw that the cause of this uproar was a band of some fifty performers costumed in black and yellow, and wearing saucy little straw hats with cheap pink ribands stuck coquettishly on one side of their heads. I wish very much indeed I could transfer to paper some faint notion of how supremely ridiculous these children's straw hats appeared in the midst of what was otherwise a rather imposing spectacle. The guard of honour was about 100 strong, uniformed in plain blue, their arms being old-pattern Mausers. These they handled remarkably well, and they stood quite steady in the ranks as I walked down the line inspecting them, and asking some of them questions which they answered very intelligently. The officers were next presented, and then we sat down on red-cushioned chairs, drank tea out of octagonal glasses, and had a much more rational conversation than we usually do with the Japanese on similar occasions of ceremony.

I was just about to take my leave when "kashi to saké"* was announced, and we were ushered into another room where vodki,

---

* Cakes and wine.

THE CHINESE GENERAL.

Russian beer, red wine and cakes were laid out on a polished table of dark grained wood. I ate cakes until I began to feel ashamed of myself, but they were delicious, and the General seemed to be well pleased at my appetite. The cakes are just like shortbread made with rancid butter. Our host now produced a Chinese atlas of the world, which was, so he told us, his favourite study. As, however, he mistook Afghanistan for England and thought India was an island, he knows hardly as much as a boy at an English public school. After all, what is a trifling geographical inaccuracy such as this compared with the monumental misconceptions I myself have cherished for the past thirty years about the men of China? I have now met several leading Chinamen, and if General Tangei and the Fenghuangcheng Taotai are exceptionally good fellows, there is not one of them that fails to strike me with surprise by his cleverness and efficiency. The farmers about here and their dependants, wives, womenkind and children, are also most admirable people as far as I can judge. They are in fact a startling revelation, and I have a feeling in their presence as if I had all my life been systematically duped and misled by the stereotyped European and American delineation of the Heathen Chinee. I think I have always felt some curiosity about these people, and I remember questioning some of my soldier friends who took part in the Boxer business as to what they thought of them. As far as I can remember, with the exception of Vincent who was in Pekin and loves them, every one dismissed them with a couple of words, dirty devils, beastly swine, or something of that sort. Possibly the Manchurian Chinese are a different race. It seems incredible that these dignified, clever, often noble-looking men and these sensible, practical, hard-working women should have served as originals to the Chinese depicted in Western literature. I admit that some of their habits are dirty. They keep the inside of their houses neatly enough, although doubtless far below the Japanese standard, but one yard outside the door is as good as a mile to them from the sanitary point of view. Otherwise I can only discover in them qualities so admirable that they fill me with alarm when I think how far we have fallen behind them. To me these Northern Chinese are an astounding set of fellows. I have never in my life even imagined a set of people so passionately, feverishly devoted to work. There is no eyewash here; no extra efforts under the eye of the master or mistress. All have some share in the profits, and they all of them put their backs into what they have to do as if their very lives depended upon it. Energy is only half the battle; these men and women possess high individual intelligence to guide that energy. To be realised, their farming must be seen. Such furrows! Such promise of crops with each sprouting corn-stalk tended like a rose-bush in the garden of a duchess! And all this energy, strength and intellect available for about tuppence ha'penny per diem!

When the Russian officials saw this beautiful land, where even the mountain crests ai'e being coaxed to bear crops; where nothing is disorderly or wasted; where the tile-roofed farms peep out from their encircling orchards, each a peaceful picture of neatness and exceeding prosperity; when they saw all this, it seems strange that they could even have imagined the plan of bringing over their own feckless moujiks to farm side by side against such competitors. To court such proximity was obvious madness. But for how long is distance going to shield any of us? Now that our poor little planet keeps shrinking, shrinking, beneath the embrace of electricity and steam, for how long is it going to remain large enough to admit of one man doing for shillings in one part of it what another man does for pennies in another part of it? When I see a Chinaman mending a road or unloading rice bags with apparently twice the energy of the Western working man and for less than one-tenth of his pay, I wonder how it is all going to end? We seem actually, like the Russians, pressing on to meet the danger.. At the mines of the Witwatersrand all artificial barriers have been removed by our own statesmanship; and now that white, black and yellow are about to tilt at one another in fair field and with no favour, it ought soon to be seen which is the winning colour.

What then are these barriers? They are the safeguards imposed by fleets and armies; by what is called militarism. What but the army and fleet serving under the Stars and Stripes lends any significance to a declaration by American labour leaders that Chinese coolies must be excluded from the States? But for those military forces the least that even a pacifically inclined China could do to retain its own self-respect would be to retaliate by ordering every American ship, concessionaire, merchant, missionary and globe-trotter to disappear from the Middle Kingdom within twenty-four hours. If a generation hence China found herself faced only by Europeans and Americans who had beaten their swords into policemen's batons she would then be j&ee to set to work and starve them to death with celestial serenity.

Under conditions of perpetual peace and that industrial and social equality of all men without which perpetual peace is a fantastic dream, the Chinaman as I have seen him in Manchuria, is as capable of destroying the white working man of the present type and driving him from the face of the earth as was the brown rat of destroying and driving out from England that excellent but less strenuous, less omnivorous, black rat who had preceded him. The Socialists who gaily flaunt the words "unity of labour" on their banners, little dream where their theories would lead them to in practice.

Is it then to be the fate of the white man ultimately to sink and disappear? It depends, in my humble opinion, on whether he has the good sense to close his ears to those who tell him that wars and preparations for wars are pure evil, and that pure unadulterated commercialism would be an earthly Paradise instead of the limbo of dead souls which I personally should conceive it to be. It is heroism, self-sacrifice and chivalry which redeem war and build up national character. What play do these heroic qualities find in the ignoble struggle between nations for commercial supremacy, with stock exchanges and wheat pits for their battlefields? It seems to me that the working men must take their choice. They must, as the world seems at present constituted, either accept militarism with its occasional wars, or else elect for one long cruel life and death struggle against a rival worker who will certainly ruin them in the end.

I suppose this is a well-worn theme, but the Chinaman is quite new to me, and it is more than likely that the simultaneous movements of Chinese to South Africa and of Japanese towards the heart of China may bring many questions to a head which have hitherto seemed exceedingly dim and remote. Everywhere I see these wise efficient Chinese, placing all they possess unreservedly at the disposal of the Japanese. I can see they look upon them much as a wise dachshund regards a bristling, pugnacious, excitable and yet rather shallow fox-terrier. Undoubtedly the Chinaman bows low before the power of the sword in the hands of a martial race, but it seems to me also as if there might be an after-thought; an idea that Japan is too near akin to be able to take upon herself the burden of directing China without thereby losing her identity and becoming herself Chinese. I must watch the trend of the relations between the two peoples. I ought to have opportunities enough if I get through all right.

Meanwhile General Tangei saw me to the door, and then, mounting one of his gaily caparisoned ponies, sat to Vincent for his portrait.

On my return from our visit I found a note from Mr. Maxwell, of the *Standard*, enclosing a literal prose translation of the Japanese war song, which the men seem never tired of singing. He has heard I can turn a rhyme at need, and he asks me if I can in any way poetise what seems to be a hopelessly prosaic composition. My attempt is deplorable, I admit, but such as it is I set it down.

> Sons of Nippon, down with Russia —
> Down with Russia! Lay her low!
> Faith and Justice Russia scoffs at,
> Russia is our mortal foe.
>
> All her kindred Christian nations
> Hate and fear the Russian power,
> Ever, like a ravenous wolf-pack,
> Seeking what it may devour.
>
> Fair Manchuria's triple province
> Scarce dismembered, ere the hordes
> Press down Southwards towards Korea
> Brandishing their bloody swords.
>
> Russia 'twas that urged, "for peace sake
> Render back the Liao-Tung!"
> Scarce had ink dried on the treaty
> Than another tune was sung.
>
> Shameless; breaking every promise,

Grasping countries far and wide.
All the world was turned against her
For her lawlessness and pride.

Comrades, can we live forgetting
Comrades — gallant comrades — slain
Ten years since? Oh, Powers ancestral,
Did your life blood flow in vain?

There must be some end to evil
Even in our life's short span:
Now is the hour — for we are marching.
Down with Russia! On, Japan!

Vaunt not Russia's vast dominions —
Boast not of her legions bold:
What is vastness in a desert?
What are hosts whose hearts are cold?

Thousands starving: traitors lurking:
Coffers empty: lack of grain,
How shall Russia stand against us,
Stand the long and weary strain?

But our own dear precious country
'Neath its Emperor can combine,
A thousand years, and more, unbroken.
Stretches back his Heaven-bom line.

We are true and we are loyal,
"Roshia," as its letters say,*
Melts before the morning sunlight;
Melts and swiftly fades away.

March then with our sunlight banner
Waving proudly in the van:
March beneath that glorious emblem.
Down with Russia! On, Japan!

---

* The Japanese characters for "dew" and for "Russia" are identical.

The Chinese General Pays a Visit 145

June 9th, 1904. — Rode round the outposts, after having bidden a sad adieu to two charming country-women who have shed the radiance of their countenances over Fenghuangcheng for the past two or three days. The visit of Miss McCaul and Miss St. Aubyn has been a delightful break in the monastic order of our life. They have not only been very clever to get here but also lucky, with a luck only equalled by ours in meeting them. Not a single Japanese soul feminine is allowed even at the base. The Imperial Princesses themselves are restricted to making charpie in Japan. The ladies of the Far East do not seem to exercise powers at all proportionate to their fascinations. I have asked Japanese officers about female influence in the army, and they simply do not understand the question. There is no such thing. It does not exist. Not that favouritism of other sorts is unknown, although it seems, judging by what Lieutenant told me the other day, to take an upside-down shape, like so many things in Japan. He said he had such a number of important friends in the army that it would be necessary to promote him more slowly than his contemporaries, in order not to give the others reason for talk. I believe he was speaking the simple truth, and it quite fits in with the fear I constantly notice amongst the Japanese of one another's opinions. I think myself that even female influence is preferable to this sort of moral cowardice.

To return to our charming compatriots, one little incident connected with their visit appeals to me very forcibly, as it gives voice to a feeling which is beginning to take possession of me, although, Heaven knows, I have struggled hard against it. A Japanese lady, Madame K., accompanied our fair visitors.

She appeared to me to be one of the most enlightened and sympathetic little women I had ever met. In her ideas regarding the raising of the status of Japanese women, the necessity for universal higher education, &c. &c., she might be described as an advanced American. She seemed fond of the two ladies she chaperoned, and certainly they were extremely fond of her. One night, *à propos* of nothing special, but apparently carried away by an irrepressible burst of feeling, she exclaimed to them, "Do tell me the truth! You do not like me at all! All your kind manners are put on; a part of a game! A foreigner is incapable of liking a Japanese. I feel in my very innermost being we are people apart!" Is this then the naked truth, seen vividly for one instant, just as, by the lightning's flash, a traveller might behold a frowning fortress barring the road along which he had till then been cheerfully marching to claim the hospitality of a neighbouring city? Or, is the forbidding obstruction a mere optical illusion, which needs only to be boldly faced to vanish like an enchanted castle at the challenge of the knight who perseveres? Perhaps it is still too soon for me to say. But of one thing I am certain, namely, that the path to friendship, trust and intimacy between a Western and a Japanese has not the smooth and easy gradients I so lightly allowed myself to believe amidst the feasting and *fêteing* of the cosmopolitanised society of Tokio. The whole scale of emotions, tastes, ideals, ambitions and wants is set to a totally different pitch, and just as a used-up Sybarite cannot expect sympathy for his sufferings from a hungry tramp, so our more complex sensations seem idle waste of thought to the Japanese soldier of comparatively few, but proportionately intense, ideas.

The outposts were interesting. They curved in a semicircle about five miles to the east, north and west of Fenghuangcheng. There is no essential difference between our own system and that of the Japanese. The approximate line to be held is designated by the General Officer commanding, who allots a section to each division; the Officer commanding the Division, in consultation with the headquarters staff; the Commander of the Artillery and the Commanding Engineer fixes his own line more definitely, and tells off sub-sections to his Brigadiers, who, similarly, decentralise portions of these sub-sections to their own Regimental Commanders. This procedure applies only to positions which are likely to be held for some time. On the march the outposts may be furnished by the advance guard, as with us.

Neither cavalry or artillery was included in the composition of the force forming the outposts I visited today. The nine available squadrons of cavalry were all pushed out far away in front, some of them as far as twenty miles, which is just as it should be. The guns were brigaded in Fenghuangcheng, some five miles behind the epaulements and pits which had been carefully prepared for them a few hundred yards behind the line of resistance. There was no field of fire for artillery, the ground being so broken and

The Chinese General Pays a Visit   147

confined that in many places they could not shoot over a mile. This was a weak point in the position, and one which was only partially compensated for by the fact that the enemy also would have had great difficulty in bringing field guns into action except along the bottom of the valleys. The line of resistance was usually identical with the line held by the supports.

A Visit from the Governor of Fenghuangcheng

The Japanese have a great deal to learn from us in the matter of visual signalling. To get their guns up in time they depend entirely upon telephones, telegraphs or mounted orderlies. With their cavalry so far ahead, and only five miles to traverse, there is not probably much danger of anything going wrong in this instance; but the advanced posts have no heliograph, and even the men on the observation posts cannot signal properly, but are only able to make two or three conventional flag-signs, such as "enemy's cavalry is approaching," &c. If there was a British army here it would be in close heliographic communication with the Second Army and with Korea, instead of relying, as the Japanese do, on that reed so easily broken, the telegraph wire. Luckily the Russian scouts are not like Afridis or Boers, and the Chinese are friendly. Otherwise their trusted wires would be cut in twenty places every single night, and their repairing parties would be sniped when they went out to put things right in the morning. There is no doubt at all that in some respects the Japanese are free from the difficulties and anxieties which have usually beset British commanders during their recent campaigns.

I thought the selection of the ground for the outposts was admirable. Facilities for observation, resistance, counter-attack, or retirement were combined with economy of men. The trenches were generally along the crest lines of low hills, the infantry in front, the gun pits a few hundred yards behind on a higher level. There were splinter-proof shelters everywhere, with tunnelled passages leading out from them to the trenches or gun pits. The soil was disintegrated sandstone, which lent itself very well to solid excavations of this sort. In all the infantry trenches there were niches cut at intervals of a yard for ammunition. Ravines were filled up where they would have afforded cover to the enemy, and woods were cut down and turned into abattis.

As I have said, there is little difference between the Japanese system and our own. With them, as with us, sketches are made by young officers of the sections or positions entrusted them. The proportion of men allotted to picquets, supports, and reserves, the detached posts, examining posts, patrols, night positions, &c., are similarly arranged in both armies. When, however, a descent is made from the system to the execution thereof it is better to confess at once that we can never get our men to do the digging work which has been put in by the Japanese since they have been here. The semi-permanent nature of these fortifications prove that the Japanese did not mind asking their men to take unlimited trouble, and to work desperately hard on the mere off-chance of an attack. Indeed, immeasurably more labour and thought were put by the Japanese into their works which were very unlikely to be seriously attacked, than were employed by the Russians, with an equal amount of time at their disposal, in preparing the Yalu position which was practically certain to be attacked.

In this respect the British resemble the Russians rather than the Japanese. Not even the imminent acknowledged approach of the most desperate danger would get as much spade work out of a British force as has been done here by the First Army since it came to Fenghuangcheng. Least of all would Colonial contingents shine

The Chinese General Pays a Visit 149

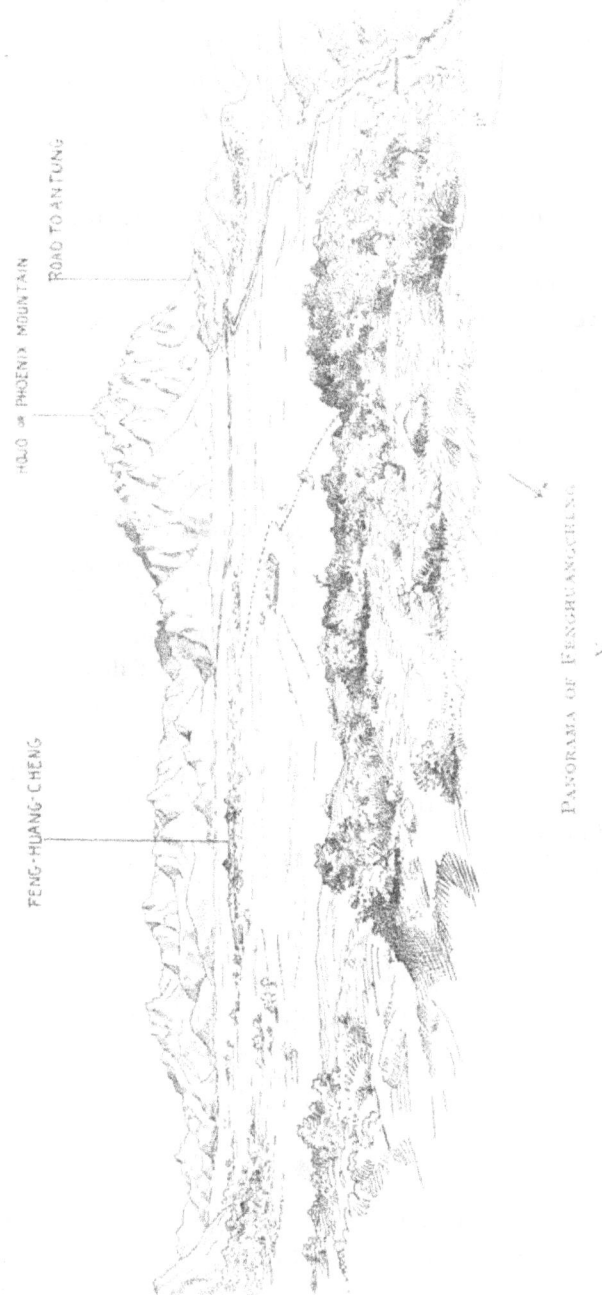

in such a comparison. In saying this it would be ungrateful not to acknowledge the enduring mark fixed by some of them on the face of the Western Transvaal at the end of the war, or to forget that those solid redoubts were dug daily, or rather nightly, for at least a week, after much longer marches than the Japanese have even contemplated making up to date. On the other hand, if the Colonials are fair, they will acknowledge freely that it was most terribly against the grain. They did it because they had excellent officers to lead and coax, drive and persuade them, and because they were good keen fellows. But they hated it like poison, considered it was outside their bargain, and if the operations had lasted two days longer they would have certainly eased off, and their prey would have escaped them. Now I say that henceforth ability to dig is going to rank high in the ever-lengthening list of qualifications demanded of a good soldier — cavalry, artillery, or line; and that although our city-bred people can never acquire the natural taste or physical aptitude for this sort of work which is possessed by the Japanese rustic, a little more practice would make them very much better. It is just as honourable for the men of a horse battery to practice digging gun pits once a month, instead of once a year, as it is to knock their horses' legs to pieces galloping over hard ground, and coming into action at the end of it with considerably more bravery than discretion. As for the Japanese, to judge by what their artillery did on the Yalu, they must be capable of sinking like moles into the earth before the very eyes of their enemies.

June 11th, 1904. — All the Press censors have come to ask me if they may make copies of my version of the war song which they have seen in Mr. Maxwell's letter when be sent it off This is highly Battering. I feel elated, and begin to realise a Poet Laureate's sensations.

(At this stage of my diary many pages are filled with accounts of petty obstructions and mortifications. No doubt the tedium of a long halt did not tend to minimise their importance, and in any case

The Chinese General Pays a Visit   151

I mean to cut them right out, on the principle that all is well that ends well. I do, however, insert some extracts from a letter that I wrote at this time, as they may throw a light upon our difficulties as they presented themselves to me then. The letter was intended much more as a convenient means of letting army headquarters know, through their Press censors, where the shoe was pinching me, than as an appeal for outside assistance. We were beyond the reach of outside assistance, and were entirely in the hands of the field army. We knew, of course, that the Press censors told army headquarters everything that we wrote.)

Extracts from my Letter.

...In the estimation of the First Army, England seems absolutely nowhere. Where the officers are at all touched by foreign influence, that influence is either German or French. The former class is the most numerous, and the clique belonging to it are nicknamed by their comrades either "Kaisermen" or, sometimes, "High Korrar."* There is no doubt in my mind that the French-speaking Japanese tend to have French sympathies, and the German-speaking Japanese German sympathies. This is only human nature, seeing that they have spent several of the best years of their life in these countries, and have been kindly treated by their instructors. On the other hand, the one or two rare exceptions who have been to England (or even to America) are our friends, and never lose an opportunity of making some reference to our alliance, which the others pointedly ignore...indeed, if it was not for the consideration always gracefully conceded to my senior rank, which can, on occasion, be so twisted by me as to serve some practical purpose, there would not have been the smallest difference of any sort made in our favour. As an example, the other day I asked a few simple questions about the lines of communication, and I was informed very politely that such information could only be given to all foreigners simultaneously. Now, in practice I do not in the least mind sharing bits of news

---

* Japanese pronunciation of the English words "High collar."

with my friends of all nations. But, if the principle is put forward as a general working principle then it is surely wrong. ...Here we come back to the language question. If we want to tempt Japanese students to England we must be content to compensate them for second-rate educational establishments by granting them increased facilities in some other direction. I am sure England could do more than she does to attract young Japan to her universities, and India could help a great deal by inviting officers to big manoeuvres and attaching them to district staffs at important military centres. It would pay us to pay them to come. What a pity Cecil Rhodes did not live a few years longer! We should have had Japanese at Oxford then, instead of some other strangers. ...I do not, of course, question the necessity the Japanese are under of maintaining complete secrecy on many points. Indeed, I should be very sorry myself to see them follow our bad example in this respect. But mystery about a question like the organisation of the lines of communication is mystery misplaced, and to say that everything I am told must also be told to every one else is a flat negation of the alliance as a factor of any significance, actual or potential! It would be quite easy for the First Army headquarters to give me some facilities. I have two Japanese-speaking officers with me — Vincent and Jardine. Several expeditions have moved out from here during the past few days, and it would help me quite a lot if I could get permission for one or both of them to go out and see some skirmishes or affairs of cavalry patrols, instead of remaining here tied to my apron strings...

Chapter X – General Fujii Talks

June 15th, 1904. — The shot I blazed off at the Press censors yesterday has brought a real rocketer tumbling down out of the troubled sky. I have had a two hours' visit from General Fujii, Chief of the General Staff I The others had gone out for a walk, and I was sitting alone in our doll's house with Jardine when I heard the clatter of a sword in the brick pathway leading down between the peony bushes, and seeing the great man I felt sure his visit was connected with my letter. I was right too, although, from first to last, no direct reference was ever made to it.

The General began with polite conversation whilst the servants flew to borrow tea and cigarettes from our friends the Americans round the corner, who were in clover just then. After a little he went on to tell me how much he had been worried that day. A foreign officer had complained to him of discourteous treatment, which turned out, as usual, to have been the result of the too literal and unintelligent reading of his instructions by a minor official. Fujii had then been obliged to go into the matter very exhaustively himself. I felt sincerely sorry for him. Here he was, Chief of the Staff to a great army, on which hung the destinies of Japan, compelled to spend his precious time, hours of it, in running around to pour oil on troubled waters; and, after all, the tempest which had troubled those waters was but the affair of a teapot.

I tried to imagine myself similarly persecute and hampered at Pretoria when I filled a similar position, and I could not but realise keenly what an intense nuisance we must all be to our unwilling but ever courteous hosts. Nevertheless, I hardened my heart by reflecting that it was their own fault for working through subordinates who are either unable to distinguish between the spirit and the letter of an instruction, or, what is more probable, will not take the trouble or responsibility of doing so. I felt that every one must consider how he can live before he can afford to consider over much how he can let live; and although I would have liked to leave the poor man alone to attend to his proper business, the instinct of self-preservation drove me to the attack. Accordingly I said, with reference to the incident of the other officer, that I had always found the Japanese soldiers of all arms extremely polite, and that I considered it a special compliment to be saluted, as I always was, by the men of another army. But as regards the officers, and especially the officers placed in immediate charge of us, and their interpretations of the restrictions placed upon us, I too had, I feared, to trouble him by making my small protest. It had been openly said to me that no distinction could be made in favour of the British attachés, but I could not but feel that the representatives of an allied nation deserved some little special consideration, even though they must be quite neutral in their actions. I was not asking to be told secrets, nor had I any desire to exclude other foreign officers from any information I might get, but I did object on a point of fairness and courtesy when —— enunciated to me the doctrine that all foreigners were alike from the Japanese point of view.

General Fujii listened to my harangue with that perfect good temper which makes it always so difficult to score off a Japanese. He proceeded to reply, with a humorous smile, that he was glad to find himself in general agreement with my views, and that I should very soon see he appreciated the special position of the British. For one thing he would send two officers of the headquarters staff to me on an early date to supply me with a full account of the working and organisation of the lines of communication; for another, he would now, on the spot, gladly give me permission to despatch two of my officers to pay visits of inspection to the columns detached on the right flank of the army at Aiyanmen, 47 miles to the north-east, and to Kuantienchen, 51 miles north-east by east, of Fenghuangcheng. Constant skirmishing was going on in these directions, so they ought to be able to see something of interest. As regards myself, he said General Kuroki would be only too pleased to authorise me to join any expedition whatsoever, supposing I cared to do so. It would only be necessary for me to express the wish, and it would be forthwith granted. Further, I might take it from him that the signboards forbidding foreign officers to enter certain gun parks and supply depôts were not meant for me, and that, if I would merely warn the general staff beforehand, I could henceforth go practically anywhere I liked. He then, probably intentionally, let the cat out of the bag as regards my letter by saying that although the senior officers of the army spoke no English, and although unfortunately there were no English-speaking men on the staff of the First Army, yet, going out to stay with regiments, I would certainly find a few of the younger officers who could talk to me in my own language.

Turning next to the map he showed me how detachments from the First Army were now beginning to press northwards. This was in consequence of two Russian Divisions, that is to say, 30,000 men, having advanced south along the railway against the Second Army. They had twenty-four guns, and had taken up an unprepared but naturally very strong position, just south of Telissu, which is a small town twenty miles east-north-east of Foochou. The position consisted of an amphitheatre of hills, having their only exit on the northern side. One of these Japanese Divisions was working wide on the west, and would endeavour probably to work round the Russian right and rear. If then the Russians could be cut off from the north we should soon hear of some heavy and important fighting. Indeed, unless the enemy had retreated, the battle would be taking place this very day. At such a crisis Mischenko ought to be employed either attacking the First Army or prolonging the left of the Russians at Telissu; but he was still in touch with our patrols yesterday and was idle, so that his force might be reckoned as having been wasted if the action at Telissu was actually taking place. Fujii went on to say: "The Second Army consists of three Divisions, one brigade of cavalry, and one brigade of artillery, that is to say, 40,000 men and 150 guns. It marched for Telissu from the line Pulienten-Shaoshiatun, and if it is victorious it should be able to join hands with our First Army. If it is not victorious, or being victorious is pressed hard after the battle by Kuropatkin with fresh troops, we must march at once to its help via Siuyen towards Kaiping, even if we have all our communications out from the Lienshankuan and Saimachi directions and have to starve on our way through the mountains. We have so far based all our strategy on the assumption that Kuropatkin must attack either the First or the Second Army. We have not thought it likely he would come to us, but I myself have never supposed he would be content to do nothing. That would have been too good to be true. You have inspected our carefully prepared outpost position. In case of attack we had hoped to hold it with comparatively few men, perhaps two-fifths of the army, whilst with the remaining three-fifths we would have delivered a vigorous counter-attack on the enemy, possibly from the left or centre, but probably from Aiyanmen or Saimachi. The entrenchments are, as you have seen, quite irregular and broken in outline, and the terrain does not admit of good artillery positions. Some of our staff officers conceived the idea of letting the enemy work close up to our entrenchments, and then delivering a counter-attack straight to our front, when they thought we could utterly destroy them in the close and broken ground of which we know every turn. However, I did not myself approve of such a plan. In the terrible confused *mêlée* which must have ensued anything might have happened. I am able to tell you all this to-day because the movement down to Telissu shows that the Russians have abandoned the idea of coming here, and that we shall have to go to them instead. Still, no one knows what may happen in the future, and I must ask you to keep these details to yourself.

"Since our flanking columns have been out they have had something like a dozen skirmishes, and in each of these the Russian Cossacks and cavalry have shown themselves pretty helpless and have been driven off with comparative ease. Although theoretically our enemy should have been able to concentrate superior forces at the point of contact it is we who have managed to do this on almost every occasion. There are 17,000 Russians at Lienshankuan on the south side of the Motienling Pass, and about 1500 of them are holding a position across the main road at Bunsuirei, ten miles to the south of Lienshankuan. No preparation is being made by the Russians to hold the Motienling, and if the result of the Second Army's fight is such as to enable us to work on the lines which seem to us strategically soundest, then, in advancing over that formidable pass, we should not meet much resistance. Facing the right column at Aiyanmen is Bennenkampf, who is at Saimachi with a mixed force consisting mainly of cavalry. Bennenkampf is always trying things, which do not seem to succeed. Still he does try. When General Sasaki went to Saimachi we had resigned ourselves to the unpleasant certitude that the Russians must succeed in occasionally cutting his lines of communication to the Yalu. Certainly we did our utmost to prevent such a contretemps by placing two battalions of Kobi at Kuantienchen, but we were not too hopeful. Nevertheless, we have up to date been entirely successful, and, far from the lines of communication having been interrupted, all attacks have been repulsed, and even the telegraph wire has so far received no injury. On our other flank Mischenko causes less anxiety than Bennenkampf, as he is much less active. In fact I might almost say that Mischenko has done nothing at all in his area. We have, however, sent a battalion out along the sea coast, five miles to the west of Antung, as a preventative measure, but so far all has been quiet in that direction. The total number of Russians in Southern Manchuria is probably eight Divisions, of whom we are keeping at least 35,000 in play, so, although we may have seemed to you rather quiescent, we are actually earning our bentos of rice. Two Japanese divisions are at Chouyuang, with a Russian mixed brigade facing them twenty-five miles to the north-west on the Haicheng road. Well, much will depend now on the result of this battle, if there is one, at Telissu. The Russians have only twenty-four guns, all of them field guns, and seeing we have six times that number I feel fairly confident as to the result. Whatever happens at Telissu the Russians are sure to fight a battle at Kaiping. It is a very strong position indeed, facing south. It can only be turned from the east, which is just what the First Army could very easily do from this base. We suffered heavily in taking Kaiping from the Chinese during the late war. As I said, the position faces south; and although light vessels can assist the assault by engaging the enemy's batteries from the west, certainly the most effective way of dealing with the problem will be for us to march across and turn the Russian left from the east. You understand I am speaking purely from the strategical point of view. When you have your conference about the line of communications you will see that you were not far wrong in applying for information on this particular subject, and that it involves other very serious difficulties, against which we are now struggling with our utmost energy. Indeed, it sometimes seems only too possible that instead of making daring and glorious strokes against the line of the Manchurian railway we may be doomed to remain stuck here ignominiously until the rainy season is at an end; but this, please, is only for yourself, and I would rather you did not tell even the other British attachés.

"Supposing Kaiping falls into our hands after a battle, the next place at which the Russians are likely to make a stand is the city of Liaoyang. The approaches from the south have already been strongly fortified, and we hear from Chinese spies that immense labour has been expended by the enemy in constructing a semicircular sunk way in rear of the redoubts for safe lateral communication. We hope the heavy rains will completely fill this up by the time we are ready to attack.

"There are 20,000 fighting men, including sailors, inside Port Arthur. There is not much danger that they will be able to cause a serious diversion. Up to date the fleet have been busily occupied in clearing Talien wan of mines. The big 11-inch howitzers for the siege of Port Arthur will all be landed there.

"Our own position at Fenghuangcheng is now becoming more satisfactory — perhaps I should say less unsatisfactory — from day to day. The tramway from Antung will be finished by the 26th inst.; when it is in working order it should carry almost one complete day's food for the army in each twenty-four hours. The tramway consists at present merely of rails, along which coolies can push the trucks by hand; hut the railway battalion has now finished its work on the Seoul-Wiju line, and we have made urgent applications for its transfer to General Furoki's command. If these applications are favourably considered, then it should not be very long before we have locomotives working on this first Manchurian section of the railway from Fusan to Liaoyang."

The General then asked me to do him the favour, as an ally, of criticising freely any shortcomings I might have noticed up to date. I replied, certainly, that I would willingly speak as a friend. The only respects in which the Japanese had so far struck me as falling short of our own standard were the quality and power of their gun horses, the uselessly close formations they adopted in the earlier stages of the infantry fight, and the dangerous reliance placed upon telegraphs and telephones to the exclusion of visual signalling. This was all I had noticed myself, but I gathered from officers in whom I had confidence that the drill and fire discipline of their artillery could not, like so many other parts of their military machine, serve as a pattern upon which our emulation might model itself.

He replied: "When the fight is raging our brains are inclined to get heated. It will be a great advantage to us at such moments to have a cool head, noticing all that passes, as a playgoer might witness a mimic battle on the stage at Tokio. Your Excellency must remember I will never resent any criticism you make, however severe it may be, for I am sure the intention will be good. You are certainly not wrong in the shortcomings you have noticed. We are not to blame for the weedy gun horses; they are our grievous misfortune. Artillery officers have long been urging that we should buy horses from Australia; but we are not rich like you, and we have not been able to meet their wishes. Nevertheless, I believe myself we shall have to come to it before we are done, unless we can capture a great number of horses from the Russians. We have already empowered divisional commanders to double the interval laid down in the drill-book if they consider it necessary, and I daresay as we go on we shall get looser and looser in our attack, especially if the Russians (who are far more inclined than we are to expose masses of men to fire) show any signs of assuming more elastic formations. The signalling certainly seems to be a weak spot. I can quite understand how useful it would be to have a heliograph on the top of Hō-ō-San (Phoenix Mountain),[*] communicating with Antung and Wiju. But Continental armies have also neglected visual signalling, and that is the reason our attention has not been sufficiently turned to the subject. No nation has practised this as much as you British, and now that we have come into a country like Manchuria we see the reason why."

The great Chief of the Staff then made his adieus, and left me filled with gaiety and exhilaration. I was perfectly well aware, of course, that his visit, including his flattering request for my criticism, was merely, or at any rate mainly, a well-considered method of smoothing my ruffled plumage. Moreover, when Fujii said that the other aggrieved foreign officer had put the sustaining power of the railway at twenty-four Divisions,[†] I realised intuitively, but with the most absolute conviction, that our conversation, which until then I had thought so delightfully confidential and exclusive, was going over ground he had already trodden stale that very afternoon in company with the representative of another Power. It is sad to be undeceived from a flattering misconception. I suffered a momentary shock, such as might be experienced by a wooer who discovers that the innocent-looking queen of his heart has already buried her second husband! But what is the use of diving into the mud at the bottom of the pool when the surface is pleasantly smooth? It is a depressing, and not a very profitable, act. Besides, I have certainly secured a very fine budget of news. A talk such as this is so valuable that I have now lost all sense of shame, and unblushingly whip out my notebook and pencil just like an American interviewer. I think Fujii likes me to do this. It reminds him of his attentive pupils sitting in a row when he lectures at the Staff College in Tokio.

The strategical position just now is certainly very interesting. I am glad we are on a broad front, a brigade of the Guards out by Siuyen, and the Twelfth Division at Saimachi. Thus we cover the north-west of Korea, Antung and the Yalu. We also dominate the

---

[*] The Phoenix Mountain, overlooking Fenghuangcheng.

[†] This refers to a portion of my conversation with the Chief of the Staff which I have thought it wiser to suppress.

coast of Manchuria at least as far as Takushan, and are in an excellent position to co-operate with troops landing at that place, or anywhere to the east of it. We are sufficiently far advanced into Manchuria to get a certain grip over its people, its supplies, and its transport — the latter a factor of supreme importance. We are also suitably placed for sending out reconnaissances and stirring up the enemy, and we have made a fair stride towards threatening the railway line north of the Russian main army, although, no doubt, we cannot do this effectively until we sit astride the famous Motienling. In short, we cover our own communications, threaten those of the enemy, and accumulate, not only supplies and carts, but also prestige amongst the Chinese. Only, the situation must not be too long spun out, or else the tide may begin to turn the other way.

This idea of Fujii's of perhaps having to halt here till the end of the rains is not only personally distasteful, I might say distressing, but a bad look-out also from the strategical and political point of view. I cannot believe it. I feel sure we shall get along somehow before very long. I think Fujii was especially interesting about Bennenkampf and Mischenko, when he showed how incapable they were of doing any harm to the communications with all their cavalry. Certainly the country is mountainous, and it gets worse to the east of the main Liaoyang road. The valleys become more contracted there, so we are told, and run mostly north and south. This, by the way, would interfere pretty considerably with Fujii's idea of rapidly shifting the bulk of the First Army to the right flank by Aiyanmen in case we were to be attacked. I don't think it could be done in any reasonable time. I should not, however, call it a bad country for cavalry. It affords a far better theatre of operations for an enterprising commander than a perfectly flat plain which many people erroneously suppose is a suitable terrain for mounted troops. It is too contracted for movements by brigades, or even perhaps by regiments, but it is what I should call a fine squadron country. I cannot help feeling a certain malicious satisfaction at learning that the cavalry has done nothing, as nothing could better bear out the correctness of the theories I have been so vehemently abused for advancing.

About half an hour after Fujii's departure I got a letter. It was from Colonel Matsuishi, the Vice-Chief of the Staff, authorising Captains Vincent and Jardine to start on the 17th instant for Aiyanmen, with an officer of the Twelfth Division who was going out to that place. I have thought it right to tell ——, who has hastened off to headquarters, no doubt to insist that all attachés must participate in the privilege. This is nothing to me. So long as my men go I don't really care myself who else does or does not, except that an individual always sees more and hears more than a crowd.

Chapter XI – The Feast of the Dead

Fenghuangcheng, June 19th, 1904. — Heavy rains have caused the departure of Vincent and Jardine to be put off until this morning, when they started in high spirits with the Italian and the Swedish attachés and an escort of four cavalrymen. I am glad they have got safely away, although their departure makes the place seem more than ever like some beautiful but inexpressibly dreary prison. I must say I am lucky in having three such attachés as Hume, Vincent, and Jardine. They are not only soldiers of high professional attainments, but thorough men of the world, who know the rough side of things, and are prepared to meet all difficulties in the proper give-and-take English public school spirit. Poor old War Office! No one will ever hear of these most excellent appointments; and yet, had they made but one real bad one, there is the machinery in the news-starved correspondents' camp over the way to blazon the fact over the whole of Europe and America. For, like a wolf, the newspaper correspondent does not become really dangerous until he is ravenous.

The day after the great interview, namely, on the 16th, Fujii sent over Captain O. to tell me that the battle had taken place all right at Telissu. The Second Army found the Russian two Divisions occupying the position Daiboshi-Joshisan, and attacked from daybreak on the 15th. At the same time the Third Division advanced along the railroad from Sukaton and joined in, whilst at 9 a.m. a brigade of the Fourth Division from Toryako, and at midday the cavalry from Kakaton, helped to envelop the Russians, with the result that they were driven back northwards after a severe fight. Several quick-firing guns, colours, &c., were captured. The Japanese casualties were 1000, those of the Russians are not yet known. No one here is in the least exultant. The victory is taken quite quietly and as a matter of course. I must say my own mental attitude coincides. I feel that the Japanese are not going to be beaten by any one just at present, and I perseveringly impress this view upon my employers and friends in nil my reports and letters home. Nakamura says that the names of the places mentioned by Captain O. are the Japanese renderings of the Chinese ideographs, so I don't quite know how we are to identify them when, some day, we get decent maps of the country.

Yesterday, the 18th, the whole army was given a present of saké and tobacco from the Empress. I was dining with Mr. Maxwell in the journalists' camp, about a mile from the city, and headquarters insisted I must have an English-speaking gendarme to escort me there and back. It spoils the great pleasure of a solitary walk in the dark to have a guardian of the law tramping after me, but there was no use trying to get out of it, and so we went. The dinner began magnificently. We had some splendid soup with dear little baby dumplings floating about in it. Then, after a long pause, some sardines, and then — nothing more. My host kept up the conversation very gaily, but I could detect a certain anxiety, which I fully shared, as to what was happening to the next dish, which was plainly set down in the bill of fare as nothing less than sausages. At last he could no longer restrain himself, and he called in loud tones of some acerbity for more food; there was no articulate answer, but we heard a sound of scuffling and remonstrance, mingled with stern, sharp orders, and looking out of the tent we saw my gendarme hauling off the Chinese cook by his pigtail. The boy who had been waiting at table had already been arrested and conveyed in durance vile to a temple hard by. The

The Feast of the Dead

infernal gendarme had got drunk off the saké sent him by the Empress; and now, in a loud voice, he announced his intention of arresting all the servants of the journalists. The only reason he condescended to give was, "He pray wrong time." I was in an awkward situation, as I felt it was a very poor requital of a generous hospitality that my gendarme should throw a peaceful camp into confusion; and yet, in Japan, a gendarme is a gendarme more rather than less when he is half seas over, and at all costs any resort to force was to be avoided. At last, after nearly being arrested myself in the process, I persuaded my irate guardian to release his prisoners and again the dinner resumed the regal tenor of its way. Never, I hope, will I be so ungrateful as to forget its sausages, chicken, tongue, and canned pineapple.

The pleasant evening wore away in much interesting talk, ranging over many subjects, for my host and I were old comrades of Ladysmith days. At last the moment came when I had to harden my heart to the task of taking my gendarme home. Luckily he was willing, and indeed as we were starting he condescended to say, "I begin to go." Eventually I got him back to my quarters, where he wound up his imperial jollification by trying to arrest one of the most conceited and self-important of the interpreters. This was a fearful joy to every one, and I gleefully left them all struggling and squabbling in the courtyard. A queer position certainly for a British Lieutenant-General; striving to bring home a drunken gendarme along a dark muddy road, dotted with sentries ready to open magazine fire at anything in the smallest degree unusual or irregular!

After Jardine and Vincent had started this morning I put on my blue serge and mounted my horse to attend the parade of the Second Division in commemoration of the dead — the "shokonsai" or "meet soul's feast" which is the literal translation of the Japanese name.

The Second Division, less one regiment, was massed on the level plain facing the green hill, on which was raised an altar laden with the offerings made by the soldiers to their dead comrades. I was in a reverential mood, certainly; but still, when I saw a large dried salmon with its tail in its mouth being set aside for men who, according to my own religion, could not possibly appreciate the gift, I could not for the life of me help raising that I was very hungry. Beside the salmon were baskets full of cakes, sweetmeats, vegetables and live fowls; altogether a very substantial repast. Standing next to the altar on the right were Prince Kuni and General Nishi commanding the Division, and I was put immediately on the left of the latter. Opposite us were the correspondents, one or two of whom were using kodaks. This seemed irreverent, but was not really more so than my thought about the salmon.

THE CEREMONY OF THE DEAD
ON THE ALTAR POST IS WRITTEN: "THE POSITIONS OF THE SOULS OF THOSE KILLED AND DEAD THROUGH DISEASE"

The first ceremony to take place was that of the Shinto religion, and it began by a venerable priest waving a wand over our heads, I believe for much the same reasons for which a priest sprinkles a congregation with holy water at the commencement of a service. Then more and more offerings of food were brought and piled upon the groaning altar, with pauses and upliftings and ceremony, until there was no space upon it for any more. Thereupon Nishi advanced, and, in the strange chaunting tones affected by the Japanese on such occasions, read the funeral oration, not so much in honour of the dead, as directly addressed

The Feast of the Dead 167

to the dead, who were supposed to be (and who shall say they were not?) actually present amongst us. He praised them "soft and low, called them worthy to be loved," and remembered for ever. In fact, he assured them of everlasting life in the memories of their fellow countrymen. This is a sentiment which appeals to the Japanese soldier. He cares, so far as I can see, nothing for the applause of crowds, or for banquets or feasts, and not very much indeed for any actually substantial reward; but to him the hope of fame after death is a very real thing. Speaking as a stranger, as one who necessarily can but see through a glass darkly, I am struck with the feeling that this sense of participation in a life after death is to the soldier an incentive in life, and makes death his great opportunity. To the Japanese soldier in fact the dead lion is one thousand times more enviable than the live dog.

At the close of the speech I was invited to follow Nishi in laying a sprig of pine-tree* on the altar. I narrowly watched the number of bows made by the General and the number of steps he took, and think I acquitted myself creditably. As the last offering was placed upon the altar the massed buglers of the Division blew the salute, and then the troops presented arms, sloped arms, and marched back to quarters. They had been too far distant to hear the funeral oration, but they could see what was going on; and I, for one, felt very conscious all the time of the reverential presence of these 10,000 Japanese soldiers.

The official ceremony was now over, but the General and his staff still lingered in the vicinity of the shrine, and as I was hesitating whether to go or stay, an officer said to me in a casual manner, "There is another informal sort of religious ceremony about to be performed; if you would care to stay you are very welcome, but you must understand that it is nothing which really matters." Naturally, I said I would stay. This informal ceremony, which did not much matter, turned out to be the Buddhist service. The chief priest, an imposing figure of a man, brought up a brazier filled with charcoal and set it down before the altar. A ceremony

---

* This sprig of pine represents, by its evergreen colour, eternity; and the white tape bound to it is typical of purity; both well-known Shinto signs.

then took place by which, though I could not follow its sense, I was far more impressed than by the preceding Shinto service. The ritual seemed to me simple and grand, whilst the singing approximated much more nearly to the European conception of sacred music. At the close I again followed Nishi to make my offering to the spirits of the dead; but this time, instead of laying a sprig of foliage on the altar, I let fall a pinch of incense into the charcoal brazier. Certainly the Buddhist ceremony seemed to me more solemn and elevating than the other, but I could hardly explain what it was that made me feel thus. No doubt Shintoism is a better military religion, exalting, as it does, patriotism and loyalty to the Emperor above any other merely civil virtues. It is strange to think that I, this afternoon, have twice bowed my head to strange gods.

If only my poor dear old grandmother could know that I have been thus participating in heathen rites it would make her turn in her grave. But, after all, there is good biblical precedent!

When the ceremony was finished I was led off to the royal tent by Prince Kuni, whilst the other attachés went to a separate tent further down the hill. Generals Fujii and Nishi asked me about South Africa and its climate; and they all laughed very heartily when I explained to them the disappointment of a horse from the northern hemisphere when it began confidently to grow its winter coat and then found summer coming on apace.

Fujii told me that he had just got a telegram to say that 5000 Russians were advancing from Saimachi to Aiyanmen. This is the very place Jardine and Vincent started for this morning, so it looks as if they were in luck. A regiment has been sent from here as a reinforcement. It is to do double marches, and they will be able to accompany it. The Generals then began to compliment me on having played my part in the ceremony as if I had been to the manner born. I wonder how much of this is politeness. I should like to think I had done it all right, as I know they attribute great importance to correct procedure in such matters.

I hope I am not doing them an injustice, but it seems to me they don't believe very much in their religion; are rather ashamed of it indeed, and anxious to make out that it is just a mere form and good for the private soldiers, but nothing more. I am aware that this is rather a sweeping deduction to draw from such a conversation.

The Feast of the Dead 169

Most people are reticent and disinclined to open their hearts to strangers on such points. The same might plausibly be said of us; how would a Japanese be impressed by the spectacle of a British subaltern marching a company willy-nilly into a church? Might he not consider such a parade as being almost the direct negation of religion? Still, as regards the Japanese, I can only give my impression for what it is worth. One of them said, "Logically the position of the priests is unassailable when they say that as the precepts of Confucius were good when he wrote them, they must therefore remain good for all time. What is once good is always good. Still, in a practical world, politics have to be considered, and politics never have been good and never can be good. No truly religious man can therefore succeed in politics. If you wish to stick by Confucius you must be prepared to be beaten by the man who carries no handicap of that sort on his back." This is the old difficulty of reconciling the worship of God with that of Mammon, put in a new form. A comment on the army made by another officer as we rode back interested me greatly; he said:

"Nos officiers sont trés bien instruits tandis que nos soldats ont encore les moeurs rudes et primitives. Cet amalgame constitue un instrument de guerre de premier ordre."*

Fenghuangcheng, June, 20th, 1904. — Went for a walk this morning with Hume, and came upon an unfortunate pony which was hopelessly stuck in a small patch of bog. It had evidently been struggling hard all night, and was now almost resigned to its fate, letting itself sink deeper and deeper into the horrible mud which would have engulfed it altogether in a few more minutes. A graas rope was lying close by, and we tried to pull the poor brute out with this, but after a little we realised that we 'Were not strong enough. The pony had now sunk down until its nose was level with the rushes and grass which grew on the surface of the swamp; and I saw with surprise that what I had once read on this subject was

---

* "Our officers are very well educated while our soldiers still have a rough and primitive way of life. This amalgam constitutes a first-rate instrument of war."

quite true, for, almost in the act of disappearing from existence it began to nibble this food with apparent high relish. I simply could not stand by and wait until only a few bubbles should show where an animal was being suffocated; nor could I pass along on the other side, as I knew I should imagine the end even more vividly than the reality. So Hume and I ran back as hard as we could for some distance to a place where we had seen a post furnished by the Second Division. At first the soldiers of the guard were doubtful and questioned us, as closely as Hume's bad Japanese would permit, as to whether the pony was a Government animal or only belonged to a Chinaman. I thought the urgency of the case justified me in going so far as to say that I thought it might be a Japanese Government pony, although I was fairly certain as a matter of fact that it was nothing of the kind. However, at last they determined to come, and when once they had made up their mind they came with a will, and ran with us at top speed, shouting and laughing like a lot of schoolboys. There were about fifteen of them. When they got to the spot they stripped stark, and never have I seen a more superb display of sinews and thews. Each man might have earned a competence as a sculptor's model. Every one says this Second or Sendai Division is the finest in the army. I well remember the bathing parades of my brigade at the mouth of the Bara valley during the last month of the Tirah campaign. There I used to watch the Royal Irish, the Duke of Cornwall's Light Infantry, and the Gordon Highlanders, splashing in the water, and amuse myself by distinguishing the different nationalities, as was perfectly easy so soon as they took off their clothes. The Irishmen were much more split up, longer legs and slighter, lighter bodies. The D.C.L.I. shorter-limbed and more sturdy; the Gordons the most square and thickset of them all. There were some very fine men in that fine brigade, but few I think to compare in muscular development and perfect proportion with these fifteen chance specimens of the Second Division. In one moment they jumped into the bog up to their waists, and lifting up the pony carried it out and stuck it under a hawthorn tree to recover at leisure, just as easily as ants dispose of a struggling insect ten times their size.

To-night, after dinner, —— came in to see me. I was pacing up and down our tiny garden, and fortunately the others were inside,

JAPANESE WRESTLING AT THE FRONT

working. He had been drinking saké or beer, and was very communicative. As he is usually quite hopelessly reticent I was greatly surprised and also very much amused by his antics. We were quite alone in the little garden, but he behaved exactly as if we were in a room filled with inquisitive people, and kept pulling me by the sleeve first into one corner and then into the other, whispering meanwhile into my ear so softly that I could hardly make head or tail of what he was driving at. I entered very heartily into the game however, walking on tiptoe and behaving as much as possible like Guy Fawkes on the transpontine stage. He must have taken an hour to tell me four or five things which might easily have been said in as many minutes, but still they were well worth a little time and trouble, provided they are not mere tipsy hallucinations, which I do not believe. He says the First Army will move in two days' time with its three Divisions on a forty-mile front. Rennenkampf is at Saimachi with five regiments of cavalry, a horse battery and a regiment of infantry, waiting to fall on the right flank of the advancing Twelfth Division, and to cut their communications so soon as they get far enough. It is so difficult for the Japanese infantry to close with the Russian cavalry that it is generally believed in the army that our advance is merely a blind to tempt Rennenkampf to make his dash, when we shall swiftly retrace our steps, and he will find himself trapped. Drawing me to another corner of the garden, to represent a change in the theatre of operations, he said that the Japanese had now four Divisions facing Kuropatkin south of Kaiping, as well as two Divisions besieging Port Arthur, making a total of six Divisions; or, with ours, nine Divisions. I am not sure, however, whether ho meant to include the Division we heard of lately as landing at Takushan. Finally, my friend, still holding me by the sleeve, led me from the last corner of the garden wall to a central position under the big tree. Looking fearfully round, and convincing himself that we were still alone, he whispered in my ear: "Don't you think we Japanese are a very wonderful people?" With all sincerity I replied: "Yes, indeed I do." He continued: "We can turn a Japanese peasant into a first-class soldier in three weeks, and the Germans cannot make their pudding-headed yokels into soldiers under three years; what do you think of that?" I said: "I think it is almost true." He replied, shouting in startling contrast to his previous conspirators' whisper: "It is quite true!" And with that he lurched out into the darkness.

> "God Lyasus, ever young,
> Ever renown'd, ever sung;
> Stain'd with blood of lusty grapes,
> In a thousand lusty shapes,
> Dance upon the mazer's brim.
> In the crimson liquor swim;
> From thy plenteous hand divine
> Let a river run with wine."

For therein obviously lies my best hope of getting news from the Japanese.

June 21st, 1904. — A message has just come in to say Oyama has been given supreme command, and that Kodama is to be his Chief of the Staff. This is good news for me, as I know them both, although I daresay Oyama and Kodama with the army will be very different persons from the Oyama and Kodama of Tokio.

The Feast of the Dead 173

June 22nd, 1904. — Hurrah! we march in three days' time. The advance is to be in three columns, each column in three sections {see Map XVI.*). The right column, which is the Twelfth Division, moves north *via* Saimachi; the central column, or Second Division, along the main Liaoyang road leading by Lienshankuan over the Motienling pass; and the left column, or Imperial Guards Division, along a track lying further to the east. The first section of each column is to march on the 24th, the second on the 25th, and the third on the 26th. All the other foreign officers as well as the journalists are to be attached to columns, and I alone am to accompany Kuroki and the headquarters, who will probably move from column to column, but at first they will keep behind the central or Second Division column. I have arranged that Jardine is to accompany the Twelfth Division, Vincent the Second Division, and Hume the Imperial Guards. This distribution of work should answer well, as they can watch all details whilst I remain at headquarters and try to keep in touch with the big questions. I shall find it lonely work I fear, but I shall be sustained by the feeling that I am doing something unique, and that, if I do not get to understand our elusive hosts a little better, I shall at least have enjoyed a chance of doing so which can full to the lot of but few foreigners.

June 24th, 1904. — All the attachés and journalists left this morning, and the half-hoped-for, half-dreaded moment has arrived when I find myself a solitary foreigner embedded in the heart of an Asiatic army in Asia. I wish sometimes I had a servant, even a Japanese soldier servant; my so-called interpreter is no manner of use for packing saddle-bags or getting things ship-shape for a march. —— came in early and proposed an excursion to the Hō-ō-San or Phoenix mountain. He suggested that this might distract my mind from solitude and regret for the departure of the others; a charming thought and a very acceptable proposition.

We started at 9.30 a.m., and rode up with a party of men of the military train who were nominally carrying our luncheon; really

---

* Publisher's note: A copy of this map can be found on pages 310-311.

coming to see the temple on the mountain top. As we were climbing the back of a steep ridge a nightingale broke into song from a thicket close on our left. All the little Japs were entranced, and stopped as still as stones to drink in every note of the *uguis*, which is the pretty liquid name they give to the warbler of the groves. Sometimes I see points of resemblance between Thomas Atkins and the Jap; sometimes I notice points like this!

At last we came to a splendid temple; a refuge lately for the women of the neighbourhood when they heard the clatter of the Cossack hoof. The priest told me there were wolves, bears, and panthers on the mountain, but that since two tigers had come and taken up their quarters in a big ravine some six months ago all the wolves and panthers had quitted. After the war is over I should like to come back here and pay my respects to these first cousins of my dear old Indian friends.

June 25th, 1904. — I took a solitary ride this morning, first refreshing my memory as to the Japanese rendering of "I am a British General, and I am allowed to ride here; I ride here everyday." It was just as well, as I was stopped several times. The new Kobi regiments, who have taken up the guards at the gates and on the roads, stared at me till their little eyes almost started out of their heads. They thought I was a Russian. These regiments have come from the wilds of Japan, and many of them have never before in their lives set eyes upon a foreigner.

I have cabled to India, telling them how I have distributed my three officers, and that I am now the only foreigner with headquarters. I have added that the troops leaving Fenghuangcheng, for what every one thinks will be a decisive battle, appeared confident and calm, just as if they were proceeding on an ordinary route march. No shouting or boasting, not even a trace of excitement. I like this trait of character in the little men. It is the old English style of ante-Mafeking days.

To-night, after dinner, an adjutant came over with a message from Kuroki. He said the General feared I might be feeling lonely, and he hoped I would come round and see him. As this was probably the last chance I would have for a long time of hearing

The Feast of the Dead 175

any music, he had sent for the Guards band to enliven the occasion. Nothing could have been more considerate or kind. I gladly accepted, and walked across to headquarters. The moment I appeared the band struck up the "Garb of Old Gaul," which is the grand march of the Gordons. I don't know how they found this out, but I was rather touched. It was a superb night. The moon was but one day from her full, and gleamed like a huge buckler of burnished steel in the silver-grey setting of the sky. I sat between Kuroki and his Highness Prince Kuni, and, notwithstanding their kindness, I felt as solitary as Marco Polo when he used to hob-nob with the Grand Cham of Tartary. We drank tea out of tiny cups of pale green lacquer. No one could have imagined we were on the eve of tremendous things; not from seeing us at least, although I confess that personally I felt impressed by the occasion. We were talkative and gay. I do like this: a few of our fellows can do it, but many of them worry and fuss until one feels that they ought to be served out with sleeping-draughts. All the same, I did notice Fujii pacing up and down in the semi-obscurity of the background like a restless spirit sunk in deep and anxious thought. As usual, we talked mostly nonsense. The Prince said to me he feared I had been terribly bored by this long halt.

I answered, yes; but that now I saw his Highness in khaki I was bored no longer, as I felt very sure that at last the battle was near. I told them about my morning's climb up the Hō-ō-San or Honourable Phoenix mountain, and of the tigers reported to be there. Kuroki asked me if I had ever shot any tigers in India. I replied, yes, that I had shot more than I had got. He inquired how such a thing could be, and I explained how I had usually gone out with men of higher rank than myself, and how the natives in those parts were so polite they had the habit of all calling out with one accord that the bullet of the most important official had killed the tiger, even if he had forgotten to fire off his rifle. Kuroki and the Prince seemed to appreciate this idea very much, and laughed immoderately. As soon as he could find breath the General said: "Never mind — never mind; you are getting very big, and soon it will be your turn to kill tigers without firing at them." The Prince inquired about Vincent's health. I said be had broken a tooth eating a fowl, and that he was suffering in consequence. His Highness observed that he feared the honourable captain must have been served with a tough morsel. I said: "Your Highness, that fowl was as old as the Hō-ō, or Phoenix, which inhabits the sacred mountain." At this also they laughed.

The band now began to play a selection of Irish airs, and Kuroki seeing that I was listening asked me whether the Irish people were fond of music. I told him, yes, that they liked simple sorts of music. He said, " I suppose this song is about some love-story?" It was "The Minstrel Boy," and I was indeed glad to be able to answer him: "Not at all, Excellency: this is no sentimental ditty: it tells of a young player on the *samisen* who left it behind and took with him instead his father's sword when he went to the wars." Kuroki was pleased; he smiled his charming smile, and said: A very appropriate air then for us to-night: we leave all our music here, and to-morrow we advance with the swords of our ancestors!" From Kuroki this is quite a long and elaborate sentiment. Shortly afterwards I made my salaams and withdrew. Now I must go to sleep, so as to be fresh for my early start tomorrow. I should love though to sit another hour in the little peony garden, of which I have grown quite fond. This last night the moon seems trying to give me an ethereal vision to carry away with me as my memory of Fenghuangcheng. Beneath the floods and floods of azure light she pours down upon the queer pointed roofs and pagodas, they borrow I do not know what of mystery and enchantment, until I could believe myself in the city of Aladdin and his wonderful lamp. Well, even if I had the fabled lamp, there are only one or perhaps two better things I could wish than to march to meet the Russians with 50,000 chosen warriors of Japan! Certainly the moon tonight has something almost uncanny about her brilliance. To my mind comes that great line by a great Frenchman:

"Les yeux sinstres de la lune."*

---

* "The sinister eyes of the moon."

Chapter XII – On the March at Last

June 26th, 1904. — Started for Hsuehliten on the main Liaoyang road at 7 a.m. The Second Division, or central column, should have arrived there yesterday. The Imperial Guards who constitute the left column are marching along the road further to the east, and the Twelfth Division, or right column, advances on Saimachi. The First Army is thus extended on a front which, with its flanking guards, covers about fifty miles, each column marching up a narrow valley separated from the others by high mountain ridges, which are practically impassable for troops in any formation. These dispositions are obviously quite necessary, but they are not on that account less dangerous. They are necessary because the roads, or rather tracks, are so narrow and bad that a Division is the maximum which can be fed for any length of time by such an artery. They are dangerous because they afford an opportunity for brilliant generalship to the Russian commander, who, if he can manoeuvre with celerity, decision, and secrecy, ought to be able to occupy two of our columns whilst he throws an overwhelmingly superior force upon the third. In any case here we are fairly off on our adventurous march, which seems even more splendidly exciting than I thought it would be, in contrast with our long and tiresome delay at Fenghuangcheng.

It was a lovely morning when we started, but it has now begun to cloud over. Now is 9.30 a.m., when I have off-saddled for half an hour in company with the headquarters staff of the army, which I caught up about about five miles from Fenghuangcheng. This headquarters seems a very small unencumbered group compared with the unwieldy staff establishments with which we began the South African War. One or two of them may be behind with the baggage, and one or two may be in advance with the troops, but altogether we have here only fifteen officers, with their "bettos," or grooms, and an escort of five gendarmes. The whole cavalcade is entirely unpretentious, quiet and businesslike; not a touch of Napoleonic pose about it. I have never given a complete list of our staff, and think this is a good opportunity to put down the components which together form the brain of the First Army of 42,000 men:

> General Officer Commanding: Marshal* Baron Kuroki, who commanded the Sixth Division at Wei-hai-wei in the war of 1894-5.

> Chief of Staff: Major-General Fujii, who was three years attaché to the French army. Later on he was military attaché at Vienna, and his present peace appointment is that of Director of the Officers' School.

> Assistant Chief of Staff: Colonel Matsuishi, whose peace appointment is that of Professor at the Officers' School, and who has served a certain time in Germany and has seen London.

> Operations Section: Major Fukuda, who has served three years in Germany; Captain Yoshioka and Captain Kinoshita.

---

* His actual rank is full General, but all ranks of the First Army speak of him by the title of Marshal.

Intelligence Section: Colonel Hagino, who has spent seven years in Russia, and Captain Hikida.

Supplies Section: Lieutenant-Colonel Kurita, who has served three years in Germany, and Captain Saito.

Adjutant Section: Major Twamitsu, Chief Adjutant; Captains Kuroda and Shibayama, A.D.C.'s to General Officer Commanding; Captain Omura, Adjutant to the Operations Section, and Captain Miage, Adjutant to the Intelligence Section.

Camp Commandant at Headquarters: Major Watanabe.

Commandant Royal Artillery: Colonel Matsumoto.

Commandant Royal Engineers: Major-General T. Kodama.

Chief Paymaster: Colonel (ranking with) Oyanagi assisted by one captain and one lieutenant.

Principal Medical Officer: Major-General (ranking with) Taneguchi.

Chief of Military Police: Captain Niire.

So far the country we are passing through is the usual river valley land of Manchuria; rounded, wooded hills 500 to 1000 feet high, covered with thick almost impenetrable scrub, low trees and bushes of an intensely vivid green. There is something very distinctive about Manchuria, and it would be impossible to imagine one's self in any other part of the world I have visited. I think this special individuality of the country is derived from the shape of the mountains, many of which are like sharp-peaked pyramids. Even the long ridges which they send down into the valleys often also terminate in a very characteristic little pointed knob. The result is to give the impression of a countless multitude of sugar-loaves of all sizes, covered with green velvet. The road lay parallel with the stream. When I say "parallel," I mean generally parallel, for our course wound in and out with the lie of the land, and continually took us across the water. Every flat place is cleared, and is now becoming luxuriant with crops of millet, beans and peas. The road bears traces of the passage of the Second Division. The culverts of light logs are broken, or else the mud and branches with which the logs were covered have been worn away into awkward ruts which increase the difficulties of the poor little military coolies who are manfully hauling away at their army carts. Here and there one of these carts lies broken, also an occasional Chinese cart; but so far we have come across no dead horses, although I expect every moment to see one or two lying there to furnish food for the crows and magpies, which are the only birds I can see.

Later. — How heartily some of my dear friends in London would laugh if they could see me now in this farm-house, sitting dusty and dejected, whilst an eloquent Chinese lady with pinched feet pours over me the vials of her wrath! She is coated with twenty years of dirt, but still she is not so unattractive as might be imagined. I have been sent on here with an interpreter, and she is anything but pleased to have me billeted upon her. However, I am submissive and meek, and I think she is quieting down, as she has just brought me a lovely pale green duck's egg, saying, "There, you lazy loafer, I suppose that's what you want?" or something to that effect. An egg is an egg, and hard words cannot make it anything else, any more than soft words can butter parsnips. And, after all, what is a woman's abuse so long as she is not your wife? It did not make Alfred the Great any smaller.

There is a strong family resemblance about these Chinese houses. They generally consist of two or three large rooms, well roofed, with big rafters and millet-stalk thatch, or sometimes tiles. There is always a raised dais on one or both sides of the rooms which is called a kong." A flue passes under each dais, and the smoke and heat of the kitchen fire being led through this, converts it into a stove. This is an excellent plan in winter, when every one is glad to sleep upon the kong. Indeed, I think it would be a good thing to utilise the kitchen smoke similarly in some damp old

Scotch houses, and to lead it in flues under the drawing-room sofas. But in summer the heat is intolerable, and the method tends to attract flies in numbers sufficient to satisfy Beelzebub, who was, I believe, prince of that obnoxious tribe, or was he merely the father of lies? When you enter a room they rise with a buzz which is positively alarming, and fi:'om that moment onward until dark, when Providence calls off this particular tormentor, and lets loose a torrent of mosquitoes, fleas, bugs and cockroaches (who are not vouchsafed the power to trouble me greatly), life is one ceaseless struggle. The flat fellows are called by the Japanese "nankin mushi," or Chinese insect, and the cockroaches are as a line-of-battle ship is to a torpedo-boat, when compared with the modest little frequenter of our English kitchen hearths. Nakamura, the interpreter, divides the world into two categories: those whom bugs devour, and those whom they do not.

To return to the house. Even the poorest dwellings are decorated with fantastic coloured prints on cheap thin paper, which is pasted on to the walls. These pictures represent scenes in ancient Chinese history or mythology. Japanese officers can usually recognise most of the allusions, which shows how greatly their education is still permeated by Chinese lore. The cards of any distinguished visitors are very conspicuously fastened to the walls, which is perhaps a more straightforward method than the corresponding English fashion of leaving them carelessly on the top of the card tray till they begin to turn yellow with age. The most awesome things hang from the ceiling, reminding one of the apothecary's shop in Romeo and Juliet, I dare not ask what they are, lest I should be told they are my supper. In &ont of each house is a courtyard, in which pigs and fowls galore are herded at night, together with such stock of mules, donkeys and ponies as the farmer possesses; and that stock is generally abundant. I must confess that both Russians and Japanese show a much higher standard of morality as regards chickens and pigs than did our troops in South Africa. Notwithstanding much newspaper reference to Russian barbarity, the fact remains that the Muscovites have not lifted so much as an egg even during the demoralisation of a retreat; whilst I can testify that the Japanese pay without a murmur whatever the Chinese like to extort. No doubt it is to the interest of both sides to please the inhabitants; but still, even so, I am astonished when I see that the war being waged here is the most fortunate thing which ever occurred to rich or poor dwelling in the theatre of operations. The British public are, however, so wedded to the convention that war means misery for all who come in contact with it, that they probably get some stories to that effect written up for them in London. The demand creates the supply.

Two soldiers have now come into the room, having been sent across from headquarters to make me comfortable. They are changing the aspect of things as if by magic. The kong has been wiped over with a wet cloth, and a clean strip of matting has been spread over it. They have torn off the dirty tattered strips of parchment from the windows, and replaced them by fresh, clean, semi-transparent sheets of paper. Whatever else may run short this seems always obtainable in any quantity. A red blanket has been spread over the table, and three peonies in a water-bottle, with each flower exactly at the true artistic height and angle from its neighbour, at once give an air of refinement to the whole place, and turn it from a barn into an apartment. Into the midst of this spring cleaning suddenly intrudes a white rabbit with pink eyes, followed at a short interval by two delicious little balls of white fur, evidently its children. They came out of a hole under the kong, which is apparently their home. Their legs are almost atrophied from being very little used. The Chinese lady, with whom I am now on the best of terms, tells me that they are not eatable. This, I suspect, is merely to put me off. The interpreter has explained that when I came in first she thought I was a Russian prisoner, and that was the reason she gave me the rough edge of her tongue.

After seeing my room put right, I walked over to call on the *étappen* Commandant. I passed several Japanese soldiers on the way, who were fanning themselves vigorously as they marched along. This association of war with what we Europeans regard as an effeminate instrument seemed rather funny. I found the Commandant seated at a small table in the courtyard of his house, a soldier standing behind him with a fly-switch. He asked me to sit by him and to partake of some tea and loll3rpops, which I was very glad to do. Another soldier came to whisk the flies off me, and I was enjoying myself enormously when suddenly I caught sight of a European looking at me out of a small barred window in the back of the house which made the opposite side of the courtyard. It was only ten yards distant, and I distinguished that the face looked heavy and stupid, and that on it was imprinted a sort of dull bovine wonderment. A moment later another face looked out, and then I realised they were the faces of Russian prisoners, evidently about as much surprised as it was in their nature to be to see a European hob-nobbing with the Japanese. This incident has spoilt my enjoyment of the sweetmeats and the tea. I confess it gave me a sharp pang — to see white men the prisoners of Asiatics. I must struggle against this feeling; but it is instinctive, and deeply rooted, inherited doubtless from the time of the Crusades, or possibly from some even earlier epoch. If these are my ineradicable sensations, I must learn to make more allowances for Japanese coldness and suspicion, as it is only reasonable that their feelings to me should be the counterpart of my feelings towards them. The Commandant told me there were four prisoners in the room, one officer and one man wounded, and two men unwounded. They had been in garrison at Tsuyenpu, a small village on the road to the Motienling, for two months, and had been taken prisoners there in a skirmish. Afterwards I saw them at the door of their house. The officer was a second lieutenant; an honest, nice-looking boy. He Lad been wounded in the ankle and arm. The men were very small: almost as small as the Japanese, and my first impression of the faces was correct. They looked very stupid — regular clods. I was told I might go and speak to them, as the officer knew a little German, but I felt shy on their account, thinking that if I myself were in such a position I should not like to be seen by any foreign officer. Vincent, however, who is passing through on his trip from Aiyanmen to join the headquarters of the Second Division, went and gave them some cigars and chocolate, and got them to line up to be photographed, an operation which they were quite pleased to undergo. The wounded man had been shot through the jaw and his teeth were knocked out, but he managed to stick a cigarette into the only corner of his mouth which he could open. They told Vincent that they got a full soldier's ration of rice, but that they felt hungry again half an hour after eating. Whatever British hearts may be, there is no doubt their stomachs are thoroughly pro-Russian.

The headquarters have sent me a long bulletin of news, but it is not worth while transcribing into my personal diary. It amounts to this. The three columns have advanced along their respective roads — the left, or Imperial Guards column, to Kyokahoshi; the centre, or Second Division column, to Kansoten; the Twelfth, or right column, to Bodoko. There has been some skirmishing, but nothing serious. The three Divisions are now in line facing north-west, and Bennenkampf at Saimachi, far from attacking the right flank of the main advance, has fallen back before the Twelfth Division, who have occupied Saimachi and pressed on beyond it. *Vorwärts!** is the word, and there is no better in the whole of the military dictionary.

June 27th. — Exquisite morning; cloudy and cool. Started at 7 a.m. This is the richest and most beautiful country I have ever seen. Fertile, cultivated valleys; constant crystalline streams winding over pebbly beds; the strange pointed hills I wrote about yesterday — the whole landscape clad in vividest emerald verdure.

After marching a few miles we came upon a wounded Russian being carried along on a stretcher by two Chinese coolies. He was a very nice-looking boy, aged twenty. One leg was broken and twisted right rounds and the other leg was also badly crushed. He had been knocked over in the Tsuyenpu skirmish, but as he fell amongst bushes he escaped notice, and had lain there for more than fifty-four hours, until found by chance by a Japanese corporal. He appeared to me to be dying, poor boy, or very near it. At the moment we came up, the litter had been put down, and some of the Japanese coolies had run up to see him. They are not unkind, but they do not feel sorry. One of them lifted up a little locket he wore round his neck with a chain, and laughingly showed it to the others. There was infinite pathos about this little scene by the roadside. One realised all the brave thoughts with which the poor young fellow had come out to fight for his country; the keepsake given him by his sweetheart, which was probably in the little locket; and

---

* "Forward!"

the fact that in all probability his bright young life was now about to end in a lonely death amongst Asiatics.

On arrival at Linchatai, where two days previously a Russian cavalry regiment had been encamped, I was told that Kuroki wanted me to lunch with him. I followed the orderly, and found five tents pitched and all the headquarters staff busy eating rice, salted plums and tea. Kuroki, Prince Kuni and Fujii were in one tent, and with distressing politeness they got up and made the staff officers in the next tent clear out and make room for me. I was sorry, as I am sure they did not like it, although I must do their manners the credit of saying that they appeared delighted. After I had gulped down rice till I felt like the frog which emulated the ox, Fujii Sent for me. I found him concealed in ostentatious mystery behind his tent, with a map spread out before him. He whispered to me that it had been ascertained beyond doubt from prisoners and the order-book of a captured staff officer, that Kuropatkin had been misled by information brought by officers' patrols into thinking the main force of the First Army was moving by its left via Siuyen on Haicheng, instead of which we are actually moving right in front via Saimachi. Fujii improved the occasion by delivering himself of a little homily on the necessity of officers' patrols not theorising or thinking, but confining themselves to seeing exactly and then reporting exactly what they have seen. At the same time he admitted that in this instance there were several confirmatory points which might have assisted in the deception of Kuropatkin. One was that he would be naturally inclined to credit the First Army with a desire to join hands as quickly as possible with the Tenth Division under Nodzu, landed at Takushan a month previously (this was the first I had heard of it), and with the Second Army in the Liaotung peninsula, instead of cherishing the bold ambition of bearing to the north and threatening the railway communication with Mukden even at the risk of isolation. Another was that we did actually send a brigade of Guards to Siuyen, to co-operate with Nodzu (this was the first I had heard of the co-operation), and that every day must have brought the Russian Commander reports of encounters between patrols in that neighbourhood. And, lastly, there were the facts of the long halt of the First Army at Fenghuangcheng, and the heavy fortifications constructed there, which may have inclined Kuropatkin to believe that only a comparatively small force had been left at that place, the bulk of the army being shifted to the south. At any rate, the great thing was that Kuropatkin had been misled and had changed all his dispositions.

During the early days of the Japanese occupation of Fenghuangcheng the Russians had concentrated at Liaoyang in anticipation of a speedy advance by Kuroki along the Pekin road, by which we are now moving. There was an excellent position five miles south of Liaoyang at a place called Chusan, where an advance of the Japanese armies from the south could be opposed; and at Bunsuirei,[*] a couple of marches ahead of us, was an equally good position, barring an advance by Kuroki from Fenghuangcheng. Kuropatkin had meant to hold these two places. Suddenly, and most fortunately, the Russian plans had been changed; the force at Liaoyang was moved south by rail and road against four Japanese Divisions, and reaped the reward of such madness. Fujii thinks this foolhardy advance must be attributed to civilian interference, as he cannot believe Kuropatkin capable of so gross a blunder. After the inevitable defeat of the two Russian Divisions at Telissu, the troops holding Bunsuirei, Lienshankuan, and the Motienling had so little left behind them that they were now falling back without any serious resistance, and an officers' patrol hod already entered Lienshankuan at the foot of the Motienling. "Against our three Divisions the Russians have only one Division and one regiment, so naturally they have to go. One brigade, with sixteen guns, is retiring in front of the Imperial Guards; another brigade is retreating before us, and in front of the Twelfth Division on the left there is only one regiment. Thus we are, after all, going to occupy the Motienling and the other debouchures in that formidable mountain barrier without having to fight." A great advantage to the Japanese, but to me a personal disappointment. The Russians had burnt their stores at Lienshankuan and the Motienling, after pouring kerosene oil upon

---

[*] Bunsuirei, or Fanshuiling, is a common name in Manchuria, meaning "Division of Waters Pass."

them to make them blaze; a trifle, no doubt, to men whose ancestors had burnt Moscow, but still not a very exhilarating performance even on a miniature scale. As regards our own stores, Fujii said that there was great difficulty in bringing the food to the front over such bad roads; but we have now so much food and material accumulated at Antung and at Fenghuangcheng that we are independent of the command of the sea for a very long time to come.

So much for our own affairs; and those of our comrades to the south are no less cheering, as to-day the Tenth Division, based on Siuyen, attacked the enemy on the road leading to Takubokujo, and drove them back to the latter place with a loss of 100, the Japanese themselves losing only a Major Oka and five men killed. I must watch narrowly to find out if these casualty returns are reliable. The difference in favour of the Japanese is certainly remarkable, but I have seen the same sort of thing in South Africa, where people, clever at taking cover and good shots, met others who were not. Any way, it looks as if we should have an unopposed march to Liaoyang, which means no battle reports for me.

After this interesting talk I rode on here to Nidoboshi, and have taken up my quarters in another farm. The village consists of about thirty houses, all thatched with millet-stalks. On our way we passed military coolies bathing literally by thousands. Probably there never was such a clean army as this in the history of the world. It is possible to march on a hot day in the middle of a battalion without any offence to the most delicate nostrils. We, I am told, are by no means equally inoffensive to the Japanese. However cleanly we may be, our habit of devouring great quantities of meat gives us a carnivorous aroma which is not at all to their taste. It is dreadful even to suspect that when we think ourselves most fascinating we may only succeed in reminding our pretty Geisha friends of a zoological garden on a hot afternoon.

July 1st, 1904. — A fine morning at last. The torrents of rain we have had since our arrival have jeopardised the whole success of our movement. Every one has been on half rations, and if it had rained to-day the army, or a part of it, must have rolled back to

Fenghuangcheng to feed itself. During the past two days, Kuroki, Fujii, Matsuishi, Kurita, and I have spent hours standing in the mud, clad in gum boots and waterproofs, gazing for a break in the dull grey of the sky, as eagerly as ever did Elijah's servant for the little cloud like a man's hand. In vain, and the rivers have risen until no Chinamen would face them, and a batch of Russian prisoners trying to cross the swollen torrent just below here was nearly drowned, and had to be brought back again. Only a few military coolies, worked up to the *kesshitai* or "determined to die" pitch, have stuck to their work and just kept us from starvation. The only happy people here have been the multitudes of frogs. When I got a crick in my neck from looking up at the heavens, I whiled away the weary hours by watching these athletic and amorous dwellers of the marsh. As soon as the stillness of the gigantic figure which had overshadowed their little world convinced them that it was inanimate they gave free rein to their feelings. I have never seen a life more full of feverish excitement; a succession of passionate love affairs and heroic combats. With all our grand ideas, how infinitesimal must be the difference between us in the eyes of the Almighty! Russians and Japanese struggling for the Motienling; two frogs contesting for an earthworm: it is all a question of degree.

However, to-day it is fine; the frogs are sad and we are glad. I had a pleasant talk with his Highness Prince Kuni, who was fishing for gudgeon with a common house-fly impaled on a bent pin. He had caught several, and I congratulated him on taking so many prisoners from the river. He says we will march to-morrow to Sokako, and that the Russians continue to fall back all along our front. A squadron of cavalry reconnoitring in front of the Twelfth Division, our right column, reports 4000 Russian infantry, 24 guns, and a regiment of cavalry to be in occupation of the heights above Chaotao; in front of our central column on the main Pekin road, there is a regiment at Towan with detachments at Tiensuitien and Yoshirei. All these places are on the far side of the mountain barrier through which the Motienling is the principal passage. Apparently then the Russians have quite definitely abandoned the idea of fighting a battle here, and the general expectation of the headquarters seems to be that we shall not have an opportunity of gaining our *victoire décisive* until we get close up to the city of Liaoyang.

July 2nd, 1904, — Marched from Nidoboshi at about 5 a.m. The "cross roads" is the meaning of the name, and here indeed the First Army paused, hesitating between the road of failure and the road which, D.V., will lead us all to fame for all time. One more night of rain and we should now have our faces turned south and be struggling through mud and torrents back to inglorious revictualment in Fenghuangcheng!

The morning is exquisitely cool and fresh. There is no time in summer to equal the dawn, and no place like the saddle in which to enjoy it.

As we rode along I had an interesting talk with X. and one of the staff. They were both very strong as to the superiority of the peasant over the city-bred man. Y. said that the extra intelligence of the latter does not compensate for the solidity and innate discipline of the former. It is not so much that the Japanese cockneys have, like ours, lost touch with nature or degenerate in physique. They have not yet had time to do this; but it is a more subtle moral change which has already distinctly deteriorated them for military purposes. If a country soldier is ordered to mount guard at a certain spot he will stand there until relieved, even if the relief be hours and hours overdue, or if the most terrible dangers threaten; whereas, if the same duty be entrusted to a cockney, he will do very well as long as the eye of his superior is upon him, or for as long as he thinks there is a chance of his return; but he is capable of quitting his post when he considers he can do so without much danger of being found out. X. warmly agreed, and said that as an artillery officer he had had the sad experience of hearing soldiers drawn from the Osaka town area suggest poisonous and essentially unmilitary ideas to good country soldiers. I asked him if he could give me an example. He said, "Many examples; when my battery was digging gun-pits and epaulements as part of its annual training, I myself heard an Osaka recruit suggest that if they had put the same amount of hard work into digging something useful in Osaka they would each have earned at least two yen (four

TAWARATODAN HIDESATO, A CELEBRITY OF ANCIENT JAPAN
ON HIS BREAST IS WRITTEN, "HE BECAME A DEMON GUARDING HIS COUNTRY"

shillings), instead of only rebuke and criticism." At this Y. let his reins drop and held up both hands, a very unusual gesticulation for an undemonstrative Japanese, exclaiming, "Why, the fellow ought to have been prepared to pay at least two yen for the honour of digging an epaulement; if such ideas find currency there will soon be an end to Japan!" He went on to give several more instances, but admitted that the Osaka men had fought well at Nanshan. That, however, he considered was only because they happened to be personally enthusiastic about this particular war against Russia, and no one can possibly calculate, he said, how long such a selfish, individualistic motive can stand the strain of hardships and long absence from home.

We next talked about the Russian threats of bringing successive armies of highly trained Europeans from the Far West, whilst the Japanese soldier would necessarily tend to become younger and less highly trained as the war dragged on. We all agreed that further victories and conquest of territory were the best antidote to this danger which largely existed in the imagination of civilians, who fail to understand how each successive army would tend to become more and more *atteinte en sa morale*,* and thus rendered progressively less effective by the defeat of its predecessors.

Finally, the discussion turned upon the terms of peace Japan should impose at the end of the war. The general opinion seemed to be that Manchuria should be given back to China, and that Port Arthur might nominally be given back also; but that there should be a clause in the treaty saying that Japan would take care of it until she was strong enough to undertake the duty for herself. Russian interests in the Manchurian Railway must absolutely be handed over to Japan, and that would be considered sufficient as a war indemnity. Korea and the island of Saghalien must, of course, become Japanese. If the war went on into 1905, then it would have to be considered whether Vladivostock must not be besieged and taken, in which case it would have to be made a free unfortified harbour. This sort of talk is like disposing of the

---

* "Undermined in its morale."

bearskin whilst its fierce owner still roams the woods. I said I did not like over-confidence, as it was not lucky. They laughed, and asked if I really believed what we thought or said could make any difference in the decision of a question involving millions of human beings? I replied I could never be quite sure — that I believed there was no sin better calculated to call forth the vengeance of the high gods than cock-sureness, and that, when the scales were very evenly poised, the action or thoughts of even one humble individual might cause the balance to incline. At this they laughed again, and said I was superstitious — a strange accusation from men who think their ancestors are as likely as not listening to every word they say.

On running my eye back over what I have just written I feel somewhat hopeless of ever conveying to my friends impressions of the Japanese which shall be even approximately true to life. If I rode with two Europeans and noted down the scenery and very faithfully recorded the conversation, I think every one who read would receive a tolerably trustworthy idea of what had happened, and of how it had happened. Here, however, unless I mistake, the picture which arises in the mind's eye, on reading my account, shows three cheerful companions riding up a lovely valley on a fresh morning, chatting gaily as they go. The reality was not so. The three travellers rode much of the way in Indian file, and for the most part in silence. The whole of the time the foreigner was trying hard to break down, or manoeuvre round, the reserve of the Japanese (which is always more impenetrable when they are two together), and to elicit some of their ideas on interesting subjects. The Japanese fenced with these inquiries as energetically as politeness would permit; but during the long march there were one or two partial successes amidst many baffled attempts. The partial successes have been fully recorded. That is the true story. Unless, with the beneficent assistance of saké or biru, it is the most uphill, exhausting work in the world to get any tangible opinion or indication of character out of a Japanese.

We reached Sokako at midday. It is a village of some twenty small houses, many of them in a tumbledown condition, showing it is on the down grade. It ought to be a fairly important place, as it stands at the junction of this main Pekin road and a road which branches off it to Mukden. This time I am billeted in the house of a Chinese physician, where I should be perfectly happy and comfortable if only I were a spider. As it is, the billions of flies which cover everything as if with a black carpet, will end, I think, in driving me clean distracted.

Chapter XIII – An Affair of Outposts

July 5th, 1904. — Some skirmishing between patrols, but no essential change in the enemy's positions at Towan in front of us; at Makumenza, in front of the Guards; or at Chaotao, in front of the Twelfth Division; but yesterday morning early there was a very bitter little fight on the far slopes of the Motienling, about fourteen miles from here. Two Russian battalions, profiting by the fog, attacked one Japanese battalion which was holding the pass. The Russkis "made the hoorah" three times; but although they fought well and got to bayonet-work, they were eventually repulsed, and fell back to Yoshirei, on the Pekin road. The Japanese battalion pursued as far as Kinkahoshi. The Japanese loss is fifteen killed, and one officer and twenty-nine noncommissioned officers and men wounded. The Russians left on the pass itself mount up to thirty dead and forty wounded. All the headquarters staff are simply bewildered as to what the enemy can be about. They say there does not seem to be any cohesion or general direction about the Russian plans. Why, it is asked on all sides, did they give up a splendidly fortified position like Bunsuirei between this place and the Motienling without firing a shot, and afterwards the fine

An Affair of Outposts

natural position of the Motienling itself; and then, a few days later, when the Japanese had firmly fixed themselves along the heights, come 'with a comparatively small force and try to retake it? Some think that Kuropatkin had determined to fall back, and that Alexieff has at the last moment got the upper hand, and has determined, after all, to hold on. This seems a plausible explanation.

Shortly after my return from headquarters, General Fuji! came in to tell me he would make special arrangements to-morrow to have me taken over the scene of the fight by the officers who took part in it. This is splendid. I call it real good of him! He went on to say: "The general situation is extraordinarily interesting, and, at the same time, very incomprehensible. Why is Kuropatkin waiting at Haicheng and Kaiping with seven or eight Divisions? To us he seems to be running the gravest risk of being surrounded. Why did he yesterday morning send nearly a regiment to try and retake the Motieiding, each man of which carried six days' supplies with him? Had he the idea under cover of this attack to shift the bulk of his forces from our front, and move them round to join Kennenkampf on our right when that leader might be strong enough to defeat the Twelfth Division and cut our communications with the Yalu? Is he perhaps contemplating the despatch of an independent column from some point to the east of Harbin which would have Saimachi as its objective, and, by its approach to that point, threaten the rear and the right flank of our army? There are certain indications which make us anxious about this, the weakest spot in our armour. But then such a movement must take several weeks to accomplish, and if, meanwhile, the first and second armies win a battle in the vicinity of Haicheng, our eastern communications with Fenghuangcheng and the Yalu will not matter a bit, as our line of supply can be shifted at once to Dalny and Newchwang. Still, there must be *some* reason which causes Kuropatkin to maintain himself in a position apparently so dangerous, for he is a clever man, and has clever assistants on his staff. So we feel a little anxious and perplexed; and out of this anxiety and perplexity only one thing emerges clearly, namely, that this is a moment for the greatest prudence on our part. I lay stress on prudence all the more because of the undoubtedly strong temptation urging us at present to make a dash forward. Here we are only two days' forced marches from Liaoyang, and the bulk of the enemy at Kaiping is now actually further off than ourselves from that tremendously important point. However, we are going to do nothing rash, and, fortunately, nothing could be better than the morale of our men, which is the best strategy of all, and also the best tactics." Fujii further told me that Nogi had now three full Divisions round Port Arthur, and that another Division was "well on its way" (he would not say if it had actually disembarked) to Siuyen to join the Tenth Division, in combination with which it would constitute the Fourth Army. So soon as this Fourth Army got into line with us, we should go right ahead for Liaoyang. This is great news, but I am to keep it to myself, and not tell any one — not even my own British officers, if I chance to come across them.

I feel I must here qualify my lament on the secretiveness of the Japanese, written on the 2nd instant, by making a brilliant exception of Major-General Fujii. He is so clever that he has no difficulty in discriminating between a matter which should be kept secret and an interesting fact which no foreigner with this army could, even if he wanted to, utilise for an improper purpose. He is thus able to appear perfectly frank and outspoken, whilst maintaining all reasonable reticence upon essentials and upon the future.

Lienshankuan, July 6th, 1904. — Left Sokako early for this place, the headquarters of the Second Division, and the last big village on the south side of the Motienling. Vincent is here with a batch of foreign attachés. At 3 p.m. started in a broiling sun for the Motienling, taking Vincent with me. Major-General Nishi, commanding the Second Division, sent a staff officer to accompany us; and at Kikahoshi we dismounted, and saw Major-General Okasaki, commanding the 15th brigade, a part of which is holding the Motienling. He had been warned of my coming, and had coffee, sweetmeats and cigars waiting for us. After partaking freely of these welcome refreshments we went on, accompanied by the brigadier and by Colonel Baba, commanding the 30th Regiment; so that, what with escort and orderlies, we made up

An Affair of Outposts 197

quite an imposing cavalcade. From Lienshankuan onwards there was a gradual rise as far as Rikahoshi, where the ascent became accentuated. The last half-mile up to the Motienling (or Heaven-reaching pass) was quite a stiff climb, and when the crest-line was reached the view was simply superb. As far as the eye could reach, in every direction, were sharp mountain peaks and countless ridges, all covered with forest and scrub jungle of a peculiarly luminous green. Standing on the watershed it was interesting to mark the general lie of the country, and the network of valleys stretching out to the north and south. From each of these issued streams which, joining together, formed considerable rivers before they got lost to view on their way to swell the waters of the Yalu or the Liao. Judging merely by eye, and by the freshness of the air, I should think the Motienling itself must be about 2800 feet above Lienshankuan, whilst the peak just immediately to its south is some 700 feet higher. A fairly good road has been cut down the western face of the pass by the Russians. It is fit for the passage of well-horsed artillery, in which category it is, unfortunately, impossible to include the Japanese.

After going about half a mile down this road we came to a temple, standing out on a bare grassy spur. It was still quite full of Russian wounded, who seemed cheerful and well tended. It was because of the potent influence of the god of this temple that, in the opinion of the Chinese, the Japanese were prevented from advancing by the Motienling route during the war of 1894-95. For the glorification of the deity they had, therefore, built a second temple half a mile further down the pass. This, then, is the old temple, and the edifice lower down is called by the Japanese the new temple. The Japanese are much amused at this instance of Chinese superstition. As a matter of fact, the southern route was the easier one by which to turn the Chinese flank in the late war; but this time the line of communication of the enemy leads northwards, and so we have to keep well to the north ourselves if we mean to threaten it. Possibly some of Kuropatkin's mistakes have been due to a conviction that the Japanese would repeat in the present war the 1894-95 strategy.

I went on to the new temple, and there met all the officers who had been present at the fight, including Lieutenant Yoshi, who is

VIEW OF THE MOTIENLING RANGE FROM A MOUNTAIN ABOVE LIENSHANKUAN

VI

said to have killed eight Russians with his two-handed sword, although he himself is modest, and only claims to have fairly split the skulls of three. He is a singularly weak-looking youth, only about twenty-two years old; but certainly his sword, which he showed me, had cut something hard and thick, for it was still notched like a saw, although a fresh edge had already been put upon it where it was not too much indented. Some Russian rifles were also shown to us with deep cuts on the wooden barrel-guard, showing how Japanese officers had parried, or tried to parry, bayonet thrusts in the dark. After talking with the group of officers we went with them a few hundred yards to the scene of the hand-to-hand fighting. It is possible to advance upon the Motienling from the west either by the path, which mostly runs along a rocky ridge, or by one of either of the small valleys which run respectively north and south of this ridge. The old temple stands at the head of the northern valley or nullah, the new temple at the head of the southern valley. The Japanese 1st battalion 30th Regiment was holding the pass, and one of its companies was stationed in the old temple and two companies in the new temple, the commander retaining his fourth company as a reserve on the top of the pass. The commander of the two companies in the new temple detached one picquet consisting of thirty-six rifles to take up a position at the bottom of the valley to the north of the ridge,

An Affair of Outposts

and sent another picquet of thirty-six rifles under Lieutenant Yoshi to hold the village of Lichaputsu at the debouchure of the valley to the south of the ridge. At midnight Lieutenant Yoshi sent out a patrol of a non-commissioned officer and four men to move cautiously down the main road towards the Russian position at Towan to see if everything was quiet. They returned at 1 a.m., and said that all was well. At 3 a.m. two patrols were sent out, one of them going down the same road. They returned simultaneously at 4 a.m., and just as the Towan patrol was in the act of reporting that there was no sign of the enemy, a shot was fired, and a heavy Russian column was upon them with the bayonet.

It seems that whilst the patrols were actually engaged in reporting to Lieutenant Yoshi, the picquet sentry, who was posted just fifty yards in front of Lichaputsu, saw a single man standing before him. He thought he was one of the patrol who had lagged behind, but, as in duty bound, he challenged him. His challenge was answered by a shot, and instantly a mass of Russians charged into the village. This is the accepted story, and no one seemed in the least inclined to question its accuracy. Personally I have had too much to do with night alarms and surprises, and subsequent investigations, to give it full credence. Any one who chooses to believe the official account must either imagine that a Russian column can move with silent, swift celerity, or that a Japanese patrol is stupid and deaf. I strongly suspect that the patrol did not go out exactly as stated, and that the picquet sentry was asleep. On a still night such as that of the 3rd and 4th a large Russian column would certainly be heard at a distance of half a mile, if only the listeners were on the alert.

As the Russians burst into the village most of the thirty-six men who composed the picquet fell back, first of all up the southern valley and then eastwards, to try and join their reserve. But Lieutenant Yoshi and a dozen men stood their ground for some time, fighting a confused fight in the darkness with a certain number of Russians who blundered up against them, whilst the bulk of the column passed straight through the village and continued their march eastwards up the spur which led to the new temple.

At last Yoshi managed to extricate himself and fell back, but only to find the Russians who had passed on whilst he was fighting in the village lined athwart the ridge and interposing between him and his supports at the new temple. How he managed to get through or round I do not exactly know, nor do I believe he has any very clear idea himself. All he can say is, that he had to fight to do so, and that the two-handed sword again did excellent service, enabling him eventually to pierce the line and rejoin his own people.

Meanwhile the commander of the two companies at the temple had heard the firing, and sent out an officer with twenty men to reconnoitre. This small party advanced down the ridge and came into collision with the Russians just at the western edge of the wood which surrounds the new temple. The Japanese, seeing that the enemy were in very superior force, fell back some 200 yards to the edge of the wood, which is a very thick undergrowth of hazel and beech. But the commander of the company stationed in the old temple was also on the alert by this time, and he advanced at the head of his men down the valley or ravine to the north of the ridge along the crest of which the Russians were moving. From this valley he could fall on the left of the enemy's force in case they persevered in moving eastwards against the new temple. As soon as this company from the valley opened fire on the Russians they formed line to the left to face it, but in doing so they exposed themselves to an enfilade fire along their entire line from the twenty men who had fallen back to the edge of the wood. It was not yet light enough to make good shooting, but still the firing of this small party, which was very shortly reinforced by the whole of the balance of the two companies from the new temple, forced the Russians to throw back their right flank. They then, as the Japanese say, "made the hoorah" three times, and, with a part of their force charged the edge of the wood with the bayonet. Bat they never actually penetrated more than a few yards into it. A corporal who had been slightly wounded told us that the Russians were "very easy to kill" when it came to bayonet work. He said they put their heads down and rushed madly forward like bulls, holding out the rifle and bayonet before them. Nothing was more simple, he said, than to step to one side and thrust at them as they passed.

Unable to force their way forward, and attacked on both sides

An Affair of Outposts 201

by an inferior but enveloping force, whose numbers could not be seen for the thick brushwood, whilst they themselves were in column of route on the open spur, the Russians gave way just as it was getting daylight at 4.30 a.m. The combatants were still so intermixed, and it was still so dark owing to fog, that some of the Russians laid hold of Japanese soldiers by the sleeve, saying, "Come along, it is time now to fall back." I asked how the Japanese could understand this, and it was explained that several of the men who did it were taken prisoners and had since been interrogated. A few minutes after the retreat. Colonel Baba arrived on the ground with two more companies drawn from the 2nd battalion of the 30th Regiment. He left the two companies from the new temple which had home the brunt of the fighting, and taking on the comparatively fresh company from the old temple, which had been fighting with the left of the Russians from the nullah north of the ridge, he started in pursuit at 4.55 a.m. The pursuit of 2000 men by these three companies, say 630 men, continued as far as Towan. Twice the Russians tried to make a stand, but each time they had to give way when pressed. At Towan a large force of Russians showed themselves, manning the trenches, and letting the beaten troops pass through. The 2000 men who had to make this retrograde movement were the 2nd battalion of the 10th Regiment and the 2nd battalion of the 24th Regiment of Siberian Tirailleurs, plus one company of the 22nd Regiment.

Thus far my story has dealt entirely with the misfortunes of the battalion of the 10th. The battalion of the 24th had advanced beyond the mouth of the valley entered by the battalion of the 10th, and, leaving the village of Lichaputsu behind them, had entered the valley north of the spur on which their comrades were already fighting. It was doubtless their intention to press up this northern valley so as to attack the old temple; but they were so long about it that before they could get into touch with the enemy, they became aware of the defeat and retreat of the battalion of the 10th. As any Japanese troops sent in pursuit of this battalion must have intercepted their own retreat to Towan, they decided to fall back also whilst there was yet time. It has been ascertained that both these Russian battalions spent the night before the attack a little to the west of Yoshirei, and that the battalion of the 10th left their quarters at 7 a.m. on the 3rd, whilst the battalion of the 24th did not start till 1 a.m. on the 4th. The precise losses are: Japanese, 18 killed and 40 wounded, including 2 officers; Russians, 55 killed and 40 wounded. The losses caused to the Russians by the pursuit are not known.

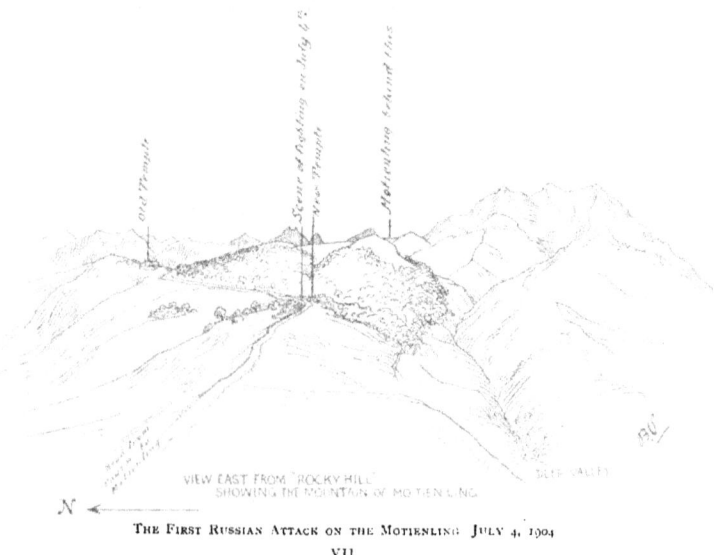

The First Russian Attack on the Motienling July 4, 1904
VII

If only the two Russian battalions had timed their attack simultaneously, it is difficult to believe that they could have failed to carry one or both of the temples, even if they did not succeed in capturing the Motienling pass itself. During what turned out to he the crucial moment of the fight, the battalion of the 10th Regiment was held fast in an exposed and unfavourable terrain by a reconnoitring party of an officer and twenty men. So small a force as this could surely never have kept hack one thousand Russians advancing with the bayonet in the darkness, had it not been that these latter were worried and distracted by a simultaneous attack on their loft from the company sent into the valley north of the ridge from the old temple. It was, however, manifestly the business of the battalion of the 24th Regiment to press so vigorously up this valley against the old temple, that the Japanese company posted there would have had more than enough to do in defending itself.

Had this been done, the battalion of the 10th Regiment must, I think, have gained the wood before reinforcements could have come to the twenty men lining the edge of it. Had the battalion once succeeded in gaining the wood, they would probably have taken the new temple, which was surrounded by jungle up to the very walls. Had they taken the new temple, it would have been difficult, without artillery, to drive them out again. "If ifs and ands were pots and pans." The long and short of it is, that the Russian attack was what the French call *décousu** to the last degree, and seemed to indicate a badly thought-out arrangement by their general staff.

On the other hand, although the Japanese outpost at Lichaputsu may not have been sufficiently on the alert, their behaviour after the surprise is worthy of the highest praise. I can think of many episodes, not altogether dissimilar to this encounter, in which a picquet of thirty-six men was suddenly overwhelmed by a thousand Russians. In some of these cases, after offering sufficient resistance to give the alarm to their comrades and to lose three or four men, the smaller force would have felt justified in surrendering to force majeure. Heaven forbid I should enter into the ethics of such a question! Much must obviously depend on the bitterness of feeling; the importance, or otherwise, from a purely military point of view, of holding out; and on local conditions generally. Only, speaking from a patriotic point of view, I feel it should be clearly understood that, *ceteris paribus*,† the surrender type of army may expect to be handsomely thrashed by the no surrender type whenever and wherever they may meet.

On the whole I think the British have every reason to feel proud and confident regarding the behaviour of their allies in this fierce little engagement, which, on the Russian side at least, appears to have been meant as something more serious than a mere affair of outposts. Allowing for a little exaggeration about the two-handed swords and the easily bayoneted Russians, it is perfectly

---

* "Disjointed."

† "All other things being equal."

clear to any one who has been carefully over the ground with all the officers concerned, that every one, from captain to private, in the Japanese companies, knew his duty to himself and to his country, and did it like a man, nay more, like an intelligent soldier.

Sokako, July 8th, 1904. — Here I am, once more in the apothecary's house, where the flies welcomed me with effusion. On my way back I went over the Bunsuirei defences constructed by the Russians between this place and the Motienling. I have sent home a good long report upon them, with drawings by Vincent, so there is no need to say much about them here. The spot is well chosen. Long spurs run out from the hills on either side of the valley and overlap, looking at a distance as if they formed a continuous steep green barrier. The field of fire is excellent, and it seems to me that had the Russians waited for us here we must have lost a great many men, or else have halted until the Guards on our left or the Twelfth Division on our right could have turned the position. The improvement in the character, concealment and solidity of the works constructed here is very remarkable when they are contrasted with the works at Chiuliencheng on the Yalu. The shelter trenches were not on the summit of the ridges, but a few yards down the first gentle slope. The object must have been to leave as little dead ground as possible; but as a result the trenches lean a little forward towards the south, as if inviting a howitzer shell to drop into them. I think myself it would have been preferable to trust the defence of the dead ground to flanking fire, and to have placed the trenches on, or very near, the crest of the ridges. There was no head cover. I question whether a soldier in a conspicuous trench without head cover possesses any real advantage over a combatant who is utilising the natural features of the ground. The bodies of the latter may not be so well protected, but there is no difference regarding that vital point, so especially sensitive to danger, the head, except that the men in the trenches are more conspicuous in this respect and, in 60 far, more vulnerable, especially to long-range artillery fire. Therefore, it seems to me, if it is worth while to dig trenches or build parapets, it is like spoiling the ship for the sake of the ha'porth of tar, to omit head cover and loopholes.

When I had gone over all these solid semi-permanent redoubts and lines of trenches, I could not but sympathise with the feelings of the men who had toiled at them for weeks, only to march away and leave them the moment the Japanese advance guard made its appearance. Short of actual defeat, I can imagine nothing more trying to the morale of an army.

On my way home I met Fujii fishing. He told me the Second Army was very probably attacking the Russians at Kaiping to-day. If this is so, and if the Russians have to retire on Mukden, we shall have lost our chance of cutting in on their rear.

July 9th, 1904. — Have been writing from dictation for four solid hours about the lines of communication of this army, Colonel Matsuishi and Lieutenant-Colonel Kurita having been sent down by the kind Fujii for the purpose. It is quite splendid. To-morrow they come again.

July 10th, 1904. — Another two hours with Matsuishi and Kurita, who gave me no end of interesting details about the line of communication work from the date the First Army landed in Korea until its arrival at Fenghuangcheng. The difficulties have been enormous, and have occasionally seemed so insuperable as to have moved the staff almost to tears. This was their own expressive way of picturing to me their frame of mind. I do not myself believe that mere difficulties and disappointments are capable of causing a Japanese to weep, although a certain sort of sentiment seems to have power to affect him in that way.

The full history of the communications will be embodied by me in an official report, and the only point worth entering here is the description they gave me of their military coolies.

In the war with China 100,000 rickshaw coolies were brought from Japan to do the transport. These men were splendid workers so long as they were in a good humour, but they had no military training and, therefore, no discipline. Consequently, they gave much trouble, and occasionally lowered the good name ot Japan by acts of violence and pillage. To put it in Matsuishi's own words: "We cannot afford to have any people connected with this army plundering or ill-treating the inhabitants of the countries we traverse, and yet there must always be some danger of this happening when masses of civilian followers take the field with an army." All Anglo-Indian officers will agree as to the truth and wisdom of this view.

It was therefore resolved at army headquarters to create a body of semi-military followers by conscription. Accordingly, every year 200,000 young men are conscripted just exactly as if they were intended to take their place in the ranks of the army. Ordinarily nothing further happens, and no attempt is made to train them in peace time; but as they know they are on the list, and as they wear uniforms when summoned to a war, they acquire the moral impression that they are soldiers and are prepared to accept without question the soldierly obligations of obedience and self-sacrifice. The worst of it is that as all sorts and conditions of men are represented in their ranks, they are not nearly so strong as the professional rickshaw coolie. This time, when they landed in Korea, it was calculated that one rickshaw coolie was as strong as three of these military coolies, besides being more adroit in manœuvring his cart amidst ruts and stones. Even now, when they have got hardened and habituated to their task, one rickshaw coolie is equal to two of them. But they are still improving daily, and certainly look wonderfully bright and healthy. Sixteen thousand five hundred of these military coolies landed with the First Army, and three of them are supposed to haul about 250 pounds of rice in their little cart. They are paid six sen or 1½d. per day, and get no meat, but are allowed ¼ lb. more rice than the soldiers. They also get warm water in which a few grains of barley have been boiled to make it look like tea. This is provided free of charge.

In addition to the military coolies, each Division has its regular transport of small one-horse carts, which I have careful measurements and drawings. They are supposed to carry 350 pounds. The provision column with a Division consists of four days' supply loaded on these carts. In addition, there is one staging column of horse carts carrying one day's supply for the Division; a sixth day is packed upon the regimental baggage, and two days are taken by the soldier; making a grand total of eight days which, always, in theory at least, accompanies each Division. Good as is the military coolie system, it would never of itself suffice to supplement the regular divisional horse transport when once the army has moved far from its sea base. For the regular line of communication work the Japanese had to rely on Korean coolies in Korea, and on Chinese carts in Manchuria. There can be no better evidence of the effort this little country is putting forth than the wages she is paying these people. A Korean coolie got 30 sen to carry a bag of rice one ri (2¼ miles). A sturdy coolie could earn, at this wage, 5 yen (10 shillings) in one day. The Chinese carters are getting 25 yen or £2 10s. a day, and there are 1000 of these carts now attached to each of our three Divisions! That means £7500 a day for local transport. English people seem to think no one can spend money but themselves. On the contrary, there are no people in the world more reluctant to pay fancy, or war, prices. In peace India is more stingy than England, but in war she realises well that her rupees are her sinews, and that the saving of a lakh may mean the loss of a battle. I must not write any more on this subject, great as is its fascination for me; I will only say that with all my admiration for the Japanese line of communications work, there is one point upon which we are greatly their superiors — that is in our road making and repairing. In Burma, in the Swat valley, and in many strange and distant lands, we also have had to lay military highways through rice-fields as bottomless as those of Korea. We have carved broad roads deep into the Himalayan cliffs, and have carried food for our armies over ranges loftier and wilder far than those of the Motienling. I do not speak without knowledge then when I say the Japanese would save the lives of men and horses, and get ten per cent, more stuff to the front in a given time, if they would only devote more attention to their roads. Not far from where I am writing there are short sections of the highway which in rain turn into sloughs of mud, peppered at intervals with large boulders. It is just possible to struggle and scramble through this when it is wet, with much cracking of whips, and when it is dry and the river is low, the carts can escape the bad bit by working along the banks. So repairs are left alone, and the ample military labour available is now being employed in making a grand avenue up to Kuroki's quarters in a Chinese house lying half a mile back off the highway, an avenue which the Chinese will plough up again the moment our backs are turned.

Every one is anxious at no news having come to hand about the Second Army, which was supposed to be fighting yesterday.

July 12th, 1904. — Good news to-day from the Second Army, which has made every one cheerful. They seem to have pushed the enemy back from Kaiping without much trouble.

July 14th, 1904. — Magic-lantern show last night. I sat between Kuroki and the Prince. A mixture of battle scenes and pretty *musumes** was exhibited, the latter being much preferred by both officers and men, not to speak of the solitary foreign attaché. Certainly all men ought to be very thankful every day and all day that there are women in the world. It is as if the Almighty had prepared an everlasting treat for them. I wonder why I never felt this sentiment until now. Probably because I have never before been so long a time without even seeing a woman.

July 15th, 1904. — Have had an intensely interesting evening, and although 11 p.m. is very late for Manchuria, I must try and jot down a few points to-night before I forget them.

Fujii dined with me alone and talked to me, seemingly, without any reserve. He says there are nearly four Divisions and 350 guns round Port Arthur, and that once Nogi fairly sets to work he ought to overbear all opposition and carry the place in one grand assault. Anything seems possible to these little fellows, and, after the American volunteers under Pepperel did something similar against France at Louisbourg in 1745; still, it is a big order against modem armaments, especially if the Russians make full use of electric searchlights and barbed wire.

---

* Girls.

An Affair of Outposts

Another item of news was that Oyama and Kodama landed at Dalny yesterday, so that we are no longer the free and independent army we have been until now. I have noticed that the weak general is inclined to welcome the advent of the generalissimo; whereas the man of strong character at once begins, in anticipation, to feel worried and hampered. I think Fujii falls under the latter category.

My friend went on to tell me that the Second Army facing the Russians at Kaiping was about equal in numbers to the army of Kuropatkin, the bulk of which was still almost certainly well south of Haicheng. In this particular case, however, any comparison based upon mere numbers would be most misleading. Kuropatkin's army contained two reserve Divisions which were not worth much; it would, indeed, be rating them very highly, in Fujii's opinion, if they were classed as the equivalent to one regular Division. The Russian army contained also two Divisions which had already been well beaten in battle, and these he does not reckon as equal to more than one and a quarter Divisions. Basing his calculations on these assumptions, Fujii arrives at the highly satisfactory result that the Second Japanese army is very much its superior.

In front of the First Army we have two Divisions, one of them the 10th — from Europe, and we shall have to fight as hard as we can to get through. Fortunately, Kuropatkin evidently still thinks that the bulk of our army is at Siuyen. It is true that two Japanese Divisions will shortly arrive there, but our army is practically all in line of battle fracing the Motienling, and the passes east and west of it. Fujii seemed pleased with our position in relation to the Russians, and thought that the situation looked promising. This time he expected that the Twelfth Division would get most of the luck in the way of fighting, and after that it would be the turn of the Second Division, which constitutes our own central column. We shall have a very nasty river to negotiate before we can strike into the Russian line of communication to the north of Liaoyang. It is called the Taitsu-Ho, and at this rainy period of the year there is always a chance that we might be held up by floods whilst the Russians were making good their escape from the direct attack of the Second Army. Fujii bemoaned the fate of our own First Army; he said it seemed to be its unfortunate destiny to be eternally fording, swimming, or bridging rivers — we might just as well be an army of ducks, so he said. Opinion on the general staff is greatly divided on the subject of Kuropatkin's intentions, and last night, after the magic-lantern show, argument seems to have run quite high in this connection. The point at issue is whether Kuropatkin is going to attack the Second Army, or intends to remain on the defensive. Fujii himself seems inclined to believe he will continue to act on the defensive. He says that if he had thought it possible to attack at all, he ought surely to have done so before the First Army got athwart the Motienling. Now that the Japanese are on the pass, almost overshadowing Liaoyang by their presence, an attack southwards on the Second Army would be altogether too risky, unless Kuropatkin weakened himself for that attack by detaching a large proportion of his force to hold the First Army fast.

No doubt it is possible that Kuropatkin, clinging to Liaoyang, and sweeping together all the reinforcements he can, might look to play the part of Napoleon at Austerlitz, and remain crouching in the plain until the Japanese come out of the mountains to cut his communications, when he would make his deadly spring. At the same time Fujii is clearly of the opinion that such a scheme would be extremely rash. He evidently finds it difficult, notwithstanding the Austerlitz theory, to account for his hanging on so long at Liaoyang. He said: "He has thirty-six big magazines at Liaoyang, and I can well understand his anxiety to cling to his communications with Newchwang as long as possible. Those communications help him enormously in provisioning his army, but still his delay at Liaoyang seems altogether too dangerous. Indeed, some of us think he is already too late to get away if only the Second Army keep a close eye upon him. He has a great reputation, and I really cannot understand him at present. The moment of his decision against holding the Motienling should also have been the moment of his issuing orders for the retreat on Mukden."

He then began to talk about provisioning the army, and I can see he is naturally anxious that the Russian magazines at Liaoyang should not be burned before we could get at them. *À propos* of magazines, he told me a funny story about the Russian commissariat. The other day the Twelfth Division sent out a foraging party from Saimachi to Kanshio; on arrival at the latter place they found that the Russians had retired, leaving behind them their magazines of food. The commander of the party got fifty carts and brought all the stuff back with him to Saimachi, where it was very badly needed at the time. As soon as the foragers had fallen back clear of Kanshio, the Russian commander returned and found the magazines empty. He was beside himself with rage, and made prisoners of twenty Chinese, over whom a court-martial was held, with the result that two of them had their heads cut off. Some of the others escaped and, flying to Saimachi, implored the Japanese to send their troops back again and turn out the Russians. The Japanese will probably do so, but the point of the story is this: The Russian commander had given explicit orders on his retirement that the stores were to be burned. The Chinese inhabitants, however, were afraid that if the stores were burned their own adjacent dwellings and *kaoliung* stacks might catch fire. They therefore subscribed money, with which they bribed the Russian intendant, who was left behind with orders to bum the stores; he took the money and spared the stores. I gathered that there was some similar arrangement on the tapis whereby the Liaoyang magazines might also escape burning when the Russian army retired.

The trial report on the captured Russian field guns has just come back from Japan. The gun is satisfactory except as to weight, which is excessive, but the bursting charge of the shrapnel is too strong. There is thus too great a dispersion of, and not sufficient depth of area covered by, bullets. The fuses are not good, and very frequently burn out prematurely. If the Japanese take these guns seriously into use they will have to make some high explosive shell specially for them, as they will not care to go into action without a proportion of this ammunition.

The present line of communication from the Twelfth Division does not run from Fenghuangcheng at all, their base is Changsong on the Yalu. Boats from Antung take up supplies to a place on the bank opposite Changsong, and they are carried thence up the valley of the Aiho by the main Aiyanmen-Sai-machi-Chaotao road.

Chapter XIV – The Battle of the Heaven-Reaching Pass

July 18th, 1904. Evening. — This is my first quiet interval since I was awakened in the grey and foggy dawn of the 17th by the solemn boom of guns being fired far away to the westwards. I slipped into my clothes; saddled up; filled my haversack, wallets and feed-bag, and rode to headquarters. There an adjutant, more excited and less discreet than usual, told me the Motienling was being attacked, and that our troops were falling back before superior numbers. I wanted to start at once, but was kept dancing with impatience for at least an hour before permission was granted. To make up for lost time, I galloped along for the Motienling, *via* Bunsuirei and Lienshankuan. The morning, though foggy, was calm and fresh. It looked as if my hopes were about to be realised in full. My horse seemed as keen as myself to lessen the distance between us and the artillery, which kept sending its messages, reverberating along the mountains, calling thousands of eager soldiers to the battle-field. Never had my prospects seemed brighter of shortly finding myself in the thick of a general action. But there is no truer proverb than that which differentiates between haste and speed. After pushing along for some twelve miles, my

The Battle of the Heaven-Reaching Pass 213

poor old Canadian horse, Montana, began to slow down, first to a jog-trot, then to a walk, until at last we came to a complete standstill; whether it was colic, or a touch of the sun, cr several touches of the spur, I cannot say; but there he certainly stood, hanging his head and pouring with sweat, obviously incapable of carrying me a single yard further. By this time a point had been reached only five miles short of the pass, and there was nothing for it but to finish the journey on foot. Accordingly, I put my "bento" of rice into my haversack, and, leaving Montana in charge of the gendarme, started off in a very crestfallen, almost despairing, frame of mind. Before long I heard the rattle of musketry, and began to meet wounded men wending their way back slowly and, as it seemed to me, reluctantly from the fight. With every step the sound of the firing increased in violence, and as I went I got mixed up in the sunken road with a battalion and a number of ammunition mules pushing their way up to reinforce. Not a single preternaturally solemn face did I see amongst the men. All were gay and smiling with joyful anticipation, and it was evident that the only anxiety which existed was lest they should be too late to participate in whatever was happening on the far side of the mountain. Such keenness was contagious, and I pressed on, running whenever I came to a bit of level ground. But the pass itself was steep, and by the time I got over it and down to the old temple, the Russians had definitely begun to retire, whilst the Japanese had left their trenches some time previously, and were now advancing in pursuit. At the old temple two Japanese companies had piled arms on the reverse side of the ridge, and were beginning to dig graves for the Russian dead, of whom there were a considerable number, scattered along the line of the main road, and on a rise of the ground immediately behind the temple. About twenty or thirty Japanese dead had been collected into a heap close to the temple walls, where they lay awaiting cremation, with their faces covered with Russian greatcoats.

Were I writing this to please any one but myself, now would be the moment to introduce some suitable reflections on that well-worn theme, the horrors of war. For the life of me I cannot see these horrors to-day. Is it horrible to see these young heroes, scarcely cold, laid by other heroes beneath the fresh green turf of the Heaven-reaching pass? The death-chamber; the associations; the callous professionals, fill me with awe and even with shrinking. Here all is natural, and if sad is yet glorious in its sadness.

THE OLD TEMPLE AT MOTIENLING

A gigantic Russian, badly wounded in the leg, was hobbling up the hill with the aid of his rifle, which he used as a support. On his face was a timid deprecating smile as if he was not sure what terrible thing might not be going to happen to him, but no one besides myself seemed to pay the slightest attention to his movements. There is something sad in this if you will, but it is not half so dismal as seeing ragged unemployed in Mayfair.

Looking westwards, the view was bounded at about seven miles distance by mountains running parallel to the Motienling range, on which the Russians had established their main position. These parallel ranges were divided by the broad Tiensuitien valley, and from each of them ran subsidiary valleys and ridges, which were subdivided again into numberless ravines, woody spurs, and rocky knolls — an admirable terrain for troops well exercised in mountain warfare, but one which provided a. series of death-traps to an army trained in the plains, which could only hope to make up for deficiencies in its education by the display of exceptional adaptability, intelligence, and initiative on the part of its regimental officers.

The firing was now notably less heavy than it had been when I was toiling up the eastern slope of the Motienling, and was restricted to the lower slopes and spurs running from the Motienling range into the Tiensuitien valley. My experience told me that I had surely missed seeing the crisis of the engagement. I felt mortified, and, like Colonel Kurita in face of Korean transport difficulties, could almost have sat down and wept. It was certainly cruel bad luck, but, considering the mischance more dispassionately to-night, it was not so bad that it might not have been much worse. I did see a good deal of promiscuous fighting during the next four hours; and Vincent, who was up in comparatively good time, has told me exactly how things stood in the earlier stages of the action. I hope, therefore, I may be able to send home a fairly complete and accurate report, and I will spend to-morrow in putting down all I saw and all the news I have been able to glean up to date, so that I may get the whole story clearly outlined in my mind before I have to spoil it by considering how much I can squeeze past the censor, and how much I must omit. Meanwhile, I shall send a cable to Lord Kitchener bringing out a few points, such as the sparing use of artillery by both sides, the dismounted fighting of the cavalry, the unsophisticated nature of the Russian attack, purely frontal, in close order, without utilising the ground and without any attempt at a turning movement. I must also draw attention to the bad shooting, and to the antique fashion of firing by section volleys of seventy rifles adopted by the Russians. Not even their companies, still less their sections or individuals, seemed to show much flexibility, dash, or initiative. On the other hand, I must remember to bear tribute to their fine indifference to danger. Everything seems to point to the Europeans being superior to the Siberians, and I think I must cable this also, as the fact is important.

It is now 10 p.m., and in our Chinese physician's house it is 93°F.

July 19th, 1904. — X. has come back from his visit to headquarters, and tells me my cable has got past the censor. He says also that our right column, the Twelfth Division, has begun what promises to be a big and bloody fight with a superior force of Russians who are barring the road to Cbaotao (Kyoto), upon which place they had received orders to advance. These Russians are said to have twenty field guns in position, rather a stiff proposition for the thirty-six little mountain guns of the Twelfth Division.

However, the first thing I have to do is to digest the fighting of the 17th. This action, which the headquarters have named the Battle of the Heaven-Reaching Pass, turns out to have been of much greater importance than was apparent to any one who, like myself, saw only the repulse of the Russians from the actual Motienling. No doubt the bulk of the Russian strength marched down the Pekin road, and then, turning east, climhed the mountain on either side of the pass to attack the Japanese entrenched astride of it. But it seems now that there was also a great deal of subsidiary, but desperate fighting, extending over a frontage of at least ten miles, which took place to the north and south of the Motienling, simultaneously with the main attack. Indeed, the success gained by Kuroki was apparently due quite as much to the fine military qualities of his detachments on either flank as to the steadiness of the defenders of the pass, who were never, in my opinion, put to any exacting test throughout the course of the action.

Another noteworthy point about this engagement is that, considerable as it was, it was limited on the Japanese side to a successful defence of its positions by the central column or Second Division. Neither the Twelfth Division on the right or the Imperial Guards on the left took any part in the fighting, hut, on the other hand, the whole of the front covered by the Second Division, extending from Gebato, some five miles to the north-east of the Motienling, to the mountain of Shinkwairei, some four miles a little west of south of that pass, was subjected to a general, and, in some cases, to an enveloping attack.

Generally speaking, it may be said that the line of resistance of the Japanese outposts ran in a curve like a half-stretched bow from Gebato on the right, along the Motienling in the centre, to, and inclusive of, the mountain of Shinkwairei on the left. For the most part it followed the crest line of the main ridge, but at Gebato it

The Battle of the Heaven-Reaching Pass 217

was pushed forward north of the watershed.

About one-half of the Second Division was immediately available to hold this defensive position; the other half were more or less concentrated in the neighbourhood of Lienshankuan. To carry further the simile by which the line Shinkwairei-Motienling-Gebato was compared to a half-bent bow, Lienshankuan was the centre of the bowstring against which the notch of an arrow pointing towards Liaoyang might figuratively be supposed to press. Lienshankuan is about seven miles by road from the top of the Motienling pass, and about the same distance, but with inferior communications, to Shinkwairei and Grebato.

It will make the somewhat confused series of actions which took place on the 17th more clear, I think, if I resist the temptation to begin with what fell under my personal observation, and start at the extreme right, or north, of the Japanese line, taking each section of the position successively until I get to the left on the Shinkwairei mountain.

The Japanese right was entrusted to the 16th Regiment, which had its headquarters at Gebato. The regiment was under the command of Colonel Taniyama, and at the time of the action he had only two of his battalions — the first and second — ^present, the third having been sent back to the extreme left of the army on some special secret mission, which is still to be a secret to me. Whatever this mission may have been, it removed the 3rd battalion entirely out of the sphere of action on July 17th.

The outposts thrown forward by Colonel Taniyama were as follows (see Map X., pages 236-237):

One company on the Cebato-Chaotao road, one company on the Cebato-Jokahoshi road, and one company on the Grebato-Shokorei road. Thus the Colonel was left with one complete battalion and one company under his personal command at Glebato.

At 3 a.m. he heard by telephone from Shinkwairei mountain, on the extreme left of his Division, that the enemy were shovring signs of activity. He at once sent word to his outposts, but it was not until 11.50 a.m. that the company on the road to Chaotao— viz., the company on the extreme right of the Division— was attacked by eight Russian companies and one squadron of cavalry, which came from the direction of Jokahoshi. As soon as the enemy developed their full strength, the Japanese company fell back slowly upon its prepared line of resistance, shown upon the map as "B," a short distance in advance of the crossing of the two roads to Chaotao. Here it was reinforced by a company of pioneers sent out by the divisional commanders from Lienshankuan, and held its own easily, the enemy showing no great determination in the attack. At 12.40 p.m. the Russians engaged at this point began to fall back in a north-westerly direction, and were allowed to draw off without pursuit.

In contrast to the foregoing rather tame affair, a great fight was put up by the next outpost — the famous 6th company, 16th Regiment — a fight which challenges comparison with that made by the 5th company, 24th Regiment, on May 1st, when they barred the Russian retreat at Hamaton by the Yalu.

This 6th company was posted to watch the GebatoJokahoshi road at a spot marked "C" upon Map X., about two and a half miles north-west of Gebato. At 8 a.m. the enemy, who had made a very wide turning movement from the direction of Okahoshi, and had probably marched all night through a most difficult and intricate country of precipitous mountains and deep, winding valleys, suddenly opened fire from height "D" upon this picquet. To reach their point, the Russians must have terminated their night march by a climb of a clear thousand feet out of the valley to the north-west of the mountain. This speaks well for their determination and powers of endurance. Not only was point "D" a thousand feet above the valley out of which the Russians had issued, but it was 150 feet above spur "C," which it completely commanded at a range of about 600 yards. The Russians were at least two battalions strong, and having so energetically and yet so secretly managed to place a very superior force in a dominating position, it hardly seemed possible that they could fail in their object, which was to turn the Japanese flank. To complete their success they had only to press on with a portion of their force to the neck marked "H." Had they once succeeded in establishing themselves there, the picquet holding spur "C" must have fallen back, thus enabling the Russians to move down the valley and envelop the whole of the Japanese right. Everything seemed to favour the attackers on this occasion.

The Battle of the Heaven-Reaching Pass 219

Their long and well-conducted night march had been rewarded by the capture of the highest ground in the neighbourhood, from which they completely overlooked the position of the 6th Japanese company at fixed sight range. They dominated ridge "C" by 150 feet, and, theoretically, it should hardly have been tenable. They were well covered also from view by scrub jungle, and could move to either flank without exposing themselves either to observation or to fire. Finally, they had not been expected from this direction, and although the 6th company had been warned that some Russian movement was in progress, they were, as a matter of fact, surprised at a great disadvantage.

The Russian force at this point, as evidenced afterwards by the numbers on the caps of their dead, consisted of men from the 11th, 12th and 21st East Siberian Regiments. Japanese headquarters do not, however, claim that their 6th company was attacked by three full Russian battalions, although the officers of the 16th Regiment do make this claim, and point to the cap numbers to support their contention. The general staff, on the other hand, are quite clear that there were only eight Russian companies, or two battalions, engaged in the attack upon "C." The 11th, 12th and 21st Regiments fought on the 1st May, and it is a plausible explanation that three of these decimated battalions may have been amalgamated into two after the retirement from the Yalu.

Owing to the strength of the enemy, and their commanding positions, the 6th company was overmatched, and their situation was becoming desperate, when, at 9 a.m., a reinforcement of two companies despatched from Gebato by Colonel Taniyama came up and checked the further progress of the Russians, just at the moment when victory had seemed to be within their grasp.

A brief reference must here be made to the 7th Japanese company. It had been detailed to hold the left of the line of outposts, and had taken up its position along a ridge immediately to the north of the road of the Shokorei mountain. Here it was attacked at 8 a.m. by several Russian companies coming from the west. Before the action had had time fully to develop itself three fresh companies of the 16th Regiment appeared upon the scene, and, joining forces with the 7th company, forced the Russians to fall back. These three companies had not been sent purposely as a reinforcement. Under urgent orders from Divisional headquarters. Colonel Taniyama had been obliged to despatch them towards the Shokorei mountain, with orders to leave a small detachment there, and then push on fast to Daidoko. It was in the course of executing these orders that they arrived in the nick of time to help the 7th company, and having made that outpost quite secure, they proceeded to march towards Daidoko.

There were now no reserves left in Colonel Taniyama's hands. Of the eight companies originally at his disposal, one was standing to arms in its position on the Chaotao road; three were fighting desperately on the Jokahoshi road; one had repulsed the enemy and was awaiting further orders at "G," on the Shokorei mountain road: whilst the remaining three companies were marching away from the scene of conflict towards Shokorei and Daidoko.

By 10 a.m. the two Russian battalions on "D" were once more beginning to assert their advantage in position and numbers; and it seemed inevitable, even to the most sanguine, that, unless some fresh troops could be brought upon the scene, the right flank of the three companies holding spur "C" must shortly be turned. Thereupon Taniyama bethought him of his 7 th company at "G." It had disposed of its own enemy and its front was now clear. With a Japanese commander the thought seems to father the act without a moment's delay, and the 7th company was forthwith moved at the double for three and a half miles from the extreme left at "G" to the spur *"K," where it formed line in echelon, behind the right of the three hard beset companies clinging to spur "C." Thus, once again were the Russians frustrated, success being snatched away, so to say, from their very jaws.

The fight across the valley between D" and "C now became very evenly balanced. Eight Russian companies wearied with a long and severe night march, against four Japanese companies comparatively fresh, and knowing every inch of the ground. From 11.30 a.m. to 1 p.m. the Russians were, by degrees, losing ground; but then, with admirable pertinacity, they appeared to recover themselves and resumed a vigorous offensive, whereby, after some hot fighting, they practically regained all that they had lost.

How all this would have ended had these troops been left to fight it out, no one can say. Probably in a stalemate. But the

Divisional headquarters were alive to the critical state of things on their right, and had sent off the 2nd battalion of the 29th Regiment from Lienshankuan as a reinforcement. At 1.30 the 2nd battalion, 29th, appeared in the distance on the hill overlooking Gebato at "B." So unwelcome a sight chilled the ardour of the Russians, and thenceforward they began to give ground before the Japanese, although still only very slowly and reluctantly. At last, at 3 p.m., they seemed definitely to accept their repulse, and at 4.30 p.m. fell back in good order to the north-west towards Jokahoshi.

Pinned on to the breast of one of their dead, who must have been a brave man, as he was lying nearer than any of the other corpses to the Japanese position, was a slip of paper, on which was written, in English, "Brave Japanese, bury our dead." I may add that the Japanese not only complied with this touching request, but put flowers upon these Russian graves.

The Russians left behind them fifty-four dead. They had no prisoners taken, either wounded or unwounded.

The Japanese losses were 135, of whom forty-one were killed. All the officers, as well as the sergeant-major of the 6th company, were killed or wounded, and the command, during the latter part of the engagement, devolved upon a sergeant.

Every Japanese I have spoken to on the subject considers that this is quite the best fight the Russians have as yet put up, whether as regards courage or intelligence.

Military bravery is the one virtue which every Japanese ungrudgingly and spontaneously admires. It is a curious result of this mental attitude that the officers and men who were engaged in this bitter little fight speak in a much more friendly tone of the Russians than any other Japanese I have yet met. If the Russians only fight well enough they will, at this rate, end by gaining the hearts of the Japanese army.

I certainly do not wish to be more critical of the Russians than the Japanese themselves. Still, even accepting that the infantry of our allies is second to none in the world, it is not very easy to explain how the eight Russian companies on "D" came to be stopped by one Japanese company for a full hour, especially when those eight companies had reached unobserved a commanding position only a few hundred yards from the line held by the outposts. As a mere proposition on the map, and, still more so, perhaps, when considered as a tactical problem on the actual ground, it seems strange indeed that the two battalions on "D" could not make short work of the little force which was all that at first opposed them on "C." It looks so simple to tell off two companies to storm the Japanese position, whilst six companies with magazine fire from "D," forced the defenders to keep down their heads until the assault came near enough to make a rush with the bayonet.

Once, however, the personal equation enters into the problem, all its simplicity disappears. On the one side were eight Russian companies, exhausted after their night march, constitutionally disinclined to display great initiative, ignorant of the terrain, and very indifferent shots. On the other was the 6th company, inspired with a most tenacious courage, fresh, knowing every inch of the ground, shooting moderately well, and displaying as its chief and winning characteristic a combination of very great mobility with a wide extension. It was this last quality which always enabled them to present a front to the Russians, thus not only checking their advances, but probably deceiving them as to the numbers opposed to them. The fight on the ridges "C" and "D" resolved itself into a series of attempts of the Russian commander to get on to the neck at "H," and thence to roll up the 6th company and at the same time to work down the valley to the north-east of " C " as far as Gebato. A few individuals did actually work their way into the valley, and had they been Boers would have punished the Japanese severely by effective shooting into their backs. But Russian soldiers are of much less value as individuals than in the mass. Had any formed body of Russians succeeded in following the handful who penetrated to the north of "C," the right of the Second Division would infallibly have been turned. Such a misfortune was only frustrated by the very rapid movements of the Japanese 16th Regiment. All day long, so I was told, sections were racing to a threatened point; repulsing the enemy, then, once again, hurrying back to make good their original position. The same characteristic was apparent in the dispositions of Colonel Taniyama. In fact, the Japanese shuffled their few cards so dexterously and swiftly that their opponents could not follow their movements, or estimate

The Battle of the Heaven-Reaching Pass

what forces were opposed to them. The 16th Regiment became indeed for a time like one of those theatrical armies which double in strength each time they march round the wings. So much for the Japanese right.

The next section of the fight concerns the centre and the Russian main attack on the Motienling itself. Here Colonel Baba, a very kind friend to the British officers, was in charge with the 30th Regiment, complete with its three battalions. Brigadier-General Okasaki was in chief command, and held the other regiments of his brigade in reserve. (See Map IX., pages 234-235.)

At 12.30 p.m. the outposts of the 3rd brigade were attacked along their line of resistance on the Shinkwairei mountain. The news was at once telephoned from one end of the Second Division line to the other, and the 30th Regiment stood to its arms and waited. The dispositions were as follows: The 1st battalion was posted along the Motienling ridge on the south side of the main road, the 2nd battalion took the right section of defence on the north side of that road, while the 3rd battalion was held in support along the actual road on the eastern slope of the pass. The outline sketch gives a clear idea of the terrain, and also of the position of the guns.

Since the action of the 4th July the picquet had been withdrawn from Lichaputsu, and the outposts had their picquets in the old and new temples.

The Russians began to scale the Motienling at 3 a.m. At 4 a.m., approximately, they arrived at the temples, and took possession of them, the outposts having been ordered to fall back on to the main line of resistance, the Motienling ridge.

At 5 a.m. the 1st battalion of the 30th Regiment opened fire from their trenches along the crest line at the Russians, who had swung forward their right until they had reached a point within some 300 yards of the Japanese left. As if waiting for the signal, the whole of the enemy's right wing, consisting at this hour of two battalions, made vigorous reply. To understand the relative positions of the opposing forces, they may conveniently be represented by a capital "V," with its point turned southwards, and its eastern or Japanese arm laid upon the line of the Motienling ridge. The western or Russian arm should he imagined as almost, hut not quite, meeting this eastern arm on the high ground to the south of the main road, whence it should run back at an angle along the spur "B," following the main road for a great part of the distance. Applying this figure to the map, it will be found that the Russian right was within 300 yards of the Japanese left, whilst their left was resting upon the old temple at over 1500 yards from the Japanese centre, from which it was still separated by a deep valley. The main road was worn away by traffic, so that its surface was about six inches below the level of the ground, and this meagre allowance of cover was available for the Russians where their line coincided with it.

As the extreme Russian right seriously threatened the Japanese line of defence, two companies of the 3rd battalion, 30th Regiment, which was still in reserve, were sent out at 5 a.m. to occupy the very highest point of the Motienling, thus prolonging the 1st battalion to the left up a piece of most precipitous mountain. The 3rd company, 3rd battalion, was at the same time sent to reinforce the centre, and only one company was kept in reserve.

From 5.40 onwards, the Russians were continually receiving reinforcements. At 6 a.m. the fire became very heavy indeed on the heights to the Japanese left, to which the two companies had been sent from the reserves. At this time also it became apparent that only the Russian right wing had so far been engaged, for at 6.5 a.m. their true left showed up on the heights north of Shokorei (marked "C" on the map) to the extent of two companies. At 6.30 a.m. the Japanese battery, entrenched on the north of the pass, shelled the enemy on this Shokorei ridge. At 8 a.m. heavy masses of Russians were seen coming up, some to reinforce their right wing and some to prolong the line to the left. The latter moved up the valley north of Rocky Hill, and offered to the Japanese battery on the heights a regiment moving in column of route by sections, for their shrapnel. Since the battle of Omdurman no such chance has probably been presented to artillery; and these six Japanese guns took full advantage of it, opening at 3000 yards, and killing 300 Russians in a very few minutes. The battery completely broke the impetus of the Russian advance up the valley north of Rocky Hill, and brought it to a disastrous full stop before a single Russian soldier on this part of the ground had fired off his rifle or even heard the whistle

The Battle of the Heaven-Reaching Pass 225

of a rifle bullet. It is hardly worth commenting on the tragic error committed by the Russian commander in advancing to the attack in such a formation when there was even the remotest chance that he might find himself exposed to artillery fire. It is true that until 8 a.m. his movements had been concealed by the fog, but a prudent soldier would have realised by the gun fire and musketry that this did not veil the entire battle-field, and that it might therefore be expected to lift at any moment. At 8.30 a.m. the companies of the 16th Regiment which, as already recorded, had been ordered to march from Gebato *via* the Shokorei mountain to Daidoko, came near enough to the scene of action to fire long-range volleys against the Russians in the valley north of Bocky Hill, and to engage the Russian left, which was now in position on the ridge marked "C," which is the Shokorei mountain.

CHINESE STRETCHER-BEARERS AT MOTIENLING

At 9 a.m. the Japanese battery turned on to the old temple and shelled the Russians out of it. The walls were nine inches thick, but the three or four shrapnel which hit them passed through them easily, and burst inside with such effect that the Russians recognised the place was untenable, and cleared out behind the spur.

At 9.10 a.m. the Russians began a general retirement, falling back first from the left, whilst their right held on obstinately to cover the line of retreat. The Japanese opened rapid fire from their guns, and magazine fire from their rifles, directly they perceived the retrograde movement, and at 9.40 a.m. their men had gained possession of the old temple and of a portion of the ridge running south from it. At 10 a.m. the whole of the enemy's line had relaxed its grasp on the Japanese position, excepting only the two companies on the extreme Russian right, which had fallen back indeed as far as the woods surrounding the new temple, but held on there for a time most obstinately. At 10.30 a.m. these two companies were forced, by the enveloping attack of greatly superior numbers, to retire to ridge "E," where they found some support, and where the Japanese, pursuing without much dash, fired at them from "D," and also from the road coming down the pass, whenever this was sufficiently sunken to afford some cover. I arrived just as the action had reached this stage. The only heavy fire in progress was that which was being exchanged between "D" and "E," and, as an old musketry man, I could not have desired a better object-lesson. The Russians had a considerable advantage in command even where they had taken up their alignment some distance down the wooded northern spur of "E." This advantage was, however, much more than counterbalanced:

(1) By the misguided, spurious gallantry which impelled the Russian officers to stand up, not only exposing themselves unnecessarily, but also disclosing the exact positions of their sections, and thus drawing fire upon their men.

(2) By the surprising fact that the Russian fire consisted entirely of section volleys of sixty or seventy rifles, a procedure recalling British methods (very quickly dropped) at the beginning of the Afghan War in 1879.

(3) By the parade-like regularity of the Russian alignment, whereby the men, in shoulder to shoulder formation, were exposed in equal numbers to fire all along the ridge, irrespective of whether good cover was, or was not, available at any given point.

The Japanese, on the other hand, were much more flexible and up to date in their formations, although, with an average of two paces per man, their extension was considerably less than we should consider suitable to such conditions. I say an average extension, for, as a matter of fact, the Japanese on "D" were clustered together in little groups wherever there was good cover to be obtained, leaving gaps of twenty yards or more where there was no such cover. In this fight between "D" and "E " the Japanese used only independent fire, although some long-range volleys were occasionally directed against Russians in close formation, who were falling back slowly down the main valley in the direction of Towan. I never saw anything to equal the contemptuous deliberation with which these Russian detachments fell back, although bullets were knocking up the dust in all directions about them. I have seen our own men stroll along with equal indifference through heavier fire when making the attack, but in retirement every one tries, as a rule, not to spin out the process longer than is absolutely necessary. Through my glasses I was enabled clearly to distinguish one man turn round and halt for purposes of nature, facing, as he did so, towards the Japanese firing line. Another dropped something, and spent two or three minutes carefully searching for it under a perfect hail of bullets. I was quite relieved when at last he seemed to find what ho had wanted, and strolled away in a very leisurely manner to rejoin his comrades. Great, however, as is the Russian *sang-froid*, I wager it would not have withstood a pom-pom for many minutes; but the Japanese have none of these unrivalled morale-destroying implements.

The 1st and 2nd battalions of the 30th Regiment were now extended in pursuit, covering the ground from Shokorei mountain ("C") to the Motienling main road, and at the same time the 3rd battalion took up its position on the Japanese left, and pressed the enemy's right, which was falling back on Towan as already described.

At eleven o'clock, the 3rd battalion of the 29th Regiment and the divisional cavalry (which had arrived on the scene of action at 9.30 a.m., and had been held back in reserve) reached the new temple. The Russian infantry being by no means routed were not of course open to any enterprise by mounted men. The cavalry accordingly left their horses at the new temple, and racing down the steep spur in open order, proceeded to attack several Russian companies ensconced on "M," who were annoying the right of the Japanese pursuit. I watched this little *entr'acte* with peculiar interest, and was glad to see that the Japanese cavalryman is just as ready and just as competent to use the rifle as the sword.

All this time a Russian battery of eight field guns had been unlimbered in the open fields just beyond Kinkahoshi. The detachments had left their guns, and it might have been imagined that the Japanese were invisible, whereas, on the contrary, they seemed to me to offer frequently most excellent artillery targets. At 2.10 p.m., however, this battery suddenly opened fire on "C," or the Shokorei mountain. The commander must have known the distance fairly accurately, as he seemed to get both range and fuse in three or four shots, and then let fly the *rafale*, clearing the hill top as if by magic of our old friends the three companies of the 16th Regiment, who had been despatched there from Gebato. At Gebato the 16th Regiment showed themselves inspired heroes. Here they appeared ordinary human beings, extra human, in fact; for, except perhaps at Majuba, I never saw men make better time down the slopes of a very steep mountain in the whole course of my life. I was then at the old temple, where there were a couple of companies in reserve, and any number of Generals and staff. Thinking that I also would take care of myself, I went and put the thickest part of the temple wall between me and this battery; for, although the gunners could not actually see us owing to the lie of the ground, we were within easy range, and a Russian observation party on "G" could have, and should have, switched shrapnel on to so good a target without difficulty or delay. However, after giving us this illustration of what it might have done had it liked, the battery fired a round or two at "M," whence the dismounted Japanese cavalry and some infantry from Rocky Hill had now driven the Russians, and then ceased fire for the day. At 4 p.m. the musketry had greatly slackened, and at 5 p.m. all was so absolutely still and peaceful that it was difficult to realise that the dead were scarcely cold, and the wounded not stopped bleeding, on all the slopes of the surrounding mountains.

As if to show that they were by no means demoralised, the

The Battle of the Heaven-Reaching Pass 229

Russians continued to hold "E," "G," and Kinkahoshi until next morning. So much for the right and centre of the Japanese defence. On the Japanese left, one company of the 4th Regiment, 3rd brigade, was on outpost duty on the ridge of the Shinkwairei mountain. It was attacked between midnight and 1 a.m. on the 17th by one Russian company, which was repulsed, and fell back to the north of Makumenza. At 6.30 a.m. another company of the 4th Regiment, which had been sent out on reconnoitring duty from the Shinkwairei mountain, fell in with a Russian company a little to the east of Makumenza. After a sharp struggle the Russians were forced back, and the Japanese, pressing on in pursuit, managed at 7.30 a.m. to gain possession of the high ground above Makumenza itself. Hardly, however, had they made good this important point, when they were attacked on their right flank by a full Russian battalion advancing from Rikahoshi. Simultaneously a detachment of Russians appeared marching upon them from the direction of Towan, whilst the Russian company, which had just been worsted, rallied on seeing so many friends, and turned back to renew the engagement. Attacked on three sides by greatly superior forces, the Japanese company was on the very point of falling back — in fact, the order had actually been issued — when help came in the shape of two companies of their own regiment, who had been sent out to reconnoitre, and had been attracted by the sound of the firing. The Japanese claim that these three companies not only maintained their ground against the six who were opposed to them, but that they managed to find time during the fighting to cause considerable loss and annoyance to some Russian troops, marching at 9 a.m. towards the main Motienling fight, by firing from the heights into their right rear. At midday two more companies were sent out from the 4th Regiment, the Russians meanwhile increasing to a strength of three battalions. Soon afterwards the three Russian battalions definitely retreated upon Yamorinza, leaving the five Japanese companies masters of the field, and securely perched upon an eminence east of Makumenza. From this vantage-ground they commanded the main road, and masses of the enemy retreating during the afternoon from the Motienling had to run the gauntlet here, and are believed to have suffered much loss.

I have now exhausted my available information concerning the battle of the 17th July. The total Russian losses are estimated by the Japanese at more than 2000, and the Japanese own to having lost over 500 themselves. The disproportionately large Russian losses are attributed by headquarters mainly to the effect of the six Japanese field-guns on the massive formations so maladroitly exposed to their fire in the valley north of Kooky Hill at 8 a.m. Also to the impunity with which the five companies of the 4th Regiment were allowed to molest the retreat of the Russians down the main valley from the high ground to the east of Makumenza.

The Russian troops engaged consisted of the 34th and 35th Regiments of the Ninth Division of the Tenth European Corps, and of portions of the Third and Sixth Siberian Divisions. At the main attack there were approximately three regiments and a battery of field artillery engaged, and adding to this the troops employed at Gebato on the Russian left, and at Shinkwairei on the Russian right, a full Division seems to have taken part in the operations. On the Japanese side, the three battalions and one field battery originally holding the Motienling were increased by 9 a.m. to three regiments, whilst one more battalion arrived from Lienshankuan at about 11 a.m. Altogether, it may be said that the battle in its later developments took place between a Japanese and Russian Division, each supplemented by one battery of field artillery. It must not, of course, be overlooked that a Russian regiment consists of four battalions, whereas a Japanese regiment has only three battalions.

Comment on this strange battle is rendered difficult at present, owing to my ignorance of the orders and intentions of the Russian commander. Possibly he may only have intended a reconnaissance in force. Japanese headquarters believe, however, that General Count Keller meant to recapture the Motienling. I will, therefore, assume that this was so, especially as such an assumption is supported by the prolonged and desperate fighting at Gebato. For it must be remembered that the Gebato fight went on until late in the afternoon, and that even if the Russians there had succeeded; they could only have hoped to hold their ground provided the main attack was successful on the Motienling. Otherwise a Japanese detachment sent out from that position could easily have cut off the

The Battle of the Heaven-Reaching Pass 231

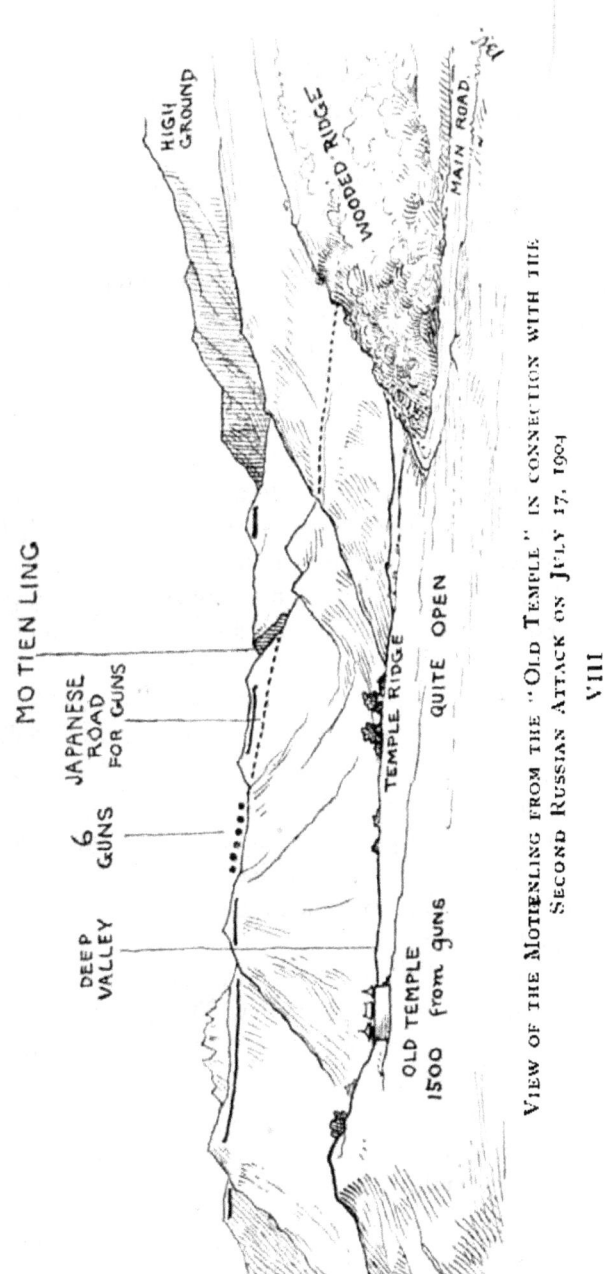

View of the Motienling from the "Old Temple" in connection with the Second Russian Attack on July 17, 1904

VIII

retreat of any Russians at Gebato.

In considering, then, the main action at Motienling, I feel exactly the same difficulty as commenting on the detached action at Gebato. I mean I cannot understand why the Russians did not make more of a push in the early hours of the engagement, when they were assisted by the fog, and when the Japanese held the pass and its approaches with only three battalions. The only Russian force, however, which ever attempted what we should call an attack, was their detachment on the extreme right. The centre, at and about the old temple, was 1500 yards distant from the Japanese, and separated from them by a very deep valley. The Russian left never got within rifle-shot until some time after the retirement had begun, although they had meanwhile suffered very heavy losses from artillery fire. I am anxious to guard myself from being over-critical of a world-famous army, especially when I was a mere onlooker exposed to no personal danger. Still, I must express my very strong feeling that, had the Russian forces been boldly led, and had every battalion commander determined from the very first to close with the enemy, and acted accordingly, then, at any time before 7 a.m., despite their dense unsuitable formations, the Russians must have pierced the Japanese line at some point or another. Whether having done so, they could have held their ground or not, is quite another matter. Just when the moment came to make the desperate, decisive effort, a strange lethargy, a sort of will paralysis, seems to have fallen upon the Russians; and it was the same at Gebato. It is passing strange that soldiers so steady and formidable in retreat should be so slow and so sticky in the attack.

The closeness of the Russian formations left nothing to be desired from the Japanese point of view. They paid the full penalty for this in the valley north of Rocky Hill. It was a mistake in any case to move up the valley, and it would have been far better to have employed these men in working up Rocky Hill, and thence, making use of the dead ground, to have prolonged the line to the north of the old temple. With the increased range of modem arms it has become mere waste of life to deploy men in valleys. Indeed, since the Tirah campaign we have, I think, learnt that, provided we hold the spurs and ridges, the valleys can be allowed to look after themselves.

The Russian marksmanship was bad, and by firing volleys they always gave away their position, even when their own officers had not already done so, by the slight haze which, from both Russian and Japanese smokeless powder, arises from the simultaneous discharge of so many rifles.

The effect of the Japanese shrapnel, and I may add of the few Russian shells fired, shows what might have been accomplished by a powerful artillery had it been employed by either side. To a British officer, accustomed to fighting on the north-west frontier of India, perhaps the most singular point in the battle was the absence of mountain guns on both sides. A brigade of mountain artillery with the Russians would have helped their attack to an incalculable but certainly very great extent, whilst in case of retreat it would have rendered them the greatest assistance. A single mountain battery with the Japanese would have enabled them to convert the Russian retirement into a rout. The Japanese field battery on the crest line remained in its gun-pits and took no part in the pursuit, although there was a good position on the ridge north of Rocky Hill, which commanded the main valley.

The Japanese pursuit may have erred on the aide of caution, but the ground admitted of whole brigades being concealed at several points along the line of the Russian retreat, and the enemy's main camp was within a few miles distance, so that it was obviously not a suitable occasion for taking any avoidable risks.

Finally, I repeat that in considering this remarkable engagement, it must be remembered that nine-tenths of the Russians never attacked at all. Some of them advanced to effective range, but many of them did not get so far. They exposed themselves for a time with admirable coolness to heavy losses in inferior positions. Then, with equal indifference to danger, they withdrew to their camp. All this, of course, is just like our Colenso. But, however greatly bravery may be admired in whatever form it manifests itself, one thing is quite certain, that since the battle of Jericho no strong position held by good troops has ever been taken by mere demonstration, however formidable this may be in appearance.

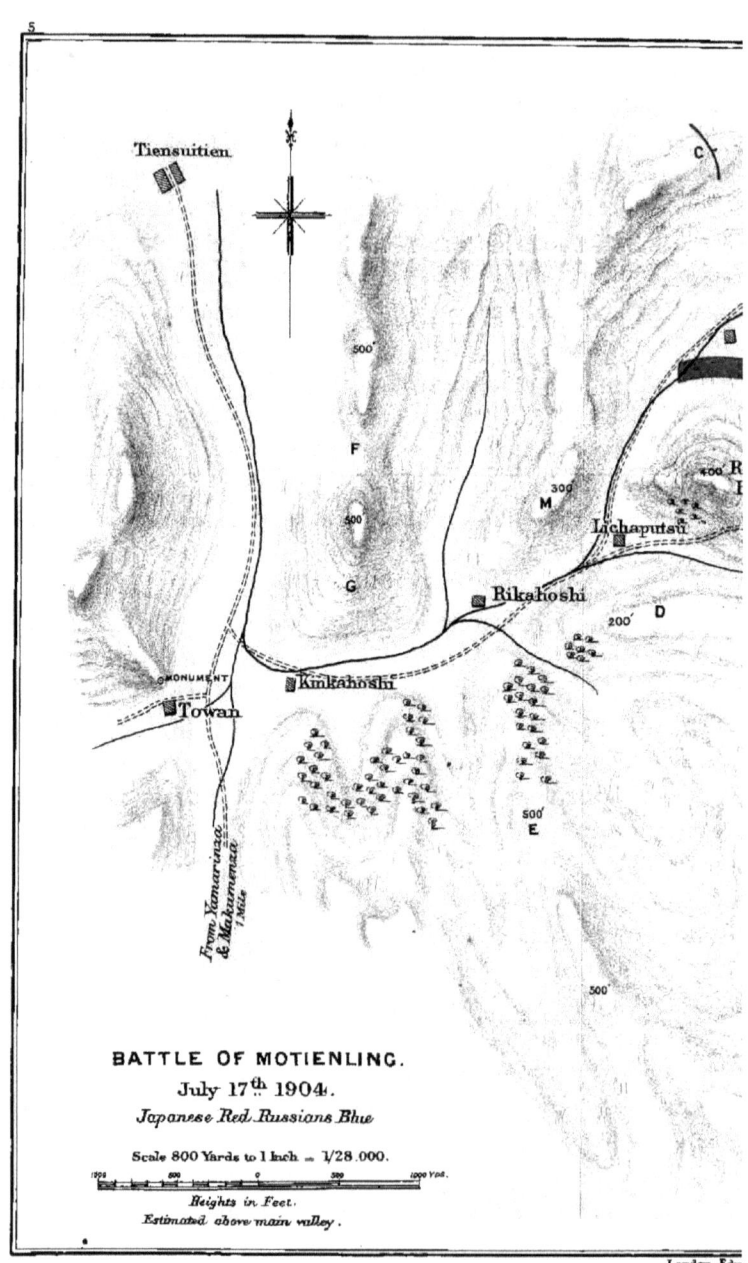

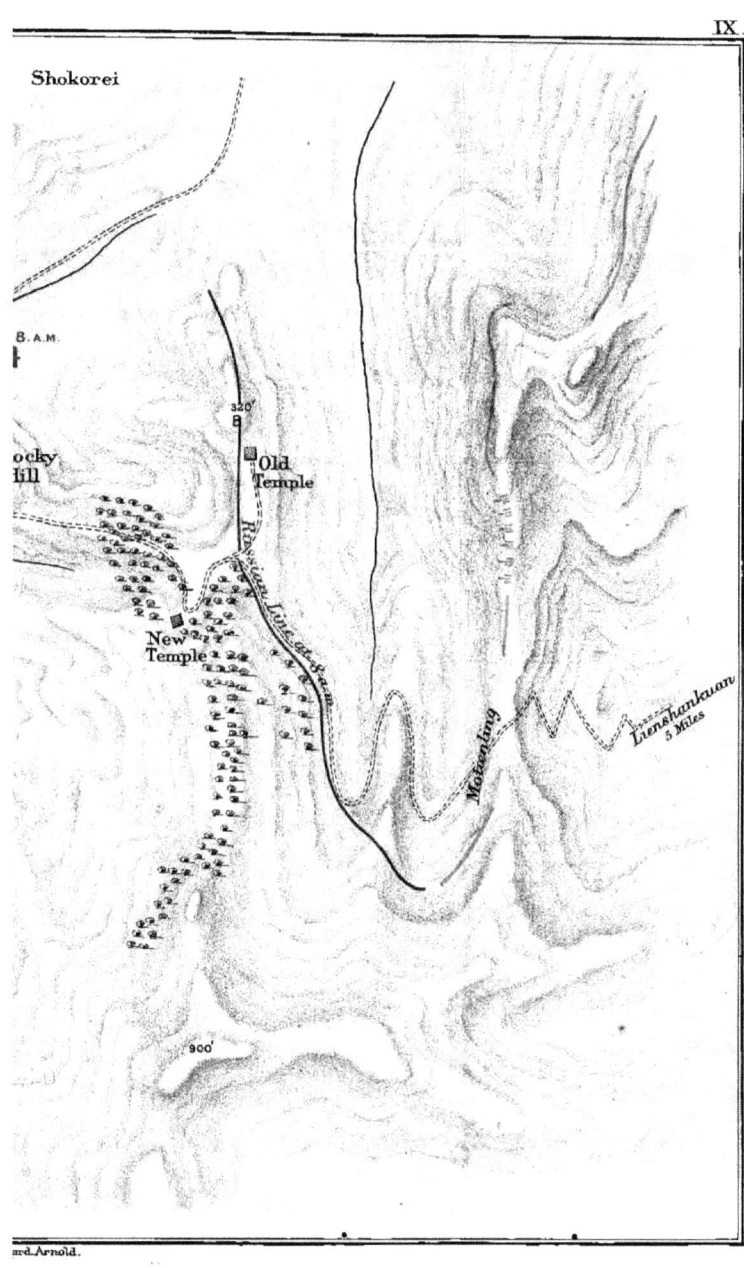

The Battle of the Heaven-Reaching Pass

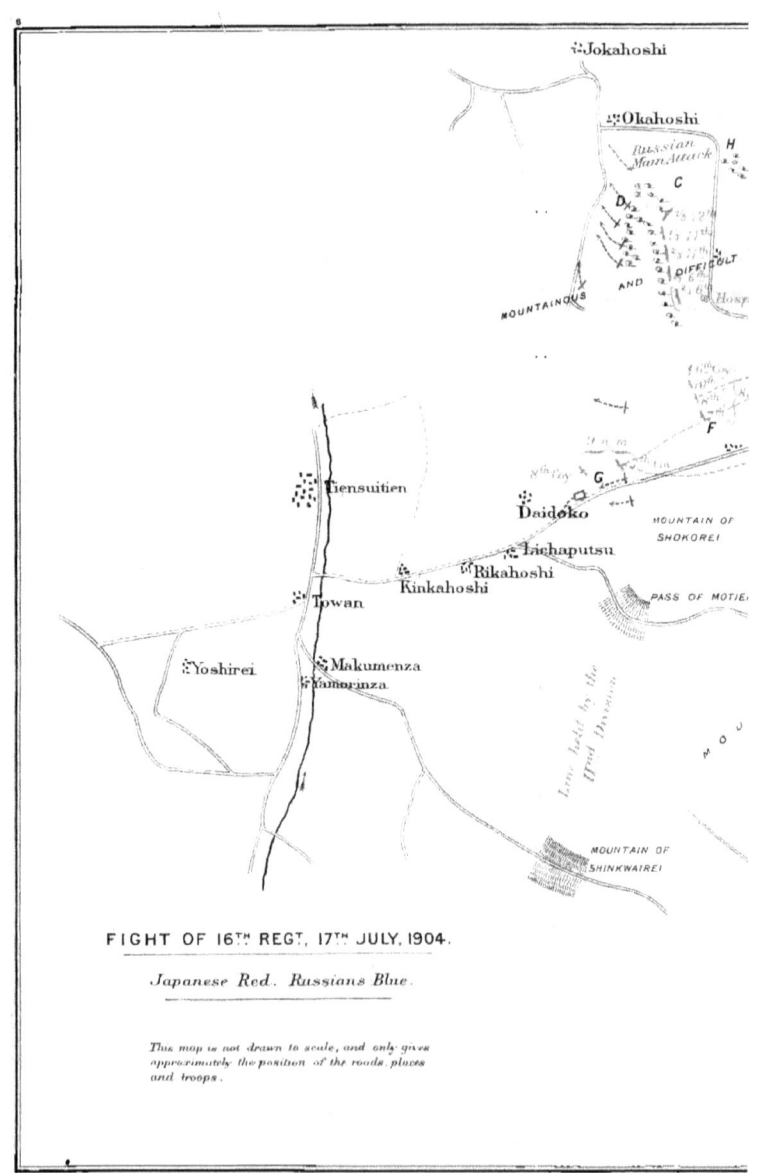

FIGHT OF 16TH REGT, 17TH JULY, 1904.

Japanese Red. Russians Blue.

This map is not drawn to scale, and only gives approximately the position of the roads, places and troops.

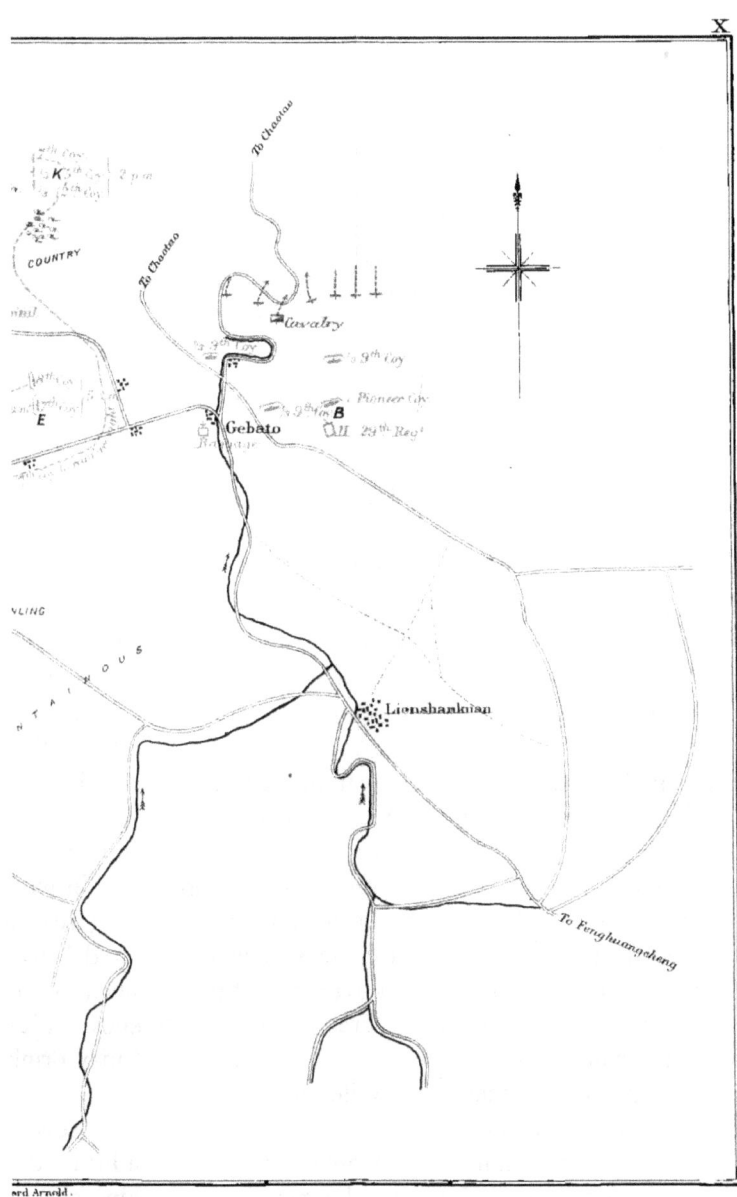

Chapter XV – Chaotao

July 21st, 1904. — Vincent rode over to see me, and has just left. He tells me that on the 17th a Japanese soldier, close beside him on Rocky Hill, got a bullet through his marksman's badge, just above his heart. He rolled over but soon sat up again, ejaculated a "Banzai," and was seen walking back to Lienshankuan that evening, showing his wound to his friends along the road. They are tough little fellows, certainly. Vincent also says that some of the other attachés and correspondents in conversation with him seemed to think that I ought to enter a protest against my position with headquarters, as it does not appear to them that I am being treated as magnificently as a Lieutenant-General ought to be treated. Why? I ride as good a horse as General Kuroki; get just as much to eat; and learn as much as it is considered good for me to know. After all, these battles are not being fought in order that I may drink champagne, or even that I may write reports.

Sergeant Watanabe, in charge of the train, is a severe disciplinarian. In fact, it is mainly owing to him that our little side-show gets along at all However, the men don't like him, and as they are being considerably worried by bugs at present, they have nicknamed him with the name of their antipathy. I heard one of them say just now, "Let us run away; here is the Nankin Mushi (*i.e.*, Chinese bug) approaching-"

Some of the military train coolies have come back from diverting the river from its bed in order to scoop up the fish left in the pools. They drove up in a cart with several baskets full. As they turned in at the gate one of them called out in an authoritative voice to his fellows, "Here you, make way at once for the Chief of the General Staff!"

There were a lot of wounded here this morning lying about under the trees, resting on their way down to the base hospital at Fenghuangcheng. One of them had an entry and exit wound in each arm, making four wounds; a graze across his forehead, which was bandaged; a bad ricochet bruise on his chest; and had also had the nerve-shaking experience of seeing his left shoulder-strap whisked off by a bullet. He was much depressed; not because of his wounds or bruises, but only because he felt quite able to go on fighting, whilst the hard-hearted doctors had taken another view of his condition, and had insisted on his leaving the front.

I got all these poor depressed little wounded fellows some tea, and it was a real pleasure to see how much they enjoyed it. I have had none myself for some time past, but luckily I was sent a present of a big tin the other day by the ever generous General Okasaki! May his shadow never grow less I

Later. — Jardine's despatch on the engagement fought on the 19th between the Twelfth Division and the Russians at Chaotao, has just come to hand by a special messenger; a cavalryman. He had first been round to headquarters, and he brought a message that the general staff would like to see the report as soon as I had read it. I know they have a high opinion of Jardine's good sense, and as he was absolutely the only foreigner in the whole world who saw this battle, I do not wonder at their curiosity to know what he thinks about it. Accordingly, after just skimming through the papers so as to get material sufficient for a cable to Lord Kitchener, I have sent them on to the censor at headquarters. I kept the cavalryman, however, and after softening his heart with tea and sugar-plums I got him to give me his own very intelligent views upon the action. I must cable and announce that Jardine was the only foreign observer of this battle, for I feel that is a great feather in the British cap. I must also add something to the effect that, although the Russians defended themselves well, they nevertheless seemed glued to their trenches, and made no attempt to anticipate or counter-attack a wide turning movement; that the European Russians are braver, better disciplined, and better officered than the Siberians; that the Japanese attacked in much wider, looser formations than at the Yalu, and that their turning march across precipitous, trackless mountains, without even a Chinese guide to show them the way, deserved the success which in very full measure it obtained.

July 22nd. — At 10 a.m. I heard guns firing from the Motienling, or perhaps from a point a little to the north of it. At 10.15 a.m. Fujii came in and said he had ridden over to have a talk. He told me I need not worry about the guns. The firing meant nothing of importance, and if anything serious did develop, I should be sent up sharp. Meanwhile, he sat down and gave me a lot of intensely interesting news, not only in the form of a supplement to Jardine's report, which he handed back to me, but also concerning the general situation.

According to Fujii, this, the general situation, is now becoming most exciting. The Second Army began its march along the main road to Tashihchiao yesterday morning. The Fourth Army at Siuyen is to advance to-day against Takutokujo. The Russians are in force behind strong works at Haicheng, and they also hold a fortified line in advance of Haicheng, and near Tashihchiao, where the Second Army may come in contact with them to-morrow. He told me that the problem now exercising the whole of our First Army staff is whether Kuropatkin will attack, or wait to be attacked? No one knows, and yet the issue of the campaign may depend upon the ability of the Japanese generalissimo to gauge the intentions of the adversary. I said I could not imagine Kuropatkin assuming the offensive at this stage of the campaign. It was already too late to strike at either the Kaiping or Siuyen forces before they could receive assistance from one another, and the First Army also was now in a position to make itself felt against the Russian line of communication. Fujii said, "Yes, we have certainly played our part by drawing away a large force from Haicheng. The enemy in front of us at this moment amounts to no less than forty-eight battalions and fifty guns. There are now no Russian troops at Liaoyang. There will be no battle of Liaoyang. The complete success of the Twelfth Division at Chaotao threatens the left of the enemy at Yushuling. Instead of the great battle of Liaoyang we have all talked about, thought about, and even dreamed about, there will now be two battles; one at Haicheng and the other along the line Tokayen-Amping. It is likely enough that, as Kuropatkin has four Divisions available he means to hold us fast here whilst he fights his battle at Haicheng. But if such a plan is made, it becomes our duty to spoil it, and therefore we must, at any cost, attack and force the enemy back from Tokayen and Amping. It is a most delicate matter, however, to choose the right moment. Some 12,000 Russians are now edging off from Yoshirei towards Amping. Perhaps they are preparing to attack the Twelfth Division; possibly they may endeavour to penetrate into the mountain between the Second and Twelfth Divisions. The first surmise is calculated to make us all anxious; the second would suit us admirably. If this latter movement was attempted, we have enough troops at Fenghuangcheng, and on our line of communications, to delay the enemy, whilst we in the front can cut off their retreat. If, on the other hand, General Count Keller orders a third advance against the front of the Motienling, we shall this time riposte by swinging up the Guards to make a counter attack on their right." He then said, "Now what is your opinion on the delicate question of when we shall get our marching orders?"

I replied to this effect: The main operation is undoubtedly the attack on Kuropatkin by the Second and Fourth Armies marching along the line of railway. Our movement, though very important, is clearly subsidiary. I should imagine, therefore, that we shall be order^ to keep quite quiet until we hear that the Second and Fourth Armies are attacking Kuropatkin at Haicheng. That is our moment, and to anticipate it even by a day would be tempting Providence, as even under the most favourable conditions it is no mean adventure for three Divisions to advance against a force of nearly four Divisions.

After expressing an opinion so unqualified, I had hoped to I m rewarded by obtaining some sign of concurrence or disagreement even from the impenetrable Fujii, but the Japanese have no idea of reciprocity in the matter of confidence. Instead of giving me the views of the general staff, which was the least I had hoped for, he looked quite blank, and made no response except that we would henceforth be stronger than three Divisions, as a fine brigade of Kobi was coming up shortly to work on the right of the Twelfth Division. He then got on his horse and rode away, I, as usual, accompanying him to the gate of the outer courtyard, to make the ceremonious bow and salute according to the code of Japanese military etiquette.

It is now only 10 a.m., and the whole day is still available for roughing out the story of the Chaotao engagement. To do this I shall piece together Jardine's despatch, the ideas I picked up from the cavalryman, and the valuable statement just dictated to me by Fujii. I shall thus get the general course of the action into my head, and shall find it easier to prepare an official report which will squeeze past the Press censor without suffering too much mutilation.

The Battle of Chaotao.

No sooner had the Central Division of the Japanese army inflicted a bloody repulse upon the Russians at , Motienling on the 17th July than Kuroki and his general staff began to consider how they could best tom this success to account by advancing the First Army one stage further on the road to Liaoyang. It was obvious that the main Tiensuitien-Towan valley could not be crossed safely by the Second Division (central column) and the Imperial Guards (left column) until the enemy opposite the Twelfth Division (right column) had been forced back from Chaotao (Kioto), where they were in a position to threaten the right flank And communications of any premature advance beyond the Motienling range. Moreover, Chaotao was in itself a place of no small strategical importance, covering as it did the line Amping-Tokayen (where Fujii has just prophesied to me the battle of Liaoyang will be fought). And commanding the Homiou Temple, whence a good road strikes off northward from the Saimachi-Liaoyang highway to the important town of Penchiho (Honkeiko) on the way to Mukden.

The actual position taken up by the Russians was about 1000 yards north-west of the village of Chaotao. Here the Aiyanmen-Saimachi-Chaotao valley, up which the Twelfth Division was advancing, narrows into a defile about a mile and a half broad, which, speaking in a military sense, is entirely blocked by a long well-defined spur running out at right angles from the mountains bordering its southern side. Geographically speaking, there is a narrow gap between the northern extremity of the spur and the northern range of mountains. The Shi river (Saiga) and the main road to Amping and Liaoyang find just room sufficient to squeeze through this gap, but no troops could do so, even by night, so long as the spur was held by an enemy. I must now describe the spur. At its northern extremity it stands sixty feet above the level of the river, and at its southern end, where it first branches out from the southern range of hills, it rises to a height of 800 feet over the flat uncultivated plain on either side of it. The eastern face of the spur is very steep, and in places precipitous. Its western face, on the contrary, slopes down gently to meet the level plain. Along the crest line the soil is sandy and well suited for the construction of gun-pits and trenches. Even at this period of the year the river was in most places fordable. The river banks were shelving, and afforded no cover. The Russian centre and left were deployed in deep Boer trenches along the crest of the spur facing to the south-east. The lateral communications and the covered ways, from front to rear, were excellent, and much labour had been expended upon them. The position of the guns is well shown in Map XI. There were twice as many pits as guns, in order to enable changes to be made whenever the Japanese had got the range accurately. From these pits the guns could fire at anything over 1500 yards, but within 1400 yards of the position the ground was dead.

As the Russians manned their trenches on the 18th and 19th July and looked towards the line of the Japanese advance, they must have seen stretching away before them a flat plain, on which only a few clusters of cottages and the valley of Chaotao interrupted their field of fire, although a fair amount of cover from view existed in the shape of fields of millet (*kaoliung*) now about five feet high. The Russian left flank was safe enough, as the hills on the right hank of the Shi-Ho descended to the river in a series of cliffs and precipices practically impassable for regular troops. Their right was posted upon the rough, bare, grassy mountains rising to the height of 1000 feet above the valley on its southern side. These troops were, for the most part, unentrenched. The Russian line of retreat on Amping or Liaoyang lay, for the first three miles, westwards over an open valley, giving even less cover than the eastern section of the same valley over which the Japanese must advance to the attack. This was the weak point of the scheme, if Chaotao was regarded merely as a convenient spot in which to fight a delaying action. Discussing the Chaotao line of defence with the Chief of the Staff, First Army, he said to me, "From the strategical point of view, the tempting thing to do was to turn the enemy's right wing; but to carry this into effect, it would be necessary to make a very wide turning movement (*mouvement très prononcé*) over a series of precipitous mountain paths. In short, this position was one so full of excellent advantages to the defence that it may be said to have been all advantages."

The Russian force holding the Chaotao defile consisted of the 35th Regiment complete with all its four battalions, the 36th Regiment (three battalions), one regiment of Cossacks (Argun), and the 9th artillery brigade of thirty-two guns (three field batteries and one mountain battery). It was commanded by Lieutenant-General Gerschelman, of the Ninth Division, who kept his other brigade of infantry in reserve,, where it remained inactive during the engagement.

The Japanese advancing against Chaotao from the east consisted of the Twelfth Division, under Lieutenant-General Inouye, with its squadron of cavalry and its thirty-six mountain guns — the latter insignificant little toys in appearance to be pitted against the heavy, comparatively modem, Russian field-pieces. In addition to the Twelfth Division complete, a battalion and a half of the 16th Regiment, which did so well at Gebato on the 17th instant, was sent out from the Second Division on the morning of the 19th to try and traverse the 15½ miles of extremely broken, mountainous country which divided them from the Chaotao defile; and they, making a marvellous march, did actually arrive in time to take part in the final stage of the action. This battalion and a half was under the regimental command of Colonel Tamiyama, also of Grebato fame. He is a very thin old man, with keen eyes. Vincent asked him the other day if he thought the war would end before the winter. He replied, "Perhaps next year; anyhow, I have come here to die, and expect to have done so before then." Fujii had quite a dispute with several of his subordinates on the general staff about sending Tamiyama. They insisted he could not arrive. I asked if Matsuishi had led the dissentients, but Fujii only laughed, and would not say any more.

It may be said, then, that as regards infantry, the Japanese were nearly twice as strong as the Russians who actually took part in the action; whereas in guns and cavalry the Russians were distinctly stronger than the Japanese. Had the Russian commander seen fit to employ all his available troops, the superiority of the Japanese in infantry would almost, if not quite, have disappeared.

On the 18th July Kigoshi's brigade of the Twelfth Division was already in touch with the Russians in their entrenchments. His outposts were furnished by the let battalion of the 46th Regiment, under Major Tachibana. At 4.30 p.m. the Russians began a feigned retirement westwards, as if to fall back on Amping. Major Tachibana promptly advanced, in order not to lose touch of the enemy; but the moment he got to the river and attempted to cross it, the Russians &eed about and reocoupied their trenches, showing a most determined front, and deploying about two battalions of infantry and eight guns. Major Tachibana had tumbled into a trap, and the 6th company of the 1st battalion (which was leading) lost all its officers in a very few minutes. Nevertheless, he only fell back four or five hundred yards, and there held on in some *kaoliung* crops, with his right resting on Chaotao village, and his line parallel to the enemy's position. Here, at 6.30 p.m., the commander of the outposts was joined by the remaining two battalions of the 46th Regiment and by two battalions of the 24th Regiment, who formed up on the same alignment. A stiff fire fight then took place, and continued until 9 p.m., but the Japanese were unable to make any impression on the defence. As it grew dark they were, therefore, forced to bivouac where they lay, keeping their fighting formations. At midnight the Russian bands began to play the accompaniment to a very heavy fire. Some Japanese say the Russians tried to make the assault; others that, although the fire was very heavy, they did not leave their trenches; but all are agreed in expressing a comical surprise at the part played by the bands. Fujii, for instance, remarked to me, "It seems a strange thing to play music during a night attack; perhaps it was the moon which made the Russians feel sentimental!" I can quite understand that if music in modern war seems old-fashioned and curious to me, it must appear supremely ridiculous to our allies, who certainly are not themselves susceptible to the influences of any "concord of sweet sounds." The casualties suffered by Major Tachibana's battalion numbered 247, and were mostly incurred in falling back from the river to his alignment on Chaotao.

On the 19th the morning broke fine and clear, and as soon as it was light enough to shoot, the 46th Regiment and the two battalions of the 24th Regiment took up the fire fight at the point where it had been interrupted by darkness. The 24th were on the left and the 46th on the right, and the frontage of each battalion was well over 1000 yards, which enabled them to hold the Russians all along their position. The Japanese guns had come up during the night, and had dug themselves in; one brigade just in front of the Homiou temple, the other on the green slope exactly facing the centre of the Russian position, at a range of 2400 yards. In all theory, the thirty-six Japanese guns should have been silenced in half an hour by the superior metal and make of the Russian field guns, but in practice it fell out otherwise. Although the defenders must have known every yard of the ground, and should have posted officers on the rough bare hills on their right, who could have commanded all the valley with their glasses, yet three-quarters of an hour passed by before they could locate the Japanese batteries. The Russians fired the first shot at the infantry at 5.5 a.m., and from that hour until 9 a.m. a heavy fire was maintained by both sides. Until 5.45 a.m., when the Russians began at last to realise the whereabouts of the well-concealed little mountain guns, the fight was as one-sided as would be an encounter between a blind man and a lynx. During that interval of forty minutes the majority of the Russian shell were bursting on the slopes of a mountain 1000 yards south-east of the Homiou temple, where there was not a living thing within half a mile of them. Meanwhile, the Japanese had put in so many effective shells that by the time the Russian gunners did locate the hostile batteries they had become demoralised to the extent at least of setting their fuses hurriedly and badly, and of shooting wildly. Thus the heavier guns never got a fair chance of asserting their innate superiority. After 9 a.m. the fire slackened as if by mutual consent, until only single occasional shots were fired by the artillery on either side. The Japanese had expended ammunition to an alarming extent, and they were forced to go slow. The communications from Changsong and the Yalu, *via* Aiyanmen and Saimachi, to Chaotao (see Map I.[*]) were so extraordinarily difficult that each round of ammunition was a very serious consideration; and now, before Lieutenant-General Inouye's infantry had gained any appreciable success, his artillery commander reported that he had only sufficient powder and shot available to continue fighting at the same rate for another two hours. He had expended two-thirds of his gun ammunition without silencing the Russians.

Meanwhile, the infantry fight had been recommenced at daylight by Kigoshi's brigade of the 46th and 24th Regiments, less one battalion of the latter corps under the command of Lieutenant-Colonel Shiba. Two companies of this battalion were detailed to furnish the Divisional and Brigade reserves, whilst the remaining two companies were pushed a couple of miles up the road, running due north from the Homiou temple to Penchiho (Honkeiko), and told to reconnoitre the twelve miles separating the battle-field from that place, where some Russian troops were known to be stationed. The 47th Regiment of Sasaki's brigade was disposed so as to meet any possible attack from the north, as information had come to hand that there was a Russian detachment of some strength at a village called Shaoshi, north-west of Saimachi. At 7 a.m., by which

---

[*] Publisher's note: A copy of this map can be found in the pages before the Table of Contents..

time it became evident that Kigoshi's brigade could not hope to carry the position on the spur by a straightforward frontal attack, the remaining regiment of Sasaki's brigade, the 14th, under Colonel Imamoura, was despatched south-westwards into a tangle of deep ravines and precipitous mountains, to endeavour to work round by the west and northwest, so as to turn the Russian right flank posted on the bare rough hills as shown in the map. As the movement had to be carried out beyond the enemy's ken, a long *détour* was necessary. In the event, the distance marched amounted to seventeen and a half miles, much of the route leading along goat tracks or across pathless gullies and crags, where each man had to make his own way and find his company again on the far side of the obstacle. Such a performance makes high demands both on science, natural instincts and physical energy. It was not considered safe to trust a Chinese guide, and the general direction was maintained by the officers with their compasses, whilst the native mountaineering habitudes of the lower ranks led them by the least inaccessible line of country. No British troops could hope to cover so much bad ground in so short a time, unless indeed it were a battalion fresh from such a campaign as that of Tirah. On the other hand, our Pathans or Gurkhas, under British officers, will do equally well when the occasion arises.

Now that the Imamoura Regiment had fairly plunged into the unknown, the Japanese commander's order of battle seemed to offer some opportunity to an enterprising foe. A fourth of his force was disposed with a view to warding off an attack on his right rear: another fourth had disappeared into the mountains, with designs upon the enemy's right, which could not bear fruit for many hours: a detachment was posted well out to safeguard his own right. All this may remind British officers of the action at Houtnek, near Thabanchu in South Africa, where half the column was similarly absorbed in the defence of its own right rear, or in attempts to turn the enemy's right, whilst less than half was available to guard the baggage and hospitals, and to make head against the front of the enemy's position. The only difference is that the Boers did press in like a swarm of angry wasps to the assistance of their friends holding the main position at Houtnek, whilst the commander of the troops holding that defile no sooner recognised that the British had detached a force to turn his right, that he counterattacked it vigorously with his foreign legion under Maximoff the Russian. The sequel will show that neither the Russians at Penchiho, nor those to the north-west of Saimachi, played up similarly to General Gerschelman at Chaotao, whilst the General himself made no attempt to counter-attack, although he had ample reserves available for the purpose.

From the time the Imamoura Regiment started on their long turning movement through the mountains, until 10 a.m., the 24th and 46th Regiments occupied the enemy's attention by fire and by feints of advancing seriously to the attack. During this period small parties of half a dozen managed, at intervals, to work their way along the broken cliffs on the right bank of the Shi-Ho and similar small parties crept through the crops to the shelter of villages. After 10 a.m. it became evident that the Russians had no idea of taking the initiative, and as soon as this was realised by Inouye, he was naturally only too glad to conform and sit down waiting till the hour grew ripe for his purpose. Thus there was a lull in the fighting, broken only by intermittent bursts of firing from the Japanese, answered by volleys from the Russian trenches.

Meanwhile, Imamoura and his men were marching through ravines and over precipitous crags, ever getting nearer and nearer to their objective, the unsuspecting Russian right.

On the field of Chaotao nothing further of importance took place until 2 p.m., when Gerschelman withdrew two of his guns from the spur, whose rapid subsequent retirement to the north-west was betrayed by the rising dust. At 2.30 p.m. more guns were removed under a hot fire from the Japanese artillery, and the Russian infantry could now be seen in leisurely fashion quitting their trenches one by one. At 2.40 p.m. Inouye got news that the Imamoura Regiment had successfully carried through its arduous flank march, and would shortly be at hand-grips with the Russian right flank. He thereupon reinforced his firing-line, and prepared to press his frontal attack upon the spur. At 2.45 p.m. the Imamoura Regiment had the good fortune, or possibly the phenomenal good guidance, to fall in with the leading half-battalion of the 16th Regiment, Second Division, which had been scrambling up and down the mountains all the way from Gebato,

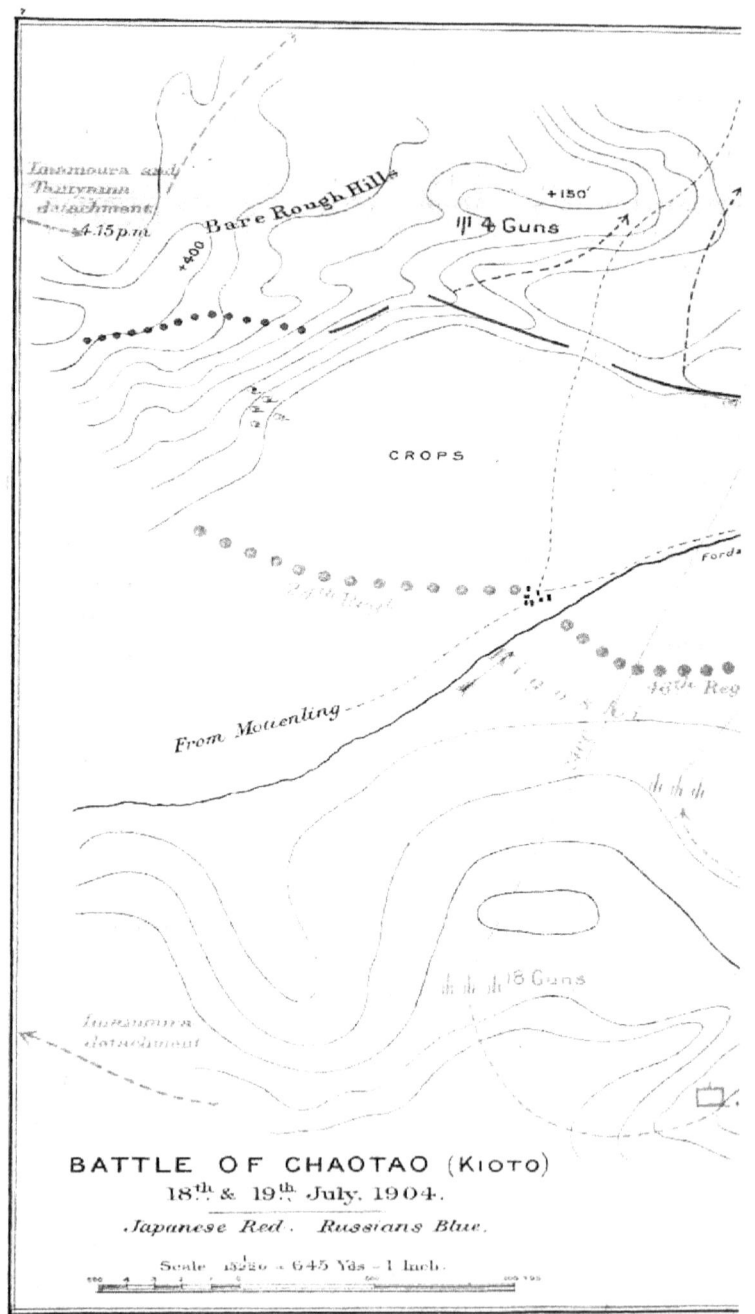

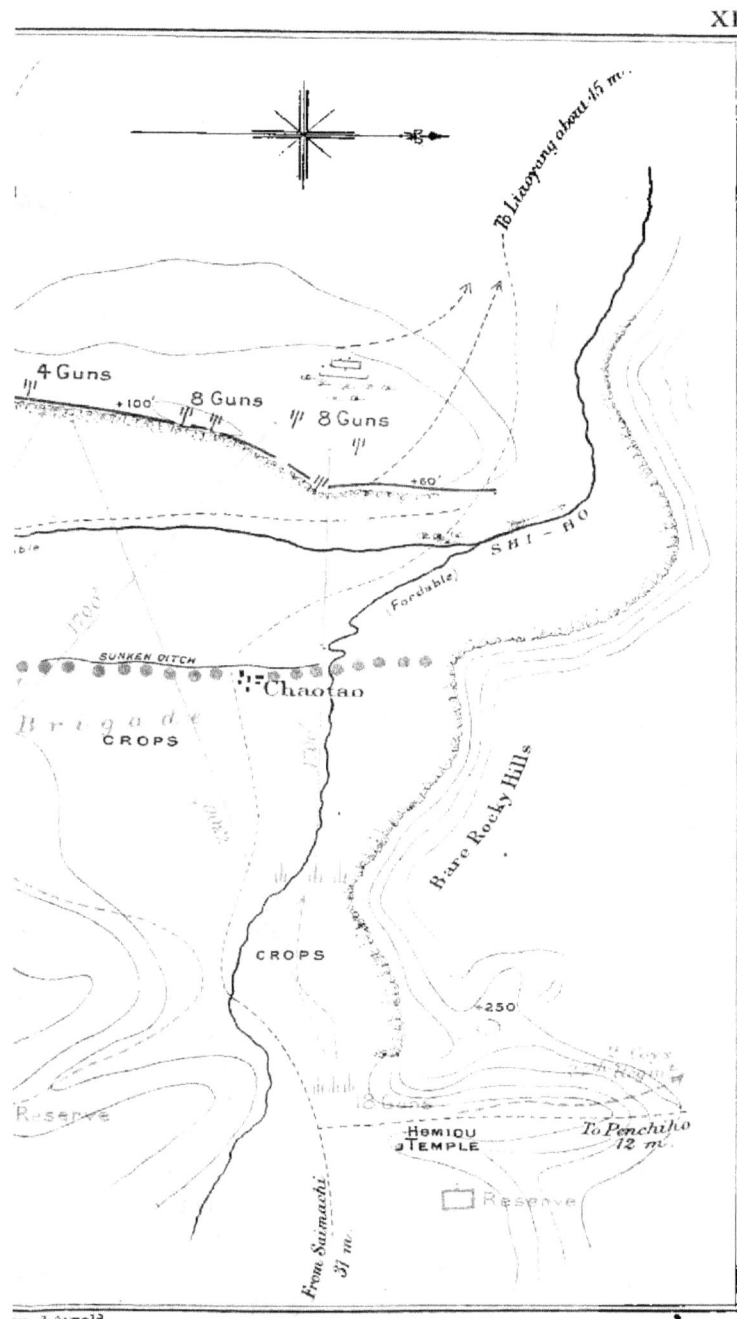

since 9 a.m. that morning. This half-battalion was being followed at some interval by a full battalion of the same regiment; but without waiting, Colonels Imamoura and Taniyama at once attacked the extreme Russian right, posted, as already described, in the rough hare hills dominating the main position. The fight became lively, and the faint sounds of the musketry reaching Inouye's ears, by the Homiou temple, confirmed the welcome news that his turning movement had, at any rate, reached its objective, and should shortly be in touch with the main body. The same sounds must have come to General Gerschelman much more clearly — as clearly, in fact, as if he were listening to hundreds of hands tapping impatiently at the door which safeguarded hie retreat. The Japanese plan of attack was now plainly disclosed. What did Gerschelman think? Did his pulses beat any the faster? To him had arrived that fateful moment when a General has to justify his whole existence — not only his past studies and preparations, but all his future career. Now was the time — now or never — to fling in his reserves to the last man and reinforce his right, or else to put his Cossacks in the trenches and on the rough bare hills, with their horses ready close behind them, so that they might hold the ground for just one half-hour, whilst he disengaged the whole of his infantry.

But nothing was done by the Russians to show any appreciation of the arrival of a crisis, or even to accelerate the withdrawal of the troops on the spur.

By 3 p.m. all the Russian guns had retired, and the two Japanese artillery brigades advanced to the positions shown on Map XI.

At 3.15 p.m. the frontal attack on the spur began to be pressed in earnest, the little mountain guns shelling the trenches heavily and the infantry closing in somewhat, and opening a heavy fire. To this the remnant of the Russian infantry, who must have been fine fellows, responded vigorously with volleys, although all the time the trenches were being evacuated by driblets.

But Inouye and his staff were less concerned with the loud fusilade to their front, or by the countless bullets which flew singing and sighing down the valley, than with the continuous hum of musketry coming to them from the west. For these fainter sounds betokened the heavy fire fight now in progress between the turning column and the Russian right, where the Japanese were enveloping their enemy and gradually forcing him off the hills and down into the valley.

By 4.15 p.m. Imamoura had practically gained complete possession of the rough bare hills, and from this point of vantage he was able to press against the Russian main position, until a moment came when the whole line of the enemy was observed to waver and shake. Then Kigoshi in front, and Imamoura and Taniyama on the flank, redoubled their efforts. The enemy now decided definitely to give way, but until 5 p.m. the trenches were evacuated systematically, and evidently by order, which is, I consider, a very great tribute to the steadiness of the Russian infantry. It is comparatively easy to be brave so long as all are in the same boat to sink or swim together. But when some are chosen to go and others are ordered to stay, then the instincts of self-preservation begin to tug at the heart-strings, and the heaviest calls are made upon discipline, patriotism, and esprit de corps.

At 5.5 p.m., this orderly retirement ceased, and the last batch of the defenders ran back in great confusion under a storm of shrapnel bullets. At 5.10 p.m., the whole Japanese line advanced at the double. At 5.14, the first Japanese flag crowned the crest of the spur, whilst clouds of dust to the north showed the direction of the Russian retreat.

The victory was won, but thus far it had been a barren victory, the losses of the attackers being probably heavier than those of the defenders. A remarkable Russian miscalculation of distance, or possibly misapprehension of the situation, was now about to offer the fruits, as well as the honours, of success to the Japanese commander. When Imamoura drove the forces opposed to him off the rough bare hills, he did not follow them down into the plain, but turned his attention first of all to pressing against and overthrowing the enemy on the spur. Meanwhile, both the Russians who had been driven off the hills and those who were falling back from the trenches on the spur were being assembled and re-formed according to the precepts of the parade-ground, only some 3000 yards from the trenches in the open plain on the southern border of the valley. Like a sportsman eager to secure a buck which has been startled, but has not yet fled beyond all hopes of circumvention, Imamoura's men withdrew from sight, and making a detour at the double through the hills, struck the valley once again well to the west of the unsuspecting enemy. There they waited, until at 5.15 Kigoshi's brigade crowned the spur and began to advance down the valley in pursuit. Then, pushing out from the cover of the hills, Imamoura occupied the village of Tayungzi, on the south side of the valley, just off the map, and fairly interposed between the Russians and their line of retreat. Such a feat seems hardly possible for infantry as against infantry; but Fujii, Jardine, and my cavalryman are all agreed about it, so I feel it must have been so. The fact is, that the Japanese infantry in mountains has, against other infantries, some of the attributes of cavalry. Attacked in front by the victorious Kigoshi, and in their right flank and rear by Imamoura, the Russians, who, it must be admitted, had had an uncommon hard, trying day of it, fell into confusion, and were completely broken up as an organised force. The main body escaped in disorder and with heavy losses towards Amping, whilst another portion fled into the mountains in what was described to me by Fujii as a "pell-mell crowd." During all the heavy fighting of the 18th and 19th, the Russians had lost 60 killed and 200 wounded, hut now in this strange surprise and the subsequent pursuit they lost 200 killed and 500 wounded in less than one hour. Thus the Russian infantry brigade, which had borne the heat and burden of the day, was destroyed for the time being as an effective military organisation, but nevertheless I do not think any fair-minded soldier can cast a stone at them. They had carried out their orders with resolution under the most trying circumstances; and although, at the last, their commander blundered into a trap which had been set before his eyes, the regimental officers and men had throughout up to that time acquitted themselves with remarkable steadiness. Sanna's Post was after all very nearly as bad an example of the same kind of thing, and it is only theorists who have not been at war who can afford to assume superior airs in discussing such regrettable incidents.

Thus ended the battle of Chaotao, leaving the Japanese in possession of the field. They had lost 54 killed and 367 wounded, against the 1,000 casualties which were suffered by the Russians.

We British officers are particularly sorry at the news that one of the killed was Major Hiraoka, commanding the 1st battalion of the Imamoura Regiment (14th). He was Japanese military attaché to our forces during the South African War, and very popular with every one.

There is not much to be added by way of criticism, as the story supplies its own commentary. It seems clear that General Gerschelman accepted battle with the preconceived idea that he was going to delay the Japanese, cause them heavy losses, and then get away himself fairly comfortably. It is improbable that he entered into the fight with any intention of staking his division and his reputation on the result of a desperate battle. At least, if he did so, it is strange that he should not have made any attempt to carry his ideas into effect. From 8 a.m. until 1 p.m. his division had only a very weak brigade immediately in front of it. The Japanese 14th Regiment was miles from the scene of action, and the 47th Regiment was also not immediately available. But the defence remained absolutely passive. Then again, when the Imamoura Regiment first made itself felt on Gerschelman's right flank, another and yet more promising form of counterattack offered itself. By that time the Japanese scheme of operations must have been glaringly obvious to a commander of any experience, even in war game or peace manoeuvres. A part of their force was holding the position in front, and had no intention of advancing to within decisive range until the other part, detached for the purpose, was ready to press against his right flank. Before this pressure began to be applied, and whilst a range of mountains separated the two portions of the Japanese force, there was time to bring up the whole of his reserve, except the Cossack Regiment, and to throw them in the overwhelming force of three or four to one against the Imamoura Regiment, and the two companies of the Taniyama Regiment.

Far from attempting any bold decisive stroke such as this, the Russian commander apparently neglected to despatch even one company from his disproportionately large reserve to help his troops on the rough bare hills whence Imamoura and Taniyama were busy driving them down into the valley.

Every student has his own views, and must draw his own

conclusions on such points. Personally, I, sitting safely in this house of the Chinese physician, find that the worst fault any general can commit is to keep big reserves bottled up in the background, whilst their comrades are being beaten before their eyes. Gerschelman wished to adopt Parthian tactics, but forgot that Russian infantry are not Parthians. When he found his front line failed to disentangle itself as he had hoped, then was the time to harden his heart, march in his reserves, and let every soldier see that he was going to put up a big fight. Had he acted thus, I believe, whatever the actual result might have been, that his good Russian soldiers would have played up for him manfully, so that even if defeated the morale of the Russian army would have gained. In any case things could not have turned out worse for him than they actually did, for even if they had gone against him it would have been late before the combat was decided, and he could have extricated himself under cover of the darkness.

The Japanese tactics were extremely daring, not to say risky, but Inouye knew his enemy, and all his calculations came off even better than he could reasonably have expected. Jardine says that the Japanese are discarding German attack formations, and approximating more to those employed by us in South Africa. He also writes that the Twelfth Division are immensely pleased with themselves at having been the first to defeat a European Division. He reports that these Russians are superior in intelligence and discipline to the Siberians, and that the Japanese officers think them distinctly more formidable.

Chapter XVI – A Pause Before the Advance

July 24th. — Rather a shock! —— has come back from his ride to headquarters and tells me that every one, including Fujii, says I was quite wrong in what I cabled to India about Europeans being better than Siberians. The general staff declare that the Europeans are more rusty, and generally less highly trained, than the Siberians. Colonel Hagino has been busy examining prisoners. He reports that the Russian recruits have only three months' instruction before passing their inspection. This is insufficient, as after that is over there comes the long winter when they can do nothing beyond barrack-square training. Hagino asked a Russian non-commissioned officer taken prisoner on the 17th to read a note-book which had belonged to one of his own officers who had been killed. He could not do it, yet he claimed to have passed his examination for non-commissioned officer. When I remember how my colour-sergeant used to write me out a beautiful little card before the General's inspection containing all the conceivable information any conceivable General might wish to have about the men, their ages, their service, the price of their socks, the percentage who could swim or who were teetotalers, underlined according to the fad of the great man, then I suspect that our non-commissioned officers are better, at any rate at book-learning, than their Muscovite brethren. It seems that many of the European prisoners do not understand the magazine rifle, being men of forty years of age, newly recalled to the colours. Hagino emphatically declares that the Siberians are more hardy, and have natural hunting and fighting instincts, which are entirely wanting amongst the rank and file of the European battalions. The best troops the Russians have are those of the army of Turkestan. —— tells me that Hagino classes their troops as follows: first, array of Turkestan; second, army of Siberia; third, army of Europe; and with seven years' service in Russia at his back, and all the resources of the Japanese Intelligence Branch, he ought to know what he is talking about. Ordinarily my chief feeling on hearing all this would have been one of intense interest. Now my interest is absorbed in annoyance, that the general staff should have let my misleading cable go through without putting me straight. I can quite understand how I came to be misinformed. Both Jardine and I have been victims of regimental officers who naturally enough were inclined to believe that the Europeans they had just defeated were the flower of the Russian army.

I have no doubt that the regimental officers are wrong, and that the general staff are correct, but it appears to me sometimes as if the latter preferred I should be inaccurate in the conclusions I sent home.

—— also says that the Second Army began to march against the Russians yesterday, and should be at grips with them very shortly.

July 25th. — The day of the great battle. None of us can talk or think of anything else.

At midday, I rode over and had lunch with the officers commanding artillery and engineers, who live in a small Chinese cottage on the fringe of the mountains. General T. Kodama, the engineer-in-chief, had made an exquisite and tiny Jappie garden all out of nothing at all, except running water and pebbles and stones. There were canals and ponds and waterfalls; there were paths and seats and a regulation central lantern, all in the space of five square

A Pause Before the Advance

yards. It was such a garden as European children might eagerly try to make, but their attempt would be comic or serio-comic, whereas General T. Kodama's garden was a gem. I confess the matter is beyond my comprehension. But they tell me that each stone is carefully chosen according to very deep and important rules of art and antique lore, and that this pretty toy has cost the commanding engineer as much anxious thought as the hundreds of yards of bridging by which, last April, he enabled the army to pass dry-shod across the broad and swiftly flowing Yalu. —— somewhat shyly hinted to me on our way home that the sight of this garden would inculcate the lesson of fortitude and endurance to any welleducated Japanese who saw it. To a Western, all such imaginings are a mystery. If I was told truth, then indeed Shakespeare is once more vindicated, and in actual solid fact we

> "Find tongues in trees, books in the running brooks,
> Sermons in stones, and good in everything."

At lunch a bottle of claret was produced: Lord knows where they got it: and I proposed the health, of the Second Army, which was drunk with much enthusiasm. A clever young German-speaking doctor sat next me. He told me our First Army had now four per cent, sick, half of whom were down with "beri beri." The reason why the army was so free from ordinary campaigning epidemics was simply because the terror of the troops lest they should miss a fight inclined even the youngest soldier implicitly to obey all hygienic rules. For instance, there was no danger at all of the men drinking bad water on the line of march. Even in hospital men would not drink water on trust, but cross-questioned the attendants as to whether it had been properly boiled before they would touch it. The doctor added that he did not consider such desperate keenness showing itself in such selfrestraint was quite normal or natural in a young Japanese. He doubted whether the troops would have developed quite the same intensely combative spirit if they had been fighting, say, Austrians or Italians. But they had been nursing their wrath against Russia for ten solid years, and now they were firmly determined not to give even disease or doctors a chance of holding them back.

10 p.m. — Fujii kindly sent me a note round to say that there was still no news of the battle.

July 26th. — Bode with Matsuishi in the early morning, and after *chota hazri,*[*] Fujii came to see me. He was in high spirits, and told me many things of interest, especially about the battle which has just been fought by the Second Army near Tashihchiao.[†] He has every appearance of enjoying our one-sided conversations, and encourages me to write them down on the spot Here is what he said: "All day long on the 24th the Japanese artillery of 250 guns carried on an inconclusive fight with eighteen batteries of the enemy. This time the Russian guns were no longer perched conspicuously on the crests of mountains, but were so well concealed that our artillery could not, in spite of its numerical superiority, silence them at all. On the contrary, on several occasions it was the Russians who silenced the Japanese guns. As long as it was light our infantry was unable to make any progress, but at 10 p.m. our right wing, consisting of the Fifth Division, carried the enemy's first line of works on the heights of Taiheirei (Erhtaoling), and then at 2 a.m. improved their success by penetrating into the second Russian position on the high ground to the north in the direction of Tapinrei (Tapinling). During the night, the Third Division, moving parallel and a mile and a quarter to the west of the Fifth Division, occupied the height east of Sanseito (Shanhsitao.)

"As dawn was breaking, the whole of our forces stood to their arms expecting an attack; but, far from attacking, the Russians had already commenced their retirement. Thereupon the Fifth Division advanced boldly in pursuit, followed by the whole of the Second Army. Judging by our losses, which are not serious, the enemy could not have made a very stubborn resistance, especially as Seisekisan (Chingshisan) fell at 7 a.m. without any fighting at all.

---

[*] "A light meal," eaten early in the morning.

[†] The names of these pieces are as given by General Fujii, but this volume contains no map showing them all.

In their retreat northwards, the Russians burnt Daisekio (Tashihchiao) and Nenkyaten. We pursued as far as Pinamfan.

"The force which the Second Army has just defeated consisted of five Divisions, and another one and a half Divisions are still facing the Fourth Army at Takubokujo. One of these six and a half Divisions, however, is a reserve Division not worth very much more than a regular regiment. The Fourth Army advanced at the same time as the Second Army, and attacked Takubokujo. As they reached tiie walls of the town, the Russians evacuated it, and took up what seemed to be a very strong position on a height to the north-west. But it does not much matter how strong their position is, for the Second Army can now detach a force to turn their right flank, when they must inevitably fall back.

"The Third Army is to advance to-day, and will try to seize a steep and lofty range of hills just in front of Port Arthur, which is held by fourteen battalions of Russians. I know the ground well, and if General Nogi makes good these hills, he should be in a position within the next few days to storm Port Arthur itself."

I said, "Your brother Generals of the other armies do you very well in telegrams"; to which he replied that all this news had come from Manchurian army headquarters.

Fujii is most anxiously debating in his own mind whether the enemy will elect to stand and fight at Daisekio or Haicheng, or whether he is likely to continue to retreat indefinitely. He puffed a great sigh and said, "If only Kuropatkin would defend himself obstinately at one of these two places, then our First Army would know exactly what to do. But I fear he will not do so, although there is one very excellent defensive position which ought to tempt him. This is Anshantien, between Haicheng and Liaoyang.

"General Count Keller, in our own front, seems nervous about his left flank, and is withdrawing troops from Toshirei, just across the Yamorinza valley, and transferring them to Amping so as to secure himself against a possible turning movement by the Twelfth Division. General Hasegawa, Commander of the Guards, has noticed this weakening of the enemy to our front, and has implored permission to cross the Tiensuitien-Yamorinza valley and occupy the hills on its western side. Marshal Kuroki would have liked to indulge him in his wish. Now, however, the First Army is no longer master of its own actions, but has to work as part of the Manchurian army under a Commander-in-Chief. We are bound, therefore, to be extremely prudent, and must do exactly what we are told to do, neither more nor less. Otherwise, certainly the enemy seems temptingly weak just now in front of our centre and left, notwithstanding that there is a good deal of digging still going on along the crest lines of the ridges.

"At the most there are four Divisions of Russians in front of the First Army. A regiment has just come down opposite our right flank to Honkeiko (Penchiho) from Mukden, and Mukden itself is quite empty. As I told you a few days ago, there will be no battle of Liaoyang, but we will do our share of that engagement at Amping and Tokayen, whilst the Second Army will probably get through its part of the business at Anshantien.

"The First Army is now quite ready to start, and Marshal Kuroki has telegraphed to Manchurian army headquarters, begging permission to advance, but has not yet received a reply. No one of us here has any anxiety about the front of our own army, but we have been anxious enough about the progress of the Second Army. All we are afraid of at our headquarters is lest Kuropatkin should get away without being brought to fight a pitched battle. This army has had the dangers and hardships of the mountains to surmount, as well as the extraordinary difficulties of its communications; and now if Kuropatkin escapes, the past efforts and victories will go for nothing, and we shall suffer everlasting shame and mortification. Whether we like it or not, we of the First Army must accept the fullest responsibility for Kuropatkin's failure or success in getting away. If the moment for our advance is well chosen, then, and then only, will Oyama be able to obtain a decisive victory. Yet it is most difficult and delicate to launch ourselves precisely at that moment. As at Gravelotte, the Saxon army fell on the French right and decided the day, so the First Army would like to fall on the Russian line of retreat. By executing our movement opportunely and precisely, we decide the first phase of the campaign. By moving too soon or too late we spoil everything, and incur everlasting disgrace. Yet here is the hard part of it: we are unable to move a yard until we get the order from Oyama although it is we and not Oyama who know the essential factor in this matter, namely, how long it will take us to defeat the four Russian Divisions at Amping and Tokayen."

I asked how long he would require. He said, " Although it is very difficult to say, owing to our having no reliable map of this part of the theatre of operations, I calculate it should take three days after making complete preparations.

"As far as our maps will carry us, the locality seems to adapt itself well to defence. We shall have to try and turn the position so as not to lose too many men. Kuropatkin has made a good road from Tokayen to Ansh^tien, and this will give him very great facilities for reinforcing his right wing against our left wing. Every northward kilometre marched by the Fourth Army tends of course to reduce this danger. Obviously if the First Army were to move prematurely by itself, although I think your Excellency would enjoy the good fun, yet it would do so with both its wings uncovered. The left would be open to an attack along a good road from Kuropatkin's main army at Anshantien; our right, to an attack from Mukden and the north. The last danger is the less serious of the two, especially as we do not intend to give the Russians much time for deliberation when once we make our start."

Sokako, July 29th. — A bulletin was sent me to-day from headquarters, but almost all the information it contained had already been given me on the 26th by Fujii. Only two of the items were new. A Russian gunboat, the *Jihouti*, of 910 tons, has steamed up the river Liao to a spot six miles above Densotai, where it must inevitably be captured, and the Third Army has succeeded in carrying the positions at Sodaiko Eikaseki, which Fujii told me were so essential as outworks to Port Arthur.

The Russians are sending up balloons to our front, and in front of the Twelfth Division. Judging by manoeuvres and South African experiences, they should now obtain a lot of misleading intelligence.

July 30th. — Went for an early ride, and met Fujii with Colonel Kurita and Major Fukuda on their way to Lienshankuan. I thought

I would accompany them a part of the way, but I saw they did not want me, and so I took the first excuse to get back. I think there is something in the wind. They had their wallets and haversacks bursting full, and three orderlies were following them. Besides, they did not seem at all pleased to see me. The only piece of news Fujii gave me was that to-day General Nogi was going to advance and take the very last line of hills which yet intervened between his army and Port Arthur.

Lienshankuan, August 3rd. — At 7 p.m. on the 30th July I got a message from headquarters to say that the army would advance next day. I packed enough food for three days on my horse, stuffed as much rice into little Mary as she could hold, and started at 9.30 from Sokako for this place. Mindful of previous experiences with Montana I rode quietly, and arrived at the house occupied by the foreign officers allotted to the Second Division at 11.30 p.m. They were all asleep, so putting the old horse into an empty shed I picked my way as deftly and quietly as I could through the recumbent forms, and lay down on a bench. The tiny room, stifling hot, was quite filled by the six slumbering officers and by innumerable mosquitoes. I could not sleep a wink. Some of the attachés began to get up at 1.30 a.m., and so I missed even that ten minutes' nap which makes so much difference next day. At 3.30 we started by the light of a brilliant moon four days past the full. Half revealed by its illusive radiance, the commonest objects assumed fantastic shapes in sympathy with my thoughts about the morrow. Near the foot of the Motienling we ourselves were strangely transfigured into a procession of phantoms groping through billows of clinging white mist, which poured down the slope in ever thicker and clammier volumes. At last, at 5 a.m., we topped the pass, and found ourselves uplifted over the shifting mysterious veil which now filled the whole of the great valley from which we had climbed. The sun was just rising very angry and red, and his light struck full against the sharp pinnacles which stood up from the mist, like great emeralds floating in a milky sea. To the westwards the foggy vapours were already rolling away their curtain from the scene of the approaching world-drama, of which

A Pause Before the Advance 265

we alone were to be the tiny group of privileged spectators. But why did the actors lag? Was it to enable us to admire the marvellous beauty of the setting of the play? Here beneath us were presumably some 80,000 men almost within shooting distance of one another. And yet, Red Indians, ambuscaded in the depths of some primaeval forest, could not have been more invisible or more deadly in their silence. This is the work of smokeless powder. No continental nation has learnt its lesson, and armies being what they are, there is not the smallest danger that they will deign to learn it until some day the little bullets, coming from nowhere, will bring conviction even to the most conservative profession in the world.

I walked to the old temple and sat there awhile, wishing I could paint a picture. Before me stretched the deserted landscape — brilliant green crops, backed by softer hued emerald mountains, which paled range upon range until they faded into faint grey-blue clouds in the far distance. I was thinking bow different would be my picture to those old-world battles so restlessly animated with gaily marching columns, glittering sabres and bayonets, waving colours and proudly prancing chargers — when suddenly, solemnly, up through the serried ranks of all the watchful mountains, reverberated the voice of the cannon. One single shot — a long pause — then another, and yet another. My blood tingled, for although I could not see them I seemed to feel that many thousand men at that mighty voice had tightened their grip on their rifles and were pulling themselves together — their bodies and their souls — for what the day might have in store.

This was at 6.15. At 6.30, Kuroki and some of the headquarters staff arrived at the old temple. Kuroki talked to me a little, and I got leave from him for Vincent to move closer up to the front. He said the misty morning had been fortunate, as it must have helped the Guards to get into their positions without suffering too much loss from the enemy's artillery. Kuroki was even more gentle and more tranquil than usual. His mere presence has a soothing effect on the more highly strung staff. I made this remark to one of the adjutants, who said I was right; that on the 19th inst. every one at headquarters had spent the day in the grip of a mortal anxiety regarding the Twelfth Division at Chaotao, excepting only Kuroki, who took things quite quietly, and thereby made them all feel better. At 6.45 a.m. I could hear the drumming, throbbing sound of heavy Japanese independent fire, as well as the tearing, ripping answer of the Russian volleys. Volleys! Good heavens, *quelle idée*! The fact is, that just as the Russo-Turkish War was fought on a lower plane of science and skill than the preceding Franco-Prussian War, so this Manchurian War is going to be fought, at any rate in its initial stages, on a lower tactical plane than the war in South Africa. What a blessing it is that the greater and prouder an army may be, the more immovably it stands rooted in its own conservatism, so that it becomes at last absolutely incapable (as a body) of incorporating the experiences of others. Thus it comes that your military attachés may discover points of training and efficiency of the most vital importance, and the bulk of their brother officers pay no more attention to them than did Napoleon III. to Colonel Baron Stöffel, the French military attaché at Berlin, in 1870.

At 7.40 the artillery fire became very heavy, although the guns of the Second Division were not yet engaged. Instead of locating the hostile batteries by their smoke, as in former days, they are now clearly designated by the cloud-balls of the shrapnel they attract. Then, looking closely through this veil, it becomes possible to see the vicious little tongue of yellow flame announcing the response of the Russian guns. Both Japanese and Russian powders emit a much brighter flash than our cordite. Fujii gave me some tea and four lumps of sugar. Two I put into two cups of tea, and the other two I rubbed together over my rice. I must say Fujii is a regular brick, and I hope I shall some day have a chance of returning his hospitality. While I was eating, he told me that our Second Division and the Twelfth Division, fourteen miles out on our right, were going to make a frontal advance westwards, but that the Guards had made a circuit during the night round the Russian right flank, and were now seven or eight miles to our left, pushing in vigorously on Yoshirei, almost at right angles to our line of advance — *i.e.*, in a northerly direction. The action now becomes too complicated and unwieldy to be put into the form of a personal narrative, and I must try therefore to weave together into one story my own experiences, as well as information which I owe to Fujii, a colonel of artillery, an adjutant, and my own officers.

Chapter XVII – The Battle of Yoshirei

This battle was fought on July 31st, 1904, by General Baron Kuroki, immediately commanding the Imperial Guards and Second Divisions, in conjunction with Lieutenant-General Inouye, commanding the Twelfth Division and one regiment of Guards Kobi;* against, respectively, Lieutenant-General Count Keller, immediately commanding the Third Siberian Division, the Sixth Siberian Division, and a part of the Ninth Division, in conjunction with Lieutenant-General Turcheffsky, commanding the Thirty-first Division and parts of the Third, Ninth and Thirty-fifth European Divisions. In all about three and a half Japanese Divisions against a nominal four Russian Divisions. I say "nominal," for prisoners after the battle told us that the average strength of the Russian companies was only 160 men and two officers. If this is true, then the Russians must have been a little weaker than the Japanese, whose companies never went into action at a lower strength than 210.

As regards the terrain, I will first describe the problem which

---

* *Kobi* means Second Reserve, the First Reserve if called *Yobi*.

lay before Kuroki, and then deal with that which Inouye had to face.

The Motienling range trends north and south. Under its western slope runs the Tiensuitien-Yamorinza-Hanchaputsu valley; also north and south. In width this valley varies between 500 and 1000 yards. It is flat, sprinkled with villages, and rich with crops. The river, which winds its way through it, averages fifty yards in breadth and two feet in depth. On its western side the valley is enclosed by another main range, very similar to that of the Motienling, running generally north and south. Along the ridges and spurs of this range the Russians had taken up their position.

There are four or five passes over the Motienling range, by which an army can descend into the Yamorinza valley; but the only roads by which that army could advance thence on Liaoyang, *via* Amping, were the road from Towan, *via* Yoshirei, and the road from Chinchaputsu, also *via* Yoshirei (see Map XII., pages 286-287, and Sketches XIII., page 288, and XIV., page 282). It was natural then that the main stronghold and key of the Russian position, which had been taken up to bar any movement towards Liaoyang, should have been in the immediate vicinity of Yoshirei.

From Yoshirei two great masses of rocky mountain run down from the main range into the Yamorinza valley. They do not splay outwards as spurs generally do, but rather draw in closer together until they almost meet across a narrow defile just by the village of Towan. In conjunction, they take a shape somewhat resembling a spear-head, and the hollow, narrowing passage into which the spear-shaft should fit is represented by the deep and narrow valley leading from Towan to Yoshirei.

The Russians holding the northern of these two converging ridges faced due north; their comrades holding the southern ridge faced south-east. At the spear-point, namely at Towan, the Russians entrenched along the crests of the two spurs were back to back, separated only by the narrow defile not more than 200 yards across. To a casual observer of the map it might seem easy to capture the points of the spurs above Towan, and then to roll up the defensive lines by an advance westwards, along the crest lines. Tactically, however, nature had made the actual spur-points almost impregnable. The southern one especially, on which is shown a battery known as the Towan salient battery, descended in a sheer precipice of smooth rock for eighty feet into the bed of the river. All the Russian guns, except this battery, the other half of which was in position further south along the same ridge, were placed at altitudes of 400 or 500 feet above the valley in the neighbourhood of Yoshirei. They are indicated on the map, and it will be observed that their positions had been so selected as to enable them to shook up and thoroughly search the several valleys coming down from the Motienling into the Yamorinza valley.

THE RUSSIAN "SALIENT BATTERY" NEAR TOWAN

South of this main position came the third ridge, occupied by the Russians. It commenced just above Chinchaputsu, ran southwards for some 3000 yards towards Hanchaputsu, where it turned south-west, thus enabling the Russians to refuse their right flank. In height it varied between 300 and 600 feet, and was steep, much of it being covered with dense jungle, about four feet high. None of the villages in the Tiensuitien-Yamorinza valley were loopholed or put into a state of defence, although they were occupied by the Russians in the earlier stages of the fight. Neither was the kaoliung and other crops cut down to give a field of fire.

The position I have described was the scene of the main battle between Kuroki and Keller. Fourteen miles due north of the Motienling stood the Twelfth Division. Fujii told me some days ago that they were on the point of being reinforced by Umezawa with a brigade of Guards Robi. At the date of the battle only one regiment of this brigade had arrived. On the 19th instant Inouye had captured Chaotao, and since then Turcheffsky had taken up a position barring any ftirther Japanese advance on Amping and Liaoyang. The spot he had selected was Yushuling, on the left bank of the Shi-Ho, and he had also detached one brigade to Penlin, six miles south of Yushuling, to block another alternative road to Amping, via Huchatsu (see Map XV., pages 304-305). The nature of the Yushuling-Penlin terrain must be described more carefully hereafter. It will be seen that the front, covered by the two armies, extended from Yushuling in the north to beyond Hanchaputsu in the south, a distance of over twenty miles of very broken country.

The fighting falls naturally into four distinct categories:

(1) The attempt of the Guards to turn the enemy's right flank and capture Yoshirei, which failed.

(2) The frontal attack made upon Towan, very late in the day, by a brigade of the Second Division which was not seriously resisted.

(3) The complete destruction of the Russian brigade at Penlin, as the results of a strategic-tactical concentration made against it by Sasaki's brigade, detached from the Twelfth Division, and by Okasaki's four battalions detached from the Second Division.

(4) The attack by Inouye on Turcheffsky at Yushuling, which was partially successful.

Before I begin the fighting I will quote some remarks dictated to me two days ago by General Fujii. They throw light on the strategical considerations of the moment.

When Haicheng and its neighbourhood became denuded of Russian troops, and when, after the lapse of a suitable interval, the general staff became aware that the left flank of the enemy was receiving considerable accessions of force, it seemed clear to

Marshal Kuroki that Kuropatkin was laying his plans to crush the Twelfth Division on our right. The probability of his making such an attempt had always been foreseen, as the great difficulty of communicating through the pathless mountains which separated the centre from the right flank of our army rendered the operation specially tempting to an enemy who could bring troops to bear upon the Twelfth Division, not only from the direction of Tokayen and Amping, but from Mukden and the north as well. There has also been a constant anxiety lest the Russian cavalry and Cossacks based on the north should have cut the line of communications of the Twelfth Division. However, so far, nothing untoward has happened, possibly because General Rennenkampf has ^en wounded. Our latest information, however, conclusively proved that whether or no the line of communication was to be attacked, the Twelfth Division itself was in some danger. It was fortunate, indeed, that we got wind of what was happening in the very nick of time. One day later might have just been one day too late! As it was, not one moment was lost; we struck with our full force all along the line, and we were just in time to catch the enemy. Not only was he caught before he had complete his movements of troops, but also whilst all his arrangements and formations had been disorganised by these movements.

"Many nice things have been said in your country about the great success of our army on the Yalu, but this battle of the 31st was an infinitely more anxious affair for the general staff than the passage of that river."

The part to be played by the Imperial Guards in this effort by Kuroki to forestall Kuropatkin was to turn the Russian right flank at some point south-west of Hanchaputsu, and then to press on and capture Yoshirei. It was hoped that Count Keller might be held in his positions along the west of the Yamorinza valley by gentle frontal pressure from the Second Division, until the Guards could get command of the Yoshirei pass at their backs. Had the scheme succeeded, it must have spelt destruction for the Russian army. The boundless audacity of the conception is certainly very attractive. The two Japanese Divisions were about to attack an equal force of Russians entrenched; a problem which might have seemed to call for exceptional caution. On the contrary, the most conspicuous quality of their plan was the daring of it. The Russians were assumed to have no General, and to be therefore immobile and incapable of manoeuvre or counter-attack. Here is the scheme. Five battalions of the Guards were to hold the right wing of the enemy, whilst three battalions were to make a very wide turning movement round that flank. Three more battalions were to keep touch between the right and left columns, whilst the one remaining battalion was to be in kept reserve. As it worked out, this meant that six battalions of the Guards would, for all practical purposes, be out of touch with the rest of the army from daylight until dark on the day of the battle. No doubt the country traversed by the turning column was worse than had been anticipated, and it was intended that it should have got into position several hours earlier, but military plans have to be judged by results. There remained the Second Division, which was detailed to make face against the Russian main division on the two ridges meeting at Towan and to play with the defenders until the Guards' turning column arrived within striking distance of Yoshirei. The Towan salient was then to be stormed, and that was to be the end of Keller and his army.

So far well and good, although the plan may be admitted to border on the adventurous. Not content, however, with the destruction, in anticipation, of the whole of Count Keller's force, Kuroki could not endure the thought of the Russian brigade at Penlin escaping with a mere ordinary defeat. Accordingly, he detached Okasaki from the Second Division to march with four battalions out of the six in his brigade so as to strike in behind the right rear of the Russian force at Penlin. This place lay full ten miles to the north of the Yoshirei battle-field. The Second Division, therefore, in front of the Russian main position at Towan was only to be represented by Matsunaga's brigade, plus the two remaining battalions of Okasaki's brigade. Thus Kuroki, in face of an equal force of Russians, had detached ten battalions, each taking their proportion of pioneers, out of his grand total of twenty-four battalions. Four of these had marched clean away out of the battle-field, the other six were lost until midday at least, and even after that hour could obviously not become available at any time on the 31st to meet any Russian attack on the Motienling. And yet the Motienling was every bit as sensitive a spot to the Japanese as was

Yoshirei to the Russians. More so, perhaps; for if the Russian communications were cut, there was still a large amount of millet meal in the country, whereas the invaders depended entirely on imported rice and other food-stuff from Japan.

When Lee at Chancellorsville sent Jackson with 26,000 men to march fourteen miles round the right flank of 70,000 Federals, whilst he himself retained only 17,000 men to hold his enemy during the movement, he displayed a boldness of conception which has always, in spite of its success, been considered akin to rashness. Kuroki's scheme for the 31st July will probably be classed in much the same category.

The detail of the part of the operations which was intended to deal the *grand coup* to Count Keller by seizing Yoshirei is best described first, as a very few words will suffice for that purpose. The left column, consisting of one battery of field artillery, two and a half troops of cavalry and three battalions of the Imperial Guards, moved by Mayapuza, which is outside the map to the southwards. After marching all night and until midday on the 31st, it had circled round to a spot some two and a half miles northwest of Hanchaputsu, as the crow flies. Here, on the prolongation of the steep and rocky ridge which turns westwards at Hanchaputsu, the Japanese found four battalions of the enemy awaiting them. Not liking the look of these Russians, who were posted behind an almost perpendicular ledge of rock, the column, which was very weary, stood fast for the rest of the day, and, beyond a little skirmishing, accomplished nothing. Its total casualty list in the operations of 31st July amounted to one man. The commander was Asada, a General held in high estimation by Fujii.

The connecting column, consisting of one mountain battery, three troops of cavalry, and three battalions, moved by Papanlin. On reaching the Yamorinza valley it found its progress barred by two companies of Russian infantry, who were holding the villages of Kuchaputsu and Hanchaputsu. Backed by their mountain battery, the infantry of the colunm soon cleared the villages and the hills overlooking them on the west side of the valley. They then proceeded with their march westwards, and at midday reached a point two miles north-west of Hanchaputsu as the crow flies. The column was here within one and a half miles of Asada's force, with which it had been ordered to keep connection, but it was now a considerable distance from its comrades on the right, as the Russian guns about Yoshirei necessitated a long *détour*. The field telephone wires had broken, the Japanese army has no arrangements for visual signalling; the country was so bad that mounted orderlies had to lead their horses; BO that, practically, this column also was lost to Kuroki for the remainder of the day. It skirmished with the Russians in front of it, but did not feel itself strong enough to assault, and at the close of the operations had suffered some sixty casualties, mostly incurred in the early morning. Thus the left and centre columns of the Imperial Guards had failed to get near enough to Yoshirei to exercise any pressure on that tender spot; they were too far from their comrades, and too entirely separated from them by the breakdown of the field telephones to be able to co-operate with them effectually, and, in fact, the mission entrusted to them by Kuroki had entirely miscarried.

The right column of the Imperial Guards was commanded by the refined and intelligent Watanabe. It consisted of five battalions, one and a half troops of cavalry, five batteries of field artillery, and two companies of pioneers. Two battalions and two batteries of this force moved by Rihorei (Lipolin) and emerged into the Yamorinza valley, opposite Suitechansa. Three battalions and three batteries moved by Shinkwairei to Makumenza. Thus it will be seen that Watanabe's right column was again subdivided into two distinct forces. As my description moves from left to right I shall call the force which issued from the Motienling range opposite to Suitechansa the Right Guards, Column A, and the force opposite Makumenza the Right Guards, Column B. The order given to Column A was to attack Suitechansa and Chinchaputsu. Column B was to keep touch with the Second Division on its right, and to hold the enemy lining the ridge due west of Makumenza. At 8 a.m. the two batteries with Column A came into action against the Russian batteries perched 500 feet up above them on the lofty ridge 1500 yards south-east of Yoshirei. For this purpose they took up positions in the bottom of the valley opposite Suitechansa, and as the ground was very limited in width one battery opened fire 300

The Battle of Yoshirei

yards behind the other. The two batteries had hardly begun to range when the Russian batteries, who had the range already, turned on them and reduced them to silence within twenty minutes. Several times during the day these two batteries pluckily tried to resume the contest, but on each occasion they were similarly silenced in a few minutes by the superior accuracy and command of the entrenched Russian batteries, which at 5500 yards were firing well within their own shrapnel range, whereas at that distance the weaker Japanese guns could effectively use only their high explosive shell.

The two battalions of infantry belonging to Column A were disposed as follows: Three companies of the 1st battalion were on the hills to the north side of the Suitechansa valley, where they remained until nightfall. The 4th company had been attached to the 2nd battalion, and was in position with it half a mile distant on the southern side of the same valley. At 9 a.m. this 4th company of the First Guards' battalion quitted the shelter of the hills and advanced diagonally across the Yamorinza valley against Suitechansa village. During the movement it was well supported by the fire of the three companies of its own battalion, who, by creeping down to the foot of the hills on the north of the Suitechansa valley, had got exactly opposite the village and within effective range of it. The attacking company, with its three sections in successive widely extended lines at 300 yards interval, moved in a north-westerly direction, and fording the river at the double, under a heavy fire from the village and from the trenches on the western hills, disappeared into the tall crops which ran from its western bank right up to Suitechansa. When the company got across the valley into the ground at the foot of the hills, which was dead to the fire of the trenches on the higher ridges, the men halted to pull themselves together, brought up their left shoulders, and then carried the southern extremity of the village with a rush and a cheer. No further progress was made here for a long time, the Russians clinging obstinately to the northern part of Suitechansa First Guards battalion stood fast, but changed their target, firing now at Chinchaputsu village and the Russian trenches beyond it. This they continued to do until nightfall, and made no attempt until after dark to move across the Yamorinza valley.

TOWAN TOWER

The moment the single company of the 1st battalion had effected its lodgment in Suitechansa village, namely, at 9.30 a.m., the 2nd battalion also darted out from the same small indentation in the eastern range of hills, following much the same line. Instead, however, of entangling itself in the village, it worked round the south of Suitechansa and ascended the dead ground at the foot of the western range of mountains which encloses the Yamorinza valley. Here the battalion swung round facing northwards, with its right twenty or thirty feet above the valley level, and its left some 500 yards further up the hillside, just short in fact of the crest of the main ridge, which was denied to them by the Russian guns on the height south of Yoshirei. Some little progress was then made in a northerly direction, but at 10.30 a.m. a halt was called to enable the men to rest and eat their dinners. Colonel Hume, who saw the action from doubtful safety on the east side of the Yamorinza valley, tells me that at this hour he noticed a curious palpitating tremor which seemed to pulsate up and down the Japanese firing line. On looking more closely, he found that each of the little fellows who composed it had pulled out his fan and was using it vigorously. It certainly was an appalling hot day.

At midday the battalion resumed its advance along the lower slopes of the ridge. It will be seen that the main ridge itself tapers out at its northern extremity into a long spur, almost touching with its tip the village of Chinchaputsu. The spur immediately south of this last one was seized by the 2nd battalion soon after they had resumed their advance. A deeply scooped-out gully separates the spurs from one another. As a bullet flies, the gully was only 200 yards broad in its upper section, where the two spurs approached the main ridge. In its lower section, where the spurs began to merge into the more level ground, the hollow flattened itself out and broadened to perhaps as much as 400 yards. The 21st East Siberian Tirailleurs held the last spur, the Japanese Imperial Guards had now gained possession of the last but one. It was half-past twelve o'clock, and the crisis of the action had arrived. One more effort would give the Japanese mastery over the whole of the ridge dominating Suitechansa and Chinchaputsu, but it was soon to be seen that the fiery energy of the attack was here destined to expend itself against an iron tenacity of defence, resolved to perish where it stood, rather than yield another yard of ground.

I have been over every inch of this ground. The little gully is mostly filled with very dense undergrowth, about four feet high. The backbone or ridge of each spur is bare of scrub, although there are some big trees scattered along the Russian position. The Japanese were defiladed from the fire of the Russian guns near Yoshirei by the crest of the main ridge. The reverse slope of the Russian spur was very steep, almost like the parapet of a redoubt, thus affording them good cover from shrapnel. The Russian spur stretched as far as Chinchaputsu, and from this northern extremity of their position the defenders were able to some extent to enfilade the gully by shooting up it from the vicinity of the village. The Japanese could not top the main ridge to turn the Russian right, as they then came under fire of the guns south of Yoshirei. On the other hand, adventurous Russians could, and did, occasionally try and creep along behind the crest of the main ridge, so as to pop up and fire a shot enfilading the Japanese line lying behind their spur.

By 12.35 p.m., the Japanese realised very well that the Russians had not the smallest intention of making them a present of this last ridge. They first reinforced with their supports, and then, at 1 p.m., with their reserves; they drew out the company of the 1st battalion from the south of Suitechansa, their guns opened rapid fire, and they themselves opened magazine fire — it was no good. One or two attempts were made by individuals and small parties to rush the last 100 yards, but the volume of the Russian fire seemed to increase rather than to weaken, and it was quite clear to onlookers from the other side of the Yamorinza valley that the Siberian Tirailleurs were not in a mood to care one button for the Imperial Guards, and that if the Japanese wanted the spur they had got to go and take it at the point of the bayonet. Colonel Hume tells me that one Japanese soldier came during the hottest of the fire fight to suggest to his company Commander that these men opposite were such marksmen, and exposed themselves so bravely, that they must be Japanese and not Russians at all. The officer told him that if that was his opinion he had better unfurl his little Rising Sun flag and stick it on the crest line. He did so, and was satisfied, by the three bullet holes with which it was promptly ventilated, that the people on the other side of the gully were no great

The Battle of Yoshirei

admirers of his national emblem.

The 21st East Siberian Tirailleurs are one of the few good shooting regiments the Japanese have until now encountered, and at such close quarters it was death to look over the crest line of the spur for more than one single second at a time. There is no more trying demand which can be made upon the soldier than to ask him to resume the advance when, after once being checked, his blood has cooled down and he has had time to realise that the first man to stand up must, in all human probability, be bowled over like a rabbit The Japanese did not make the attempt, not seriously that is to say, and confessed by the languor of their fire that the ardour of the attack had now burnt itself cold.

I have described this abortive affair at length. It is not only the closeness and obstinacy of the fight which has so profoundly impressed me, nor oven its bearing on the fortunes of the day. The struggle between the Guards and Tirailleurs appealed to me, as a British General, more particularly because the configuration of the terrain and all the surrounding circumstances reminded me so very vividly of a similar tight corner at Waggon Hill on the 6th of January 1900. Throughout this campaign I have been anxiously watching, I trust in no spirit of envy, hut simply with deep professional interest, to see if the moment would arrive when I could honestly exclaim, "Our fellows could have gone one better!" Thus far, except as regards a few mechanical details, such as road making, heliographs, &c., and certain tactical matters which must always remain matters of opinion. I have had to answer my own question negatively, in so far at least as the infantry is concerned. But — when I viewed this little hollow, where the lines of the opposing marksmen were clearly marked out to a man, by the piles of empty cartridge cases — then at last I was able to recall with pride the prolonged fighting at 100 yards range; the bayonet charge of the Devons across just such an interval and such a piece of ground — the loss of all the company officers and a third of their men in a few seconds — the piercing of the enemy's line and his complete overthrow. On this occasion at any rate, then, I feel we have no reason to shrink from a comparison.

The Russians made one small attempt at a counterattack on the Japanese spur during the afternoon, crawling through the undergrowth from their trenches just above Chinchaputsu. This was repulsed, and after that nothing happened in the Guards Division until 4 p.m., beyond the persevering attempts of the Japanese artillery to make head against the enemy's well-posted guns. The turning column, the connecting column, and now the left half of the right column, had all been brought to a complete standstill. It will be understood then, that Kuroki's plan of operations had failed. The turning and attacking portion of his force, consisting of the three columns whose movements I have described, had ceased to turn and to attack. There remained only the portion with which he had meant to hold the right wing of the enemy whilst it was being turned, namely, the column of the Guards which had marched down the Makumenza valley and now stood opposite Yamorinza, and the Second Division holding the main body of the enemy opposite Towan and Kinkahoshi. I will take the Guards first and finish with them.

At 3 p.m., General Hasegawa, commanding the Division, got a message from his left, which had been brought round by a foot orderly over the mountains, and had thus taken several hours in transmission. It told him of the complete failure of the turning movement, and warned him that the enemy were increasing in threatening strength in front of the isolated left and connecting columns. The only chance of relieving the pressure on his left was to try and press onwards himself with his right. Accordingly, Hasegawa promptly sent in his Divisional reserve to reinforce the Japanese oil the ridge above Chinchaputsu, and implored them to make one more effort to clear the last spur. Their bolt was shot, however, and they could not, or would not, respond. It is human nature: that poor human nature against which officers in war time and priests in peace time have constantly to struggle. Struggle as they may, it is never quite defeated, and is sore to break out just at the most critical moments. When men have been glued to the ground for three mortal hours, during which time continuous streams of bullets have been passing just over their heads, it is very difficult to get them to rise simultaneously and dash forward with the bayonet. A few specially brave individuals get to their feet and are instantly shot, which encourages the secret idea in each man's breast that he will make his start just one moment after his neighbour. As the neighbour cherishes precisely the same private intention, the result is that nothing can be done unless fresh troops are brought up and led right forward without any pause or hesitation at all. It was, perhaps, natural then ^at this order to advance had not the slightest effect. So the last column lying opposite Yamorinza was ordered to cross the valley and capture the high ground south-west of that village. Covered by a tremendous artillery fire from all the Japanese batteries, it advanced and forded the river at 6 p.m., capturing Yamorinza and the knoll 500 yards south of it. Here, however, the attack was brought to a full stop, and the enemy remained in possession, not only of the main ridge, whose crest line was about 1000 yards north-west of Yamorinza, but also of the knoll only two or three hundred yards away to the south-west.

The failure of the Guards was now complete. They had put in all their reserves, and if the battle had been between them alone, and the Russians immediately in touch with them, I believe their situation would steadily have gone from bad to worse.

Kuroki's right wing, consisting of the Second Division, less Okasaki's four battalions, was posted on either side of the Motienling road, about half a mile before it debouches into the Yamorinza-Tiensuitien valley. Two battalions and two batteries were to the south of the road, and six battalions and four batteries were to the north of it; but the disposition of the troops (which I got from an artillery colonel) is so well shown on Map XII. that there is no need to describe it very elaborately. The Second Division, being intended merely as a holding force, furnished at first no thrilling episodes. At 9 a.m., the four Japanese batteries to the north of the road, which were posted just behind a ridge, began to search the Russian trenches with shrapnel. Some clumps of wood on the side of the northern ridge of the Towan-Yoshirei valley also received a good deal of their attention. They then lengthened their range and fuses, and attacked the Russian battery on the top of the high ridge 2000 yards north-west of Yoshirei. At this time the Guards artillery was making one of its furious but spasmodic efforts against the ridge running southwest from Chinchaputsu, and the continuous rumbling roar of these discharges with the beautiful white puffs of smoke from the bursting shrapnel were wonderful to hear and to behold. At 9.45, the Russian guns 1500 yards south-east of Yoshirei, which had hitherto been firing into the Yamorinza valley, suddenly switched on to the four Second Division batteries to the north of the Motienling road. They got their range in an instant; let fly the *rafale*, and in a couple of minutes every Japanese gunner, not killed or badly wounded, had cleared fifty yards back under cover of a road cutting, whilst the twenty-four guns, until now so aggressively noisy, were left standing by themselves, silenced I As soon as the Russians were satisfied of their victory they too ceased fire; and then, instead of tumult and uproar, there reigned perfect quiet, which seemed rather accentuated than disturbed by the low throbbing murmur telling us that the Guards and Russians were still hard at it with musketry about Suitechansa and Chinchaputsu.

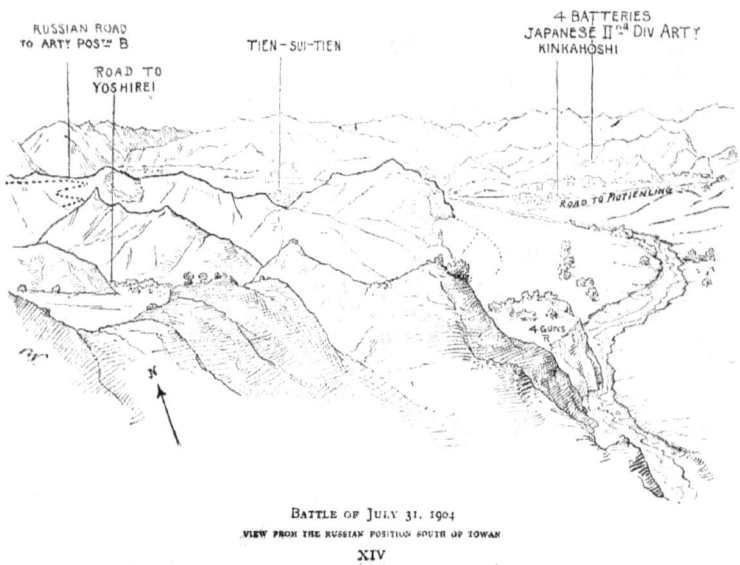

BATTLE OF JULY 31. 1904
VIEW FROM THE RUSSIAN POSITION SOUTH OF TOWAN
XIV

By-and-by the Japanese gun detachments came creeping back, and I could clearly see them handling their guns and changing their position so as to baffle the Russian ranging next time they opened.

At 2.45 the duel opened again, the Japanese using mostly high explosive shell, with which they fired at their old enemy the battery north-east of Yoshirei, and also at the salient battery near the point

The Battle of Yoshirei 283

of the spur a little south of To wan. This time the Russians on the high ground near Yoshirei were not able to repeat their first conspicuous success, the slight changes of position of the Japanese guns having probably puzzled them. On the other hand, I could see for myself next day that the Russian guns just above Towan were quite safe from shots fired from the north-east as they were most cleverly sandwiched in between a small steep knoll and the main rise of the hill. In front of them was a sheer precipice of eighty feet dropping into the river, so a more perfect position could not be conceived.

The following extract from a statement made to me by Major-General Fujii will form a good preface to an account of the last stage of the battle:

"You can best appreciate the anxiety of the general staff when I tell you that, owing to the superior strength of the enemy, we had to dispense with a general reserve to the army. It was not long before the want of this began to make itself felt. Although we were well aware that the ground in front of the Guards was difficult, we expected them to be in possession of Yoshirei by midday at the very latest. As, however, the terrain was more unfavourable than we expected, admitting of no good artillery positions, these expectations were completely disappointed. In fact, as you are well aware, the Guards' attack was everywhere brought to a complete standstill When this was realised, headquarters had to admit to themselves that the situation was critical. If only the Guards bad been able to carry out their instructions and make good their attack on Yoshirei, then the Motienling itself, and our main line of communications which crossed it, were practically safe. For even if the Russians advanced in force against it, we bad always the Second Division available to hold them on this side. But as the Guards' attack was checked, and success or failure in that section of the field of battle seemed to hang in the balance, we could no longer continue to act with all the prudence to which we constantly aspire. This is a very important point, and I would like to make it clear even at the risk of repetition. So long as the Second Division remained inactive, or active only to the extent of cooperating with the Guards by its left wing, we could enjoy the security of possessing an army reserve, although in our orders for the battle we had not expressly set apart any troops to perform that function. Any threat against our centre, where we were most sensitive, could be met by the employment of the right wing of the Second Division, who could, in the long run, be reinforced by the recall of Okasaki and his four battalions.* But the moment the light wing of the Second Division had to be used to co-operate in the attack against Yoshirei, it was entirely lost as a potential reserve, and moreover in the very process of making such an attack it must turn its right flank towards Seisekirei, and as it moved forward uncover the Motienling itself.

"At this period the Marshal Kuroki did not yet know of the great success on his right which would have relieved him of all anxiety regarding Generals Okasaki and Inouye. As a matter of fact, however, he did not believe there was any imminent danger of a forward movement being made by the enemy in the northern section of the battle-field, as he knew their preparations for their intended advance against the Twelfth Division were not complete, and be felt confident therefore they would be too fully occupied in endeavouring to defend themselves to be able to think of much else. For our left wing and the southern section of the battle-field the Marshal suffered no active anxiety; for although the Japanese could not make good their point, the ground was just as bad for counter^ attack as it was for attack, and the general staff felt quite certain the Guards could hold on to what they had gained. Therefore, feeling that the risk must be taken, the commander of the First Army gave the order at 1 p.m. to the Second Division to begin to press upon the enemy as a preliminary to attacking seriously and taking Yoshirei. After that you know what happened. Headquarters had done what it could, and had nothing more to do, as there were no more men to do anything with. They were all in action in so far as the commander of the army was concerned."

In consequence of these orders the two battalions on the south of the Motienling road moved down at 4 p.m. in extended attack formations towards the village of Kinkahoshi. The four battalions north of the Motienling road also shook themselves out, and moved

---

* The run must have been a very long one. — I.H.

The Battle of Yoshirei 285

over the ridge behind which they had been lying as if with the intention of crossing the main valley at Tiensuitien. From this time on I lost sight of both the columns, until, at 4.50 p.m., I saw the firing line of the right attack advancing in very extended order and in a south-westerly direction just to the south-west of Tiensuitien. At 5.10 p.m. the Russians began to remove guns from the battery on the point of the spur 300 yards south-east of Towan, and I watched the battery, less one gun which had turned over coming down the hill, gallop westwards up the Towan-Yoshirei valley. At 5.20 p.m. I got a beautiful view of the development of the attack. At this moment the two battalions which had started from the south of the Motienling road were advancing in very wide extension across the big valley directly on Towan, heading due west. The four battalions from the north of the Motienling road had swung round until their direction was almost due south, and were pressing up the northern slope of the big spur which forms the northern limit of the Towan-Yoshirei valley. Individuals could be clearly distinguished, and they all seemed to be working their way up in widely extended groups even smaller than sections. Whenever these groups got into dead ground they closed up, but directly they came under shrapnel fire they opened out to anything from five to twenty paces. The Russians were searching the whole face of the hill with shrapnel, but did not seem to have any luck. I believe that by this time the Russian infantry had left their trenches. At least there was comparatively little musketry fire on either side. At 5.30, amidst the intense excitement of the headquarters staff, a Japanese soldier, with a flag, climbed hands and knees up the steep hillside and fixed the emblem of the Rising Sun upon the ancient Towan tower. He and two or three of his friends who joined him were evidently under fire, as they remained close behind the tower for protection. At 5.45 the unchecked advance of all the Japanese troops visible to us, and the characteristic dropping shots which denote the close of an action, made it clear that the Russians

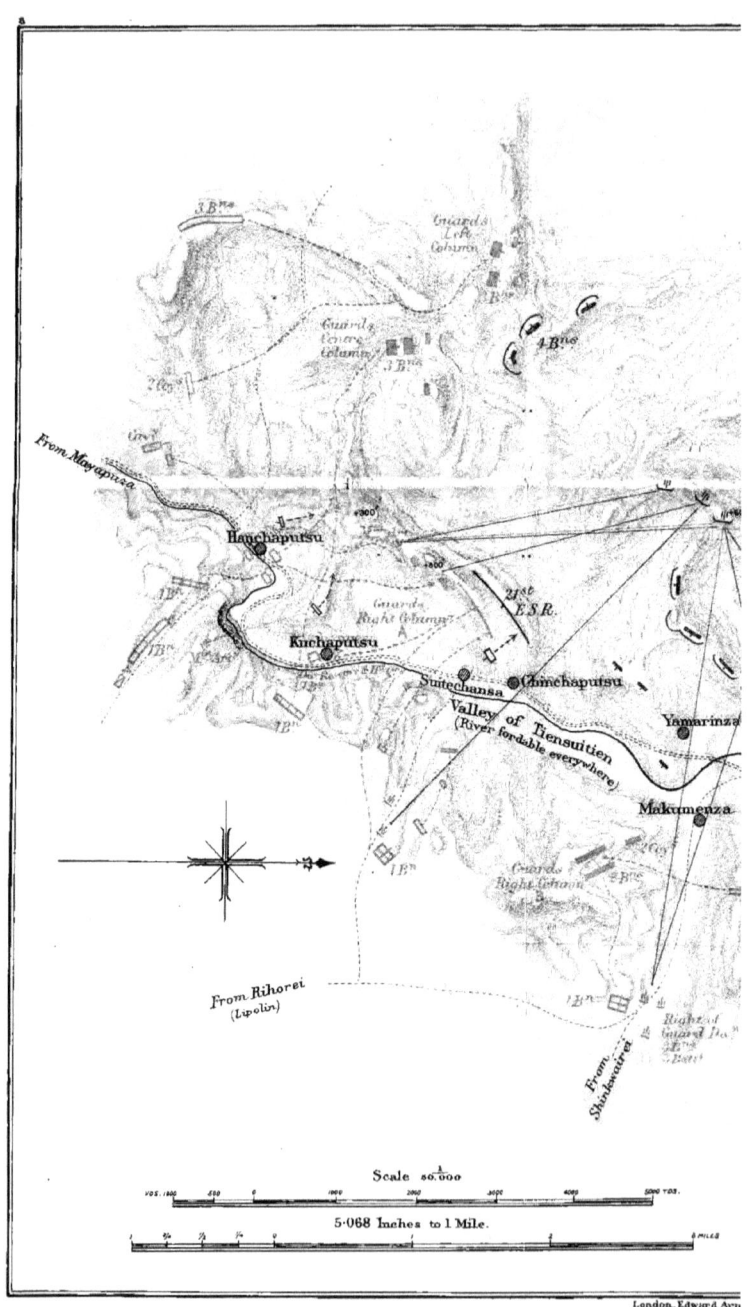

The Battle of Yoshirei

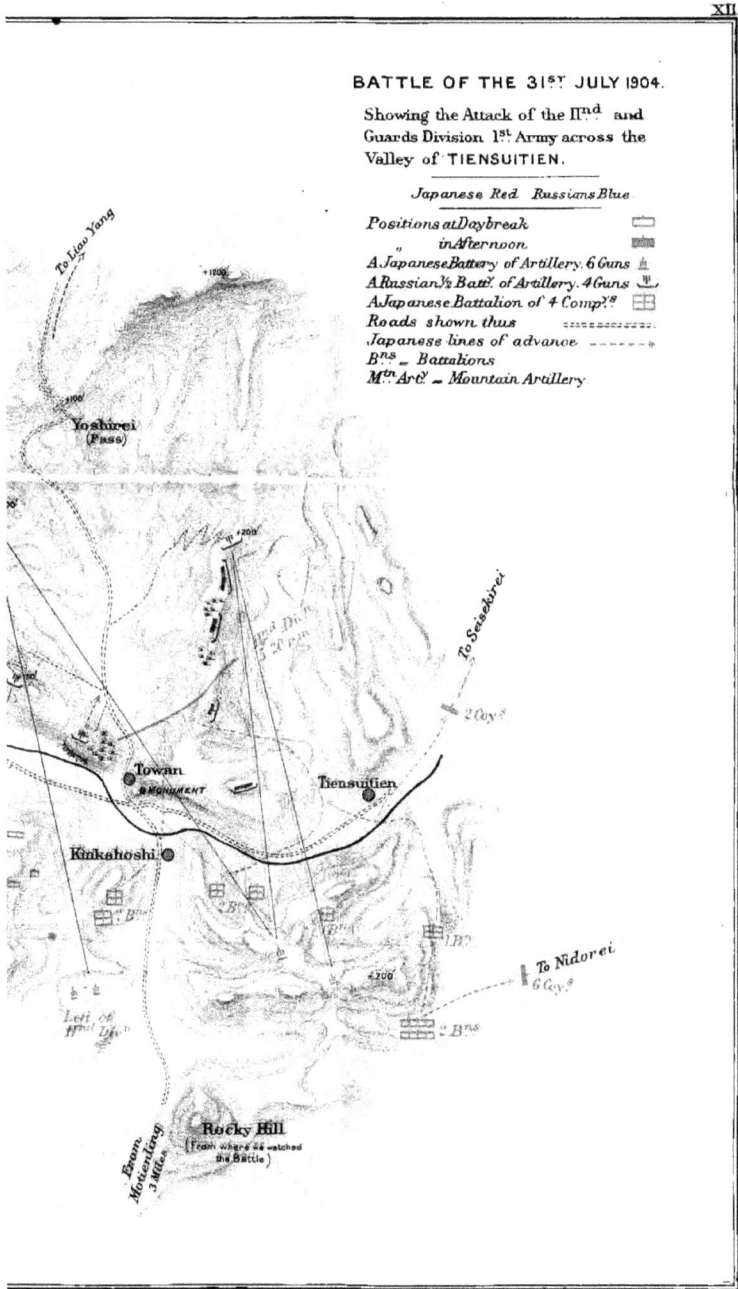

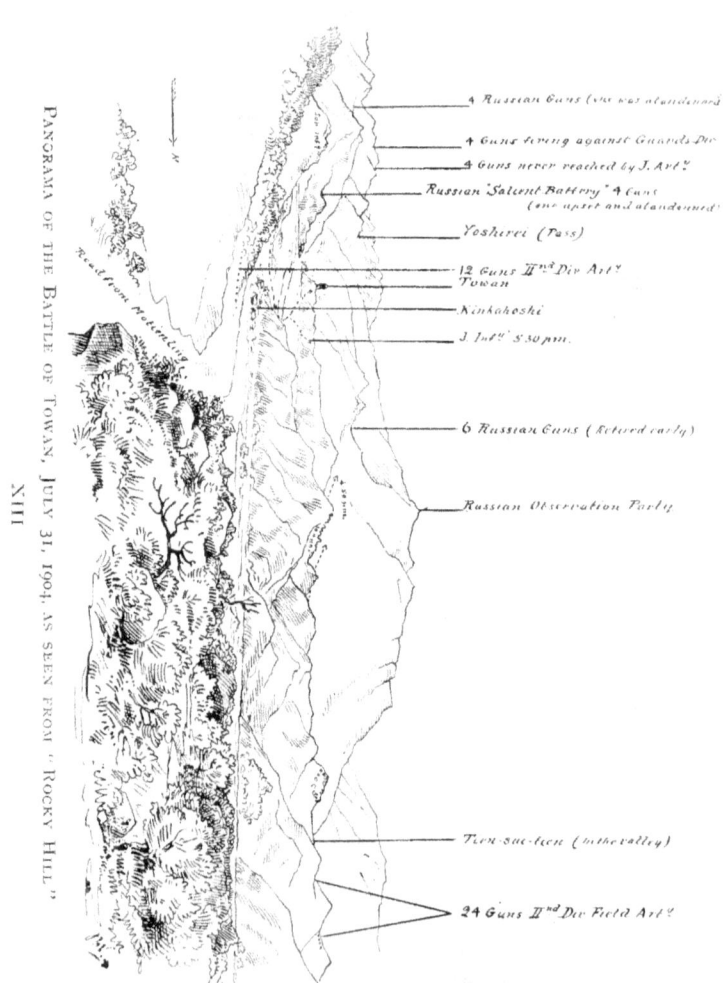

The Battle of Yoshirei

opposite the Second Division had decided to abandon the field. Why they should have done so it is impossible to say until accounts are given from the Russian side. Perhaps because of the death of the brave General Keller. Perhaps because they had received reports of them misfortunes in the northern sphere of action. However this may have been, it was certainly not because the troops of Kuroki had defeated the troops of Keller.

Onlookers are always seeing great chances missed, most frequently because of their own want of knowledge and consequent want of appreciation of the actual conditions. Yet, though keenly aware of the danger of discussing a battle whereof I have only a one-sided impression, I cannot refrain from drawing attention to the great opportunity of a counter-attack from the direction of Seisekirei straight on to the Motienling itself. It is said that the Russians had a Division in reserve at Tokayen. Had it marched thence after the men had eaten their breakfasts it would have appeared over the Seisekirei ridge at about 4 p.m., and had it then marched on to the Motienling there was practically nothing but the headquarters staff and the foreign military attachés to stand in its way unless it had preferred to strike the widely extended Japanese right full and fair on the flank.

Chapter XVIII – The Disastrous Retreat from Penlin

There now remains to be told the story of the encounter between Inouye and Turcheffsky, which, although it took place ten to fifteen miles to the north of Kuroki's right flank, was just as much and as essentially a part of the battle of Yoshirei as was the turning movement of the Guards to the south.

The battle of Chaotao had taken place on the 19th October, and since then the Twelfth Division had been held in leash and prevented by Kuroki from pursuing its advantage, as far as some at least of the young bloods of that force thought desirable. After fortifying the Chaotao position so as to have something to fall back upon in case things went wrong, Inouye, on the night of the 20th, advanced westwards two miles up the open valley of the Shi-Ho and dug a deep and solid line of entrenchments across the level cultivated plain only 2000 yards to the east of Makurayama mountain, and 3000 yards east of the Shisan ridge. He might have occupied these two positions without trouble or loss then and there; but, first, this was further than Kuroki wished him to go, secondly, neither position was very easy to defend against an attack from the west, although they were certainly very formidable against an attack from the east. Admitting the cogency of these reasons, still it was a comical idea, and probably a procedure unprecedented in modem war, for a commander to leave a strong place like Chaotao, advance two miles, and then plump himself down in the open plain before a formidable vacant position which the enemy in all likelihood would very shortly occupy. It would have seemed almost better to stay at Chaotao, whence he could easily have marched to the attack in three-quarters of an hour at any time, rather than deliberately to put himself under the command of heights on which the enemy's forces would, in all human probability, eventually put in an appearance. It was not as if the Shisan ridge and the Makurayama mountain could in any possible sense be considered a trap into which it was desired that the Russians should entangle themselves. As will appear from the narrative, they constituted a very formidable barrier to a Japanese advance westwards. I can only imagine then that General Inouye felt he would like to get a close springing-off place for his assault, as well as a rallying ground near at hand in case the assault failed. Otherwise, if he had been repulsed the enemy's guns could have shrapnelled his retiring troops all the way up the straight open valley as far back as Chaotao itself.

Sure enough, on the 26th, the enemy occupied the Shisan ridge, and on the 29th three Russian battalions drove the Japanese outposts off Makurayama and held that mountain, whilst a Japanese detachment, posted at Penlin, six miles to the south of Yoshirei, was also forced to retire.

The Russian Commander-in-Chief had in the interval since the battle of Chaotao gauged the strength of Inouye, and had determined to concentrate against Kim a superior force, so as, ff possible, to overwhelm him before assistance could reach him from the other two Divisions of Kuroki's army. The opportunity was certainly most tempting. Only half the Kobi brigade which Fujii told me several days ago was going to reinforce Inouye had as yet come to hand in the shape of a regiment of Guards' reservists. I think I can rely upon my information in this particular, although certainly Fujii again, in his statement about the battle which I have quoted, speaks of Inouye's brigade of Kobi. The Division and this regiment stood very much alone. They were a long day's march from Lienshankuan, which may be taken as the centre of the

Second Division, and the roads were only practicable for infantry without transport. In addition to its isolation, Inouye's force was specially tempting to the Russian generalissimo, from the fact that its right flank lay open to an attack from Mukden, via Penchiho, which lay only fourteen miles north of Chaotao, and was already held by a regiment of infantry and two regiments of Cossacks. Accordingly, he instructed his general staff to set to work on a scheme for an attack upon the Twelfth Division at Chaotao. By this scheme, Chaotao was to be held in front by an advance in force from Yushuling, whilst the Japanese left flank was to be turned from Penlin and their right from Penchiho. No fault can be found with such a conception of the situation, or with the plan, which was based upon that conception. Only, in front of a watchful enemy well served by innumerable Chinese spies, the two essential conditions for the success of any plan, good, bad or indifferent, were secrecy in preparation and promptitude in execution. A trifling but perhaps significant indication of the Russian interpretation of these essentials may be found in the fact that they sent balloons to their left flank, and launched them thence into the heavens. Now a balloon can give points to an American sky-sign as a method for attracting attention. Be this as it may, one thing is sure: the standard of promptitude and secrecy adopted by Kuropatkin was neither prompt enough or secret enough to deceive the intelligence of Colonel Hagino, that earnest, thoughtful man, for seven long years a sojourner in European Russia, and a close observer and student of all the Muscovitish idiosyncrasies.

From Chaotao to the vicinity of Yushuling the valley of the Shi-Ho river runs east and west — a flat, cultivated plain 2000 to 3000 yards wide (sec Map XV.). At Yushuling, the Shi-Ho takes a sharp bend to the north, and runs for a mile and a half in that direction through a valley about 1500 yards broad. The eastern side of the valley is formed by the mountain called by the Japanese Makurayama (Pillow Hill). This mountain juts out southwards from the range bordering the Chaotao-Yushuling valley to the north. It is a semi-detached ridge, some 850 feet in height, joined on to the northern range by a saddle or neck which is about 200 feet high. The mountains lining the valley on the north are from 450 to 500 feet high, and very difficult and rugged, mostly of a sugar-loaf shape. Makurayama is very steep indeed on its eastern face — so much so, that infantry armed and accoutred had to climb on hands and knees in many places during their ascent; on the west it slopes down much more gently. There is a good deal of short scrub on the knoll itself, but the neck which joins it to the mountains is quite bare.

So much for the eastern wall of the Shi-Ho defile by Yushuling. Its western wall is formed by the Shisan ridge, an offshoot from the range bordering the Chaotao-Yushuling valley to the south, just as Makurayama runs out from the northern boundary of the same valley. The Shisan ridge rises quite precipitously out of the river to a height of 100 feet. Westwards it slopes away gently. The Russians had taken up their main position along the top of the precipitous eastern face of the Shisan ridge, where they had aligned two batteries of artillery — in all, sixteen guns. This position would have been extraordinarily strong had it not been for Makurayama, on the other side of the defile 1000 yards distant. For the Shisan ridge must speedily become untenable if once an enemy coming from the east succeeded in placing artillery on that mountain which dominated the ridge by 250 feet. It was, therefore, absolutely necessary for the Russians to include Makurayama in their scheme of defence, for the position, as a whole, was bound to stand or fall in accordance with their success or failure in denying its possession to the Japanese. It might have been expected, then, that this mountain would have been held by a strong force; that it would have been thoroughly well entrenched, and that a bright look-out would have been kept up by the battalions who had been entrusted with its defence. The sequel will show clearly how Kuropatkin was served by his subordinates in these particulars.

Some six miles south of Yushuling was Penlin, where a brigade of Russian infantry on a frontage of about a mile were holding the hills on the western side of a small valley, so as to command the road from Chaotao *via* Penlin and Huchatsu to Amping. There was a good field of fire, and no crops to bar the view. I have seen some freehand sketches done of this part of the country, and the terrain is, generally speaking, exceptionally rugged and impracticable even for Manchuria. If the. Russians had dug themselves in during the 29th and 30th, after driving off the Japanese detachment, the Penlin position must have proved a very hard nut to crack; but, unlike their ancestors at Borodino, they contented themselves with a short length of trench giving very little shelter from rifle fire, and none at all to the descending bullets of shrapnel, especially when fired from a low velocity arm like the Twelfth Division mountain gun. The Russian brigade at Penlin had no artillery, but half a battery was posted to the west, at Lipyui, whence the fire of its four guns might assist, to some extent, in covering a retreat.

On the evening of the 30th July, Inouye issued orders to Major-Oeneral Kigoshi to attack the Yushuling position with his full brigade of six infantry battalions, supported by four batteries of mountain artillery and one battery of field artillery. At the same time, Major-General Sasaki was ordered to march with his brigade, at a strength of five infantry battalions, one squadron and one mountain battery, to attack the enemy at Penlin. Two battalions of the Guards Kobi Regiment had been left at Chaotao to watch the Russian force known to be fourteen miles north of that place at Penchiho, and on the morning of the 31st the remaining battalion was moved out to the right rear in readiness to fend off the same danger. This left Inouye only one line battalion; a few pioneers and some other odds and ends as his Divisional Reserve.

I will first describe, very briefly, the attack on the Yushuling position. As at Yoshirei, an attempt was made to turn the Russian right, and the 24th Regiment occupied the spur above Linsha during the night, without encountering any opposition. It had thus gained a foothold within 1000 yards of its objective, but when day broke it was realised that a further advance across the open valley would be desperately dangerous, especially in face of sixteen guns in position along the precipitous Shisan ridge. The 24th Regiment, therefore, contented itself with holding on to what it had gained, and, following the example of the Guards' turning column at Yoshirei, took no further part in the action. One half of Kigoshi's brigade is now accounted for, and may completely be dismissed from further consideration. The other half-brigade, or regiment, with two of its battalions in advance and the third in support, issued from its trenches 2000 yards east of Makurayama at 4 a.m.

The battalion on the left marched direct upon the big Makurayama hill; reached Fuchaputsu quite unobserved a short time before daybreak; extended on either side of Fuchaputsu and lay down there, covered by the dead ground, awaiting developments in other parts of the field. It had not to wait long. The battalion on the right climbed the hills on the north side of the valley, and, moving westwards along them, rushed a weak Russian picquet just as day was breaking. The picquet was posted on a steep and lofty spur about 300 yards east of the spur running out to form Makurayama neck or saddle. It was caught napping, and the enemy was upon it before the men could be formed up to defend themselves. A dummy sentry, made of straw and clad in a cast-off Russian uniform, was found on the spot where the picquet had been surprised. Any one inspecting the outpost line in a perfunctory manner from the next spur to the west from Makurayama might have been led to believe by seeing this dummy that a good look-out was being kept up by the troops. This man of straw strikes me as being a very emblematical personage.

Three hundred yards to the west of the advancing Japanese was the spur of Makurayama neck, and 250 yards behind that spur (although they did not know it) were the two infantry battalions entrusted with the defence of this part of the Russian position, snugly sleeping in their camp. Had the Japanese been omniscient, however, they could not have acted with greater promptitude; and, without one moment's delay, they pressed eagerly, like a pack of hounds, after the flying picquet, on towards the Makurayama neck. On the far side of the hill the shots fired at the picquet had given the alarm; and in a confused crowd, half dressed, half awake — just exactly as the British reserves were brought into the firing-line at Majuba — the Russians were now hurrying up the neck from the west. Even at such a critical moment a great deal still depended on chance. As in the race for the ridge which took place between our cavalry and the Boers at Welcome Farm, in South Africa, the side which first reached the crest, even if it were only by ten yards, would have an immense advantage. The Japanese had the luck, as usual, and just gained the summit by that very distance of ten yards. As they topped the neck, to their amazement they found themselves face to face with a half-clad, disorganised crowd of

Russian soldiers, breathless, apparently without leaders. In a moment the Japanese had flung themselves down, and were firing for dear life into the fully exposed mass just beneath the muzzles of their rifles. The Russians, although two to one in numbers, had everything else against them. Their men were in confusion; there seemed to be no leader generally known to every one who might have given orders. The private soldiers could not exactly realise what was happening, and had got separated from their own company officers. The Japanese, on the contrary, were in good order, wide awake, and knew precisely what they were about. Under these conditions it is very much to the credit of the Russians that there was no panic, and that they actually disputed the possession of the neck (though without ever gaining the crest line) for at least half an hour. Such of the Japanese as were not absorbed by this conflict on the hillside were free to fire into the camp, which lay conspicuously beneath them, at rather less than 300 yards' distance. Luckily for the Russians, the Japanese do not shoot like the Boers, or else there would have been but few of them left.

The headquarters here confirm the story told me by Jardine that these Japanese soldiers were in fits of laughter and shouting out to one another like a pack of schoolboys. "There, my friends, fire at the old officer pulling on his breeches!" "No! no! no! There is a fat major buckling on his sword!" "The horse! the horse! Shoot the horse quickly!" Cries like these were heard all along the neck. I must add that the Russians who found themselves in this unfortunate quandary seem also to have shown, in most cases, commendable equanimity. One young officer in particular was observed washing his face and carefully brushing his hair, whilst the air was simply alive with the whistling and the cracking of the bullets. The whole thing reminds me of an incident during the first Waziri expedition under Sir Neville Chamberlain. The tribesmen had rushed the picquets, and were charging through the camp waving their bloody swords. A terrified khidmatgar rushed into his master's tent shouting, "Waziri log arte hain!" ("The Waziris are coming!"), to which the young dandy, who was buttoning on a high collar, replied, "Bolo darwaza band hai" ("Say the door is shut" — Anglo-Indian for "Tell them I am not at home").

At the same time that the large confused crowd of Russians left camp for the purpose of anticipating the Japanese in seizing the neck, a smaller party rushed southwards to reinforce the big knoll, or hill, of Makurayama itself. It was only held by a picquet, but the Japanese battalion, lying concealed at the front of the eastern slope, could not know this, and so lay still biding their time. The Russian picquet also, feeling its weakness, did not, by fire or otherwise, intervene in the fight that was taking place on the neck.

By 5.45 a.m. the Russian reinforcement had reached the top of the Makurayama, and at the same time the Japanese battalion, which had by then made good the neck, turned south and, working along the ridge, attacked the hill from the north. The Russians on the top were making an effective resistance to this movement, when the Japanese left battalion, lying 300 feet directly beneath them, seeing the small defending force fully occupied, began to scale the steep eastern face of the mountain, pulling themselves up hands and knees through the almost impenetrable brushwood by which it was covered. Progress was slow, for the Russians, although in small force, bad on this side had time to recover from their surprise and offered stout opposition. But at 7 a.m. the Japanese gunners were, for the first time, able to make out clearly what was going on, and all five batteries opened on the summit of Makurayama from their gun-pits. The Russians were now obliged to keep their heads down, and m they had no deep trenches on the summit to shelter them from the shrapnel, it did not seem as if they could resist for many minutes more. So great was the natural strength of the position, however, that it was not until 8.30 a.m. that the Japanese finally got possession of the hill, the defenders falling back on to two spurs immediately west of their camp, where the majority of their comrades, who had previously been driven off the neck by the Japanese right attack, had already taken up a new position. The Russian artillery answered the five batteries, but failed altogether to locate them, some of the shells falling on to the old Chaotao position, a mile and a half beyond the Japanese gun-pits.

As soon as Makurayama had been carried the little mountain guns had to creep forward to get within effective range of the Russian second line on the Shisan ridge, and on the spurs west of their camp where the Russians from Makurayama had rallied. Six field guns and six mountain guns came into action immediately to the south of the Japanese trenches, and one mountain battery came into action immediately to the north of those trenches, as shown on the Map XV. As usual, all that provision and preparation could do had already been done to enable this advance to be carried out without any hitch or unnecessary loss of life or of time. Boads had been cut through the *kaoliung*; gun-pits had been dug; bomb-proof trenches had been constructed for the men; a suitable spot had been marked out for the teams; wooden logs had been fixed up to shield the gun detachments when in action; nothing, in fact, had been neglected; least of all concealment. A Japanese officer has told me he had, from curiosity, gone over to the Shisan ridge next day, and he could not make out where his own guns had been; he was an artilleryman. Wherever the guns were not entirely covered by the ground, they were shielded from view by a double row of *kaoliung* stalks planted a few yards to their front. As a reward for all this trouble, it is worth recording that the two batteries on the left did not suffer so much as a scratch either to personnel or material during the artillery fighting, which lasted from 7.10 a.m. until dark. The mountain battery on the right had, however, to cross the Shi-Ho to get to their pits on the north of the trenches, and even Japanese ingenuity was unable to improvise cover across running water. Whilst fording the river, the Russian guns were switched on to them, and one shrapnel bowled over fourteen men in midstream, and killed quite a good number of horses. This was unfortunate, as the dead horses at once sank under the surface, carrying with them essential parts of the guns, which had to be recovered before the battery could go into action. Not many minutes elapsed, however, before everything had been fished up and carried into the *kaoliung*, which grew right up to the bank of the river. The Second Division artillery officers are inclined to criticise the action of the Twelfth Division in giving the Russians such a chance at a range of under 4000 yards, and hold that the Russians ought to have destroyed a battery making such an attempt.

The Russian guns were, as shown in Map XV., posted all along the eastern edge of the Shisan ridge. They were for the most part

The Disastrous Retreat from Penlin 299

in very fair gun-pits, but there were no deep trenches for the detachments. Nor was there any attempt at indirect laying, and each gun could at once be accurately located by its flash and by the immense cloud of dust which rose with the shock of each discharge. The Japanese think that the comparatively unprotected, very conspicuous Russian gunners must have suffered cruel losses. It may be so. We shall some day hear the other side of the story. But troops are always inclined to be over sanguine about the effect of their own artillery.

A MOUNTAIN GUN COMING INTO ACTION

At 9.30 a.m., and at noon, the Russians made rather half-hearted counter-attacks down the Penchiho road against the right of the troops holding Makurayama spur. Reinforcements of two companies from the supporting battalion were sufficient to check any untoward development in this direction. After midday, the situation afforded an interesting exemplification of stalemate. Although Makurayama hill commanded the Shisan ridge by 200 feet at from 1000 to 1500 yards, the Japanese infantry were unable to establish that preponderance of fire over the Shisan ridge which was absolutely indispensable if any further advance was to be attempted, either from Makurayama hill or Makurayama spur. The gun and rifle fire from the Shisan ridge so swept the smooth and rocky face of the Makurayama plateau that the Japanese had to crouch down behind the eastern crest line and do all their firing in a very hurried "Jack-in-the-box" manner. Had the Russians possessed a couple of big five-inch guns posted on a mountain half-way to Penchiho they would have made the Japanese on Makurayama exceedingly uncomfortable. Next day it might have been otherwise, as the Japanese would have dug, and did dig, all through the night, making deep lines of entrenchments and solid gun-pits along the crest of the hill. But for this day, the 31st July, the Russian guns alone were able to hold the Shisan ridge, and the bulk of the Russian infantry might very well have been used in concert with the troops at Penohiho against the Japanese right, where only two battalions were available to oppose a simultaneous advance from the north and from the north-west.

It cannot, I think, be gainsaid that, if the situations had been reversed, a Japanese Okasaki at Penchiho would have brought down every man he could lay his hands on, including the slightly wounded and sick, and would have thrown them from the north against Chaotao or Makurayama; not in any dribbling, ineffectual manner, but as wholeheartedly as an avalanche on its way to the foot of the valley. No such enterprise was attempted on a large scale, and at dark the relative positions of the two forces was practically the same as at 9 a.m. Judging merely by what had taken place on the battle-field of Yushuling, the issue of the battle was still on the knees of the gods. A mortifying surprise had signalised the commencement of the action; had damped the Russian spirit and had entailed the loss of the camp with all it contained, and, far more important, the first and most commanding line of the position. But since that preliminary misfortune had befallen them, the Russians had quite held their own, the best proof of which may be found in the fact that the Japanese were very uncertain whether they were going to attack or be attacked next morning.

One incident gave the latter great hopes. It was the removal of several guns from the Shisan ridge just before dark. It was argued that, as nothing on the actual battle-field seemed to render this necessary, Sasaki and Okasaki must have scored a triumph at

The Disastrous Retreat from Penlin 301

Penlin. It was so. Next morning the Russians had withdrawn, and the cause of their withdrawal was doubtless the bad news from Penlin, which deprived them of their last hope of being able to retake Makurayama, and made them anxious about their own communications.

The story of the bloody reverse suffered by the Russians at Penlin has been reserved to the end. Not for many months to come will it be possible to say positively why the troops of Count Keller and Turcheffsky acknowledged their defeat by an abandonment of the battle-field during the night of July 31st, but the Penlin disaster may have been, nay, probably was, the final determining cause.

Leaving the vicinity of Chaotao at three o'clock in the morning, General Sasaki by 7 a.m. had reached the high ground on the east side of the valley through which runs the road from Yushuling to Penlin. On the bare hills immediately opposite and west of him was posted a Russian infantry brigade,* without artillery, and practically unentrenched. Sasaki had his mountain battery and five battalions of infantry, as well as a squadron of cavalry. He knew that Okasaki, with four battalions of northerners, was very shortly due to assist him, but the southern clansmen of the Twelfth prefer to be beholden to nothing but their own prowess,† and Sasaki lost no time in preparing for the encounter with he knew not what, on the other side of the valley. Four battalions advanced slowly and cautiously westwards in very open attack formations. At 8 a.m. they drew the enemy's fire, and at the same time the Japanese mountain battery came into action against the opposite crest line over the heads of its own infantry. It was a relief to every one when minute after minute passed and no deep-throated retort broke forth from the distant hills, or scream of the answering shrapnel. The attack was greatly facilitated, especially in its preliminary stages, by this absence of hostile artillery; but still, for a considerable period, not much progress could be made.

---

* According to Jardine, headquarters here declare that the Russians had twelve battalions, or a brigade and a half, at Penlin.

† The men of the Second Division come from Sendai district, in the north-east of Japan. Those of the Twelfth Division are Kyushiu men, from the south.

A sunken road ran for a short distance parallel to the Russian position, and from it a very troublesome fire was maintained which crossed with the fire of two companies detached on a height to the left of the enemy's main position, making any advance to close quarters in this part of the field temporarily impossible. Meanwhile, the Russians prolonged their right, and made a very threatening attempt to turn the Japanese left. Fortunately for Sasaki, his troops managed to put a better complexion into the fight on the other flank before this enveloping movement became so serious as to force him to renounce the offensive. To the mountain battery belongs the chief credit for this favourable change in the situation. Attentively watching, the commander of the six little guns was at last enabled to locate the exact position of the intractable sunken road by a fortunate accident. A company of the enemy's infantry, inefficiently led, showed themselves on the crest line in close order, and on being scattered by shrapnel some of them were observed to step down and disappear entirely from view. After South Africa, it ought not to be necessary to inculcate the value of concealment. Still, this example is perhaps specially convincing. The battery commander now knew what ho had to do; and his fire, which had so far been random and ineffectual, immediately became concentrated and deadly. Shrapnel whistled over the sunken road, and high explosive shells dropped into it until, in a very few minutes, the musketry was dominated by the gun fire. As soon as the sunken road grew silent, a handful of Japanese — Jardine says the party consisted of seven men — managed to work round the Russian extreme left and established themselves in such a position as to enfilade the two Russian companies detached on that flank.

The effect produced by those few men is the first practical exemplification of a theory I have several times had the temerity to put forward publicly. It is to the effect that the power of the magazine rifle is now so great against anything fairly exposed to its action, that if even half a dozen men can penetrate and enfilade the line held by an army, they may cause such local loss and confusion as to enable a frontal assault to be delivered. This view has been considered fanciful, but I have always felt happy about my theory, since I found it was shared by a man of genius. The ideas of a soldier may be despised, especially by the more conservative of his brethren; but the words of Tolstoi cannot be despised, and here they are; "One of the most obvious and advantageous infractions of the so-called rules of war is the action of isolated individuals against troops crowded together in a mass." In the present instance, the Russians fell fast; the tiny group firing into their serried ranks from cover at 300 yards range could not be located; the men began to waver, and ultimately the frontal attack grasped the situation; seized the opportunity, delivered the assault and drove the two companies headlong off the hill.

Misfortune upon misfortune was piled upon the Russians, for as they dashed down the steep declivity, they fell directly into the arms of three more of their own companies, who were marching up to reinforce them, with a magnificent brass band at their head. Naturally, these reinforcements were thrown into the worst disorder, and the whole mass, including the big drum and the trombone, were riddled with bullets as they rolled back in a confused mob across the deep gully which separated them from the next steep spur some 300 yards distant. Ninety Russians were buried next day in this little hollow. As the distance was so short, most of those who were not shot dead must have got away; and it is therefore not unreasonable to suppose that their casualties here were 500 out of an effective of, at the most, 1000. If people will have music, then they must be prepared to pay the piper. A stall at the opera costs a lot to be sure, but a band on the battle-field can only be paid for by blood.

Thus was the Russian left completely overthrown by 10.30 a.m., and now it was to be the turn of the Russian right. For some time this wing had ceased to press their advantage against the Japanese left, and it was noticed by several officers that the Russians were continually looking back over their right shoulders as if they momentarily expected to see something appear from the south-east. Soldiers who look over their shoulders have ceased to be formidable, and soon the entire line began to retreat over the ridge which had formed their first position, and into the defile through which runs the road from Penlin to Lipyui and Huchatsu. It was then that the cause of the preoccupation of the Russians became apparent. Okasaki had left Kuroki's force at 1.30 a.m., and

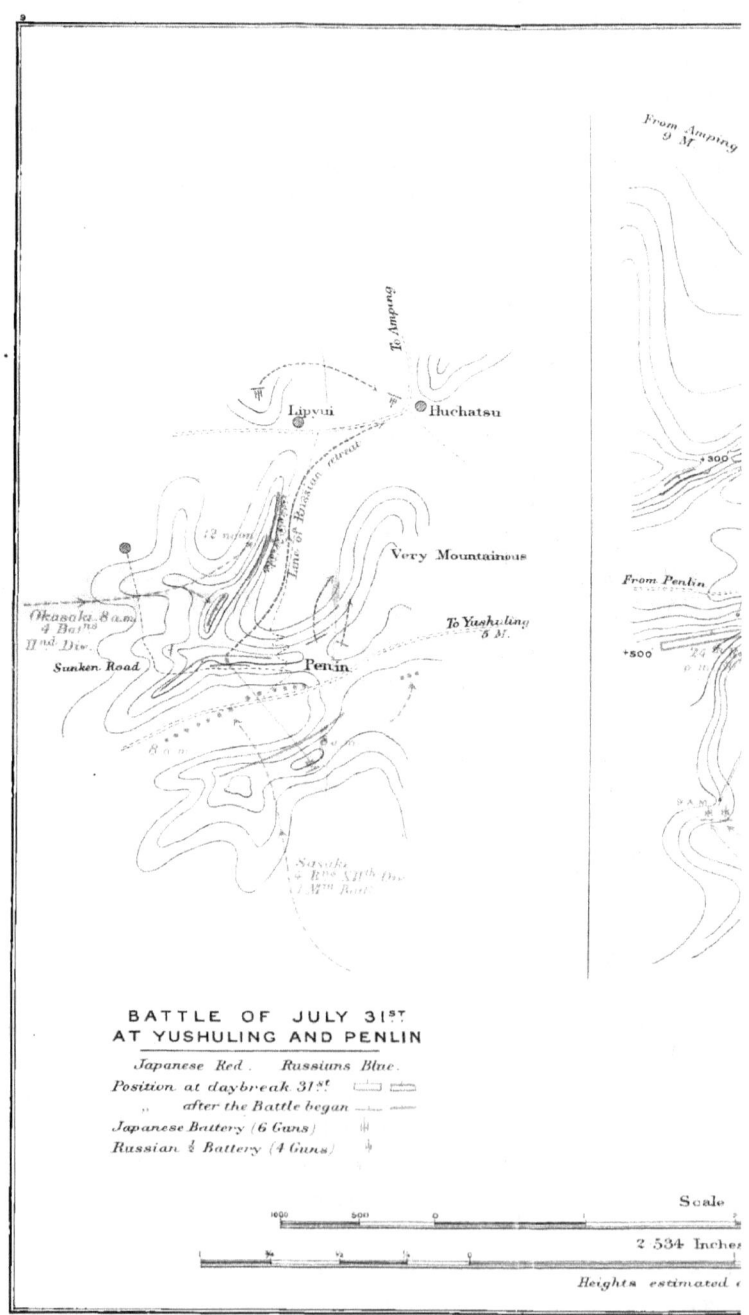

The Disastrous Retreat from Penlin

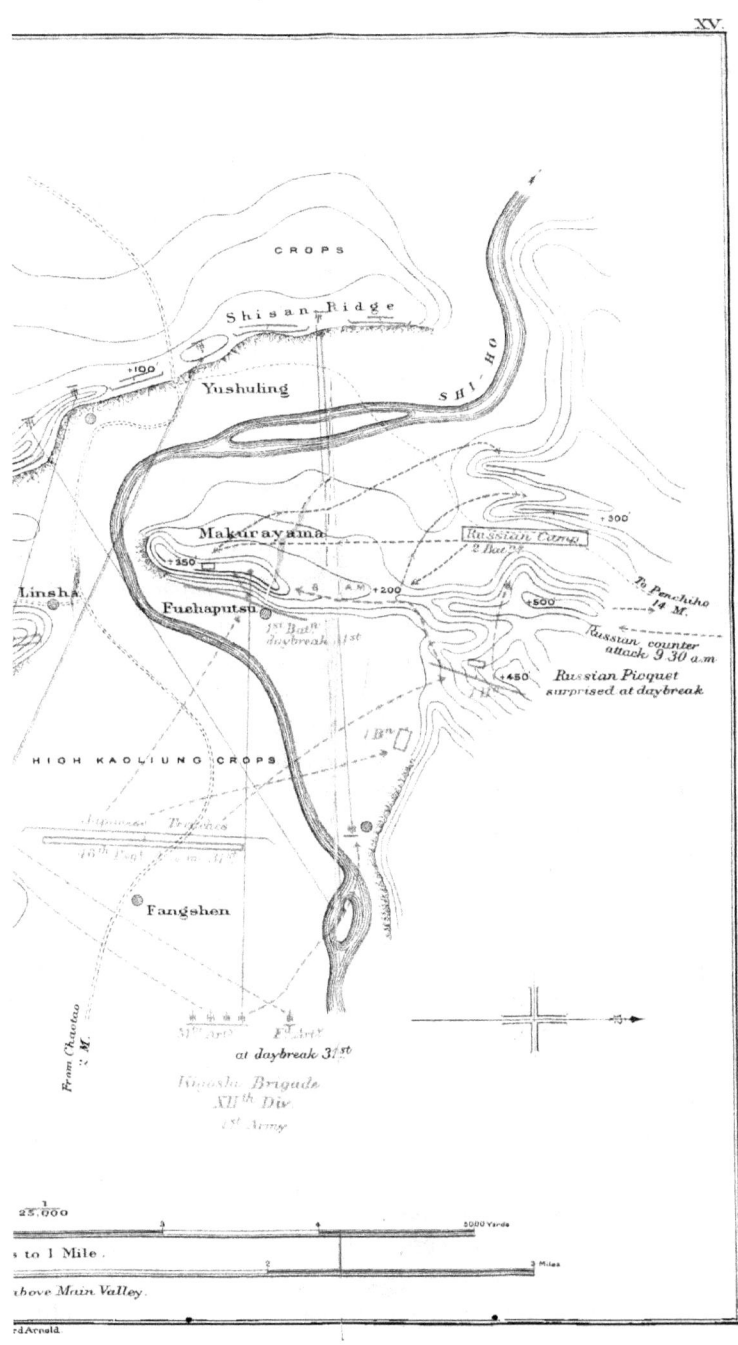

marching northwards as fast as he could, he had got so near to Sasaki by 8 a.m. that in one more hour he could have joined up on the latter's left and made practically sure of turning the Russians out of their position. With all the assurance which should characterise one good General acting in combination with another, Okasaki preferred to play for bigger stakes. Certain that Sasaki, if he did not defeat the enemy single-handed, would at least hold his own without assistance, he bore away westwards, and driving off some weak Russian picquets, occupied a lofty mountain overshadowing the ravine through which lay the enemy's line of retreat. At midday the retiring column appeared, wending its way along the bottom of the defile, which was so narrow in places that the men could not march on a greater front than four abreast. Into this long winding mass the Japanese, posted along the precipitous cliffs to the south, fired with as much impunity as a sportsman in a machan shoots at a driven tiger. The Russians could not climb up the precipitous walls of the defile, and the Japanese exposed themselves so little in shooting over the edge of the cliff that it was hardly worth while pausing to fire up at so small a mark. So the ill-starred column continued to run the gauntlet, seeming to writhe uneasily like a wounded snake where the bullets took heaviest toll, until at last the agony was past. One particular stretch of 400 yards was piled quite thick with corpses and desperately wounded men. The Russians sent out a *parlementaire* with a flag, to inquire if the ambulances might set to work at once removing the casualties, and permission was duly granted. Afterwards, there was a good deal of talk amongst Japanese officers as to whether the Russians were entitled under such circumstances to carry off rifles and ammunition. The Japanese claim that the Russians lost at least 500 killed, and no one can say how many wounded, in the passage of the defile. They maintain that, with good shooting, every Russian ought to have been wounded, but that their men got excited. Here is another version of the affair given me by Fujii:

"The Okasaki detachment got behind the enemy's right and, occupying a very high and precipitous mountain, fired a long time upon the Russians, who were quite hopelessly entangled in the narrow gorge down which they were being driven by the Sasaki brigade. The mountain on to which Okasaki had managed to climb was the highest in that part of the country, and was so precipitous that, whilst he could not go down to the Russians, neither could they climb to him. The distance of the Japanese from the Russians varied from 300 to 1000 yards. Unfortunately, Okasaki had no guns. The enemy struggled through the bullets in pell-mell disorder, and were very effectively cut about. To get a chance such as Okasaki got can only be compared to gaining the *gros lot** at Homburg!"

In this sentiment I do not quite agree. Better, I think, if chances, when they come, do not so completely exclude the chance of the enemy. Otherwise, where is the glory? I prefer, in fact, Sasaki's part at Penlin to Okasaki's, fond as I am personally of the latter General. Yet another officer, who visited the scene of action several days afterwards, told 'me that for a distance of 400 yards the whole of the road through the gorge was one mass of bloody bandages and rags. The engagement of Penlin practically closed with this ghastly slaughter, which, distressing as it must be to a Russian, yet, negatively, is glorious to the rank and file, inasmuch as very few unwounded prisoners were taken. I know several commanders who, finding themselves in such a *guet-apens*,† would promptly lay down their arms. Perhaps they might be right, perhaps they might be wrong; but certainly the Russian method of seeing the thing through appeals much more effectively to patriotic sentiment.

If, however, the Russian soldiers fought bravely and died gloriously, I think even the most ardent patriots of St. Petersburg or Moscow must admit that at Yushuling and Penlin, the quality of generalship was wanting to their arms, and that, apparently, it was not compensated for by the automatic working of any thoroughly effective brigade or regimental system. I am fully conscious that a British General spends his life in a glass house. The public are pleased to think that because their army is often happy-go-lucky in its methods, this is a military characteristic. It is useless to tell

---

* "Jackpot."

† "Ambush."

them that the profound belief in itself which encourages the army to think it can dispense with taking much preliminary trouble, is a national, and not at all a military, characteristic. But I never could see myself that the man with the beam in his own eye did an3rthing but a friendly act, when he relieved his brother of a mote; and so I venture to say that, big as my beam may be, it does not in the least prevent me from seeing quite clearly that the Russians were remarkably casual at the Makurayama mountain, and by their arrangements seemed to court disaster.

Probably most people will think the British were on occasion even more careless and less watchful in South Africa. It may be so; I am not a fair judge. But the only instance I can think of as being fairly comparable was that of the Yeomanry and the pom-pom at Tweefontein, between Bethlehem and Harrismith in the Orange River Colony, who were cut up by Christian de Wet on Christmas Eve, 1901. But the Yeomanry had stronger outposts in proportion to their total force than the Russians, although they had not been like them actually and visibly in contact with the enemy throughout the previous day. Moreover, the Yeomanry were attacked at midnight, whereas the Russians were rushed in a perfectly orthodox manner, just as dawn was breaking, an hour at which every army, by immemorial precept, should have its outposts doubled by their reliefs, whilst all the men in camp should be standing to their arms prepared for any eventuality. Even now it sends a cold shiver down my back when I think of that long black hour before dawn. Especially does that shiver associate itself with the Nile Expedition of 1885. It is not that the procedure there differed essentially from that pursued during the Afghan War of 1879-1880, but because General Earle did not allow us to put on our greatcoats lest the enemy should attack and find us hampered thereby; but, oh, that awful cold!

In Manchuria at this time the weather was warm and perfect. The Russian camp was pitched in the valley between two lofty ridges whose crests were some 800 yards apart. For the past two days the bulk of the Japanese troops had been entrenched only 2300 yards to the south-east of the camp. The Makurayama ridge was the only protection of the camp, not only from view but also against fire. None the less this vital bulwark was only held by a

The Disastrous Retreat from Penlin 309

weak picquet, whilst the main body of the defenders was content to turn into its tents, which were pitched just where, ordinarily, the picquet supports should hare found themselves. It is quite certain that neither in India or South Africa would troops have been allowed to "doss down" under canvas within such dose proximity to the enemy. At the most a hospital tent and an office might have been pitched, but as the weather was good even this is not likely. There is nothing more awkward, or more apt to lead to confusion, than an alarm when the men are ail broken up into separate small groups by their tents. If they bivouac lying down in lines by companies they are ready for handling the monent they start up out of their sleep.

At Makurayama, however, the commander trusted everything to his picquets. How did the picquets then respond to this confidence? It is obvious that they did not patrol the thick crops which ran up to the very foot of the ridge on which they were posted. It is, of course, equally obvious that the Japanese were well aware of this slackness, and counted upon its continuance. Beneath the Makurayama mountain, a Japanese battalion lay for that vital last half-hour before dawn at the very feet of the picquet on the summit, and yet no patrol came down to give his own outposts or the sleeping camp behind them a chance of getting ready to defend themselves. Not much is gained by discussing what might have been, but it seems dear enough that the observance of elementary precaution would have enabled the men in camp to occupy the crest line of Makurayama in an orderly regular manner. They could then have been reinforced as occasion demanded from the Shisan ridge, and it is certain that three battalions of Japanese would have found it very hard to make them quit their hold.

As a result of the battle of July 3lst, the First Army has gained possession of the positions previously occupied ly the Russians, who have retreated to the line Tokayen-Amping, where they appear to have halted. By thus forcing back the enemy, the Japanese have succeeded in shortening their distance from Liaoyang by some twelve miles. From the line held by Kuroki before the battle, it would have taken him three days to march upon Liaoyang; whilst, even upon sanguine estimates, he could not have reckoned on defeating the enemy and opening a free passage for his army under

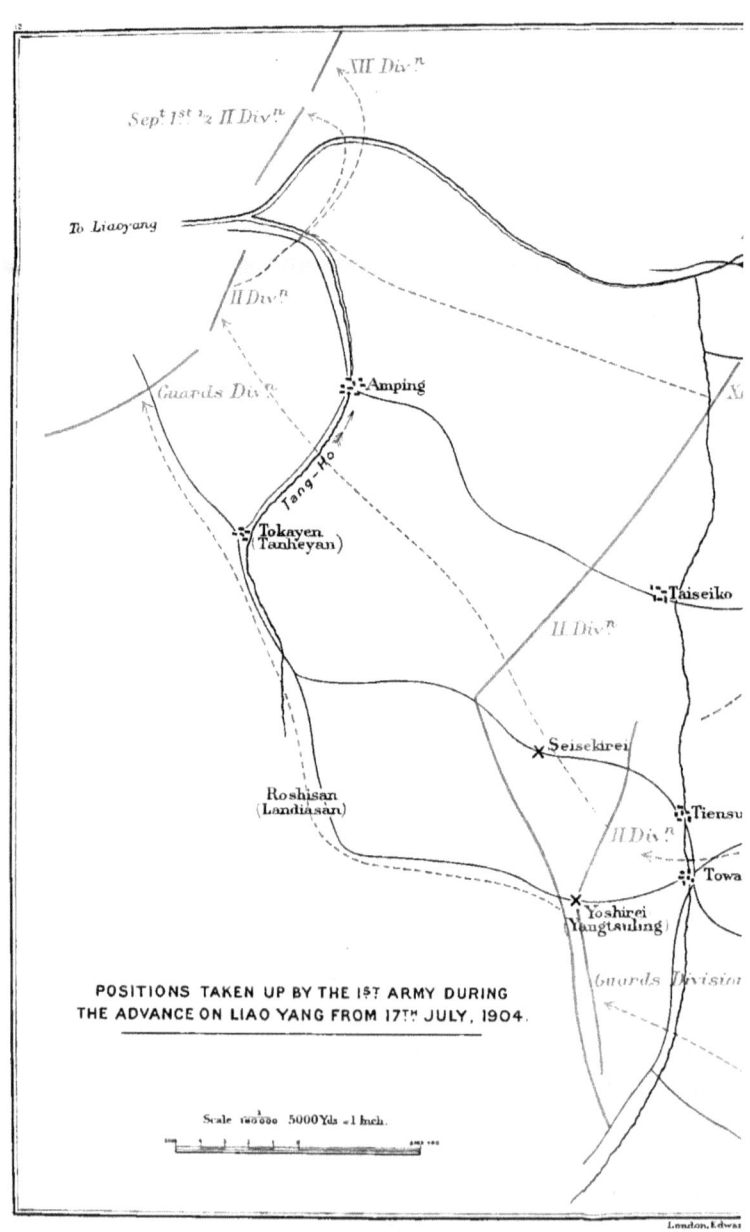

POSITIONS TAKEN UP BY THE 1ST ARMY DURING
THE ADVANCE ON LIAO YANG FROM 17TH JULY, 1904.

The Disastrous Retreat from Penlin   311

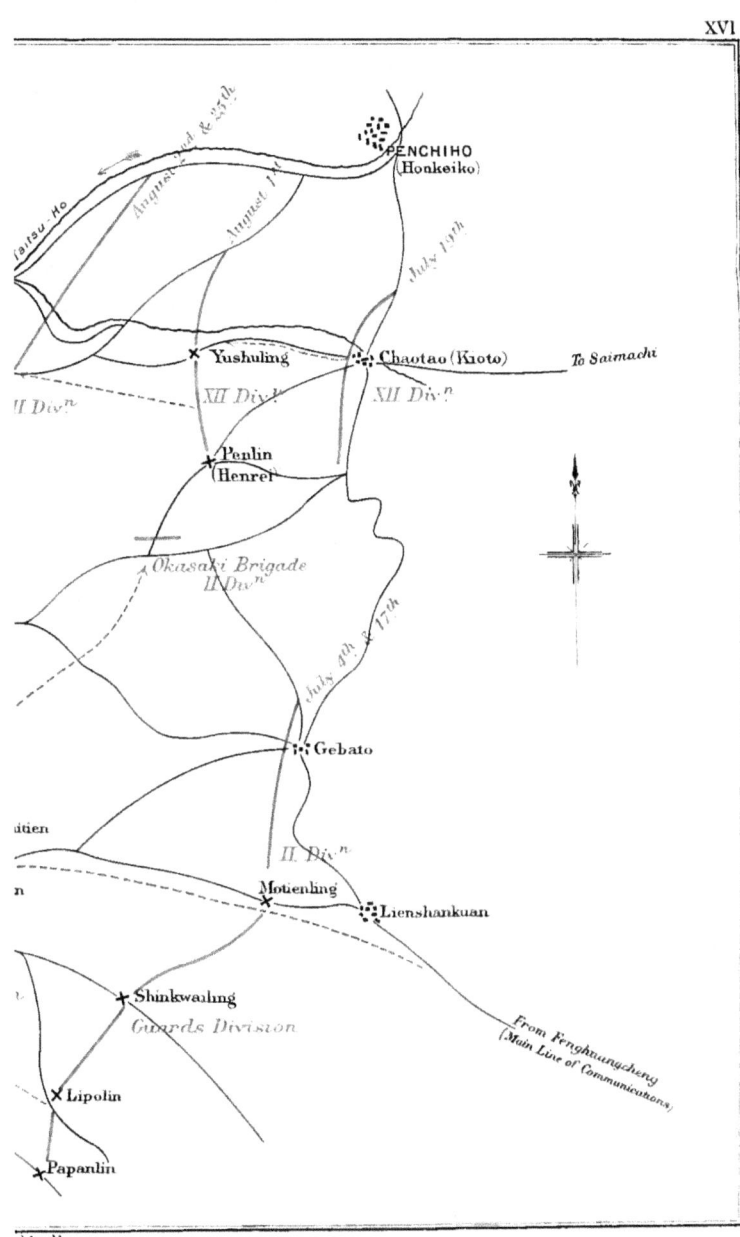

another four days. Accordingly, seven days was the minimum period within which the Japanese commander could have previously expected to enter Liaoyang or to begin to besiege it.

Since the Yoshirei engagement, however, Kuroki has shortened the distance which separates him from his goal by one day's march, whilst it is only reasonable to suppose that it will now take him less time than he had previously calculated to overcome the Russian resistance. No doubt the relative situations of the combatants may be entirely changed at any moment by the arrival on the line Tokayen-Amping of heavy reinforcements, detatched by Kuropatkin from his armies south of Liaoyang. But in that case the First Army will have played its part by weakening the forces in front of the Second and Fourth Armies and, even if defeated, will have effectively done its duty to Oyama and Japan.

Index

6th Company... 218, 219, 221, 222, 245
Abyssinia... 11
Afghan War... 13, 226, 308
Afghanistan... 11, 140
Aiho, river... 56, 72, 76, 77, 80-82, 84, 87-89, 95-100, 102, 109, 111, 131, 132, 211
Aiyanmen.. 87, 155-157, 161, 162, 168, 183, 211, 243, 247
Alexieff, Admiral..... 71, 136, 195
America.. 4, 36, 37, 51, 63, 68, 124, 131, 132, 151, 163
American Civil War 71, 110
Amping... 241, 243-245, 254, 261-263, 268, 270, 271, 293, 309, 312
Anju............ 51, 69, 115-117
Anshantien............. 261-263
Antung... 53, 56, 58, 72, 75, 76, 82, 83, 88, 99-101, 113, 115, 157, 158, 160, 187, 211
Appointments 25, 163
artillery .. 27, 43, 44, 61, 68, 70, 72, 75, 76, 79-81, 86, 89-96, 98, 101, 102, 104, 108-112, 123, 124, 127, 131, 146, 150, 156, 159, 179, 189, 197, 203, 204, 212, 215, 224, 225, 228, 230, 232, 233, 244, 247, 249, 252, 258, 260, 265, 266, 273, 274, 280, 281, 283, 293, 294, 297-299, 301
Asada, Major-General.. 72, 73, 125, 273
attachés 6, 31, 60, 63, 120, 124, 126, 130, 132, 154, 158, 162, 163, 168, 173, 196, 238, 264, 266, 289
attack.... 12, 26, 29, 56, 71, 75, 81, 84, 86, 88, 89, 94, 96, 99-101, 104, 105, 110, 111, 117, 118, 120-123, 130, 132, 148, 154, 156, 158, 159, 195, 201-203, 209, 210, 215, 216, 218, 219, 223, 225-228, 230, 232,

233, 240, 241, 244, 246-249, 252, 256, 260, 263, 270-272, 274, 277, 279-281, 283-285, 289-292, 294, 297, 300, 301, 303, 308
Baba, Colonel 196, 201, 223
balloons 263, 292
Barstow, Captain 48
battalions ... 13, 26, 68, 82, 99, 100, 102, 103, 157, 194, 201, 202, 217-220, 222, 223, 227, 229, 230, 232, 241, 244-246, 258, 261, 270, 272-275, 281, 284, 285, 291, 293-295, 300, 301, 309
battle of Liaoyang ... 241, 243, 262
bayonet charge 118, 279
bayonets 122, 265
Boers 10, 11, 40, 54, 80, 89, 94, 96, 111, 147, 222, 248, 295, 296
Buddhism 167, 168
Bunsuirei .. 157, 186, 194, 204, 212
Burma 207
caste 37, 63
cavalry ... 49, 60, 68, 72-74, 82, 83, 87, 100, 102, 112, 114, 124, 127, 132, 146, 147, 150, 152, 156, 157, 161, 164, 171, 185, 188, 215, 217, 227, 228, 244, 245, 254, 271, 273, 274, 295, 301
Chaotao ... 188, 194, 211, 217, 218, 220, 238, 239, 241-247, 249, 254, 265, 270, 290-294, 297, 300, 301
Chemulpho 43, 45, 46, 52
China .. 16, 17, 25, 28, 60, 132, 133, 140-143, 191, 205
Chinchaputsu ... 268, 269, 274, 275, 277, 278, 280-282
Chinese .. 24, 26, 27, 51, 57, 58, 60, 63, 69, 71, 77, 86, 87, 118, 132, 136-138, 140-143, 147, 158, 161, 164, 180-182, 184, 193, 197, 207, 208, 211, 215, 239, 240, 248, 256, 258, 292
Chinnampo . 44, 47, 50, 52, 87, 113
Chiuliencheng .. 65, 69, 72, 77, 79-82, 90, 92, 97, 99, 102, 103, 108, 113, 121, 131, 204
Chiuliencheng-Sheechong 82
Chouyuang 157
Christmas 50, 308
Chukodai 81, 89, 93, 94
Chulsan 52, 69, 73, 87
Chusan 186
Civilisation .. 10, 11, 15, 17, 19, 68
coal mines 71
Colenso 80, 233
Colonial 148
commanders .. 58, 71, 82, 101, 114, 146, 148, 159, 218, 307
companies .. 18, 105, 122, 198, 200, 201, 204, 213, 215, 217, 219-222, 224-226, 228-230, 247, 255, 267, 273-275, 299, 302, 303, 309
conscription ... 14-16, 50, 132, 206
coolies 27, 47, 50, 54, 115, 134, 141, 158, 180, 184, 187, 188, 205-207, 239
Cossack .. 32, 53, 63, 134, 174, 255
countrymen 59, 124, 132, 167
courage 13, 15, 25-27, 52, 128, 221, 222
cover, ... 79, 97, 105, 108, 110, 111
Crowder, Colonel 43
Daiboshi-Joshisan 164
Daidoko 220, 225
Dalny 195, 209
Demidrovitch, Lieutenant 74
disembarkation 47-49, 73, 88
Doornkop 97
Dundee 71
education ... 10, 15, 16, 18, 19, 145, 181, 214
Emperor 8, 36, 46, 144, 168
entrenchments 79, 80, 92, 111,

Index

fan, the, in firing line 156, 245, 290, 300, 277
Fenghuangcheng 58, 60, 70, 72, 88, 102, 113, 116, 120, 133, 140, 145, 146, 148, 155, 158, 160, 163, 169, 174, 176, 178, 185-189, 195, 205, 211, 239, 241
firing ... 93, 96, 117, 122, 123, 164, 175, 194, 200, 213, 215, 227, 229, 233, 240, 249, 275, 277, 282, 285, 295, 296, 300, 303
First Army... 58, 66, 69, 74-76, 88, 90, 91, 97, 103, 113, 115, 124, 126, 148, 151, 152, 155, 156, 158, 161, 171, 177, 178, 185, 189, 205, 206, 209, 210, 240-242, 244, 259, 261-263, 284, 309, 312
flags 129, 130
flexibility 215
formations ... 96, 98, 120, 121, 159, 227, 230, 232, 240, 246, 256, 271, 284, 301
Formosa 29
fortifications 148, 185
Fourth Army ... 196, 240, 261, 263
Franco-Prussian War 266
Fredericksburg 83, 110
frontal attack ... 100, 101, 248, 249, 252, 270, 303
Fujii, Major-General S 60, 61, 136, 153, 154, 156, 160, 161, 163, 168, 175, 178, 185-188, 196, 205, 208-210, 240-243, 245, 246, 254, 257, 260, 261, 263, 264, 266, 270, 273, 283, 291, 306
Fukuda, Major 126, 178, 263
Fukushima, Maj.-General 22, 30-33
Fusan 46, 159
Gebato 216-219, 221, 222, 225, 228, 230, 232, 244, 249
Geishas 38, 39

Gerschelman, Lieut.-General ... 244, 249, 252, 255, 256
Gravelotte 262
guns .. 10, 24, 27, 42, 46, 49, 63, 68, 70, 72, 73, 76, 79, 82, 86, 89-95, 97, 98, 101-103, 105, 108-114, 124, 132, 136, 137, 146, 147, 155-157, 164, 186, 188, 208, 211, 212, 216, 223, 224, 226, 228, 230, 233, 240, 241, 243-247, 249, 252, 260, 266, 269, 274, 275, 277, 278, 280, 282, 283, 285, 291, 293, 294, 297, 298, 300, 302, 307
Gurkhas 13, 248
Hagino, Colonel 126, 179, 257, 258, 292
Haicheng .. 157, 185, 195, 209, 240, 241, 261, 270
Haimun 46-48
Hamaton . 57, 65, 76, 77, 83, 97, 99, 100, 102-104, 121, 218
Hanchaputsu 268-271, 273
Harbin 195
harbour 42, 44, 46-48, 191
Hasegawa, Lieut.-Generla 125, 129, 261, 280
Headquarters 30, 42, 47, 51, 58, 60, 72, 73, 90, 93, 100, 114, 115, 124, 126, 128, 146, 151, 152, 154, 162, 164, 173-175, 178, 179, 182-185, 188, 194-196, 206, 212, 215-217, 219-221, 230, 238, 239, 257, 261-265, 283-285, 289, 296, 301
health 30, 38, 175, 259
Hikida, Colonel 179
Hiraoka, Major 255
Hlangwane 80, 89
Honkeiko 243, 247, 262
horses ... 9, 42, 43, 49, 68, 76, 136, 137, 159, 180, 207, 228, 252, 274, 298

Houtnek................ 248
howitzers.... 42, 72, 90, 91, 93, 98,
    101, 109, 113, 158
Hsuehliten............... 177
Hume, Lieut.-Colonel.. 43, 52, 163,
    169, 170, 173, 277, 278
Imamoura, Col.. 248, 249, 252-255
Imperial Guards.. 43, 47, 84, 87, 89,
    100, 125, 173, 177, 184,
    186, 216, 242, 267, 271,
    273, 274, 277, 278
Indian.... 12, 32, 33, 59, 174, 192,
    206, 296
Indian troops................ 32
infantry. 27, 44, 49, 50, 68, 70, 72-
    74, 89, 93-96, 98, 99, 103,
    104, 108, 110-112, 115,
    118, 119, 123, 124, 132,
    148, 159, 170, 171, 188,
    221, 227, 228, 244-247,
    249, 252-254, 256, 260,
    273, 275, 279, 285, 292-
    295, 299-302
Inouye, Maj.-General . 65, 126, 129,
    244, 249, 252, 256, 267,
    268, 270, 284, 290, 291,
    294
insect................ 170, 181
Ishido, Sergeant-Major....... 134
Ishiko................. 77, 89
Ito, Marquis.......... 21, 24, 25
James, Captain.............. 48
Japan... 8, 9, 15, 19, 21, 23-25, 28-
    30, 33, 36, 38, 45, 46, 48,
    63, 66-69, 76, 87, 95, 127-
    129, 133, 143-145, 152,
    153, 165, 174, 176, 191,
    205, 211, 273, 301, 312
Japanese Army.. 6, 7, 10, 13, 14, 45,
    46, 51, 60, 72, 83, 121,
    209, 221, 242, 274, 322
Jardine, Captain..... 43, 45, 52, 56,
    152, 153, 162, 163, 165,
    168, 173, 240, 254, 256,
    258, 296, 301, 302
Jokahoshi...... 217, 218, 220, 221
jokes....... 29, 35, 127, 130, 133

Kaiping.... 69, 156-158, 172, 195,
    196, 205, 208, 209, 240
Kakaton.................. 164
Kanjo.................... 117
Kanshio............... 210, 211
Kansoten.................. 184
Kaschtalinsky, General.. 65, 72, 75,
    89, 113
Katsura, Maj.-General, Count... 24
Keller, General Count.... 230, 241,
    261, 267, 270-273, 289,
    301
key of a position, the.... 13, 60, 66,
    80-82, 268
Kigoshi, Maj.-General.... 126, 253,
    254, 294
Kinkahoshi.... 194, 228, 229, 280,
    284
Kinteito Island... 77, 81, 84, 86, 91
Kitashirakawa, Prince........ 129
Kitchener, Lord..... 101, 215, 239
Kobi.. 157, 174, 242, 267, 291, 294
Kodama, Lieut.-General Baron.. 22,
    28, 29
Komura, Baron........... 21, 22
Korea.... 8, 45-47, 54, 69, 70, 115,
    133, 135, 143, 147, 160,
    191, 205-207
Korean coolies........... 54, 207
Kuantienchen.... 76, 77, 86-88, 97,
    155, 157
Kujo, Prince M............... 24
Kuni, Prince.... 60, 129, 132, 166,
    168, 175, 185, 188
Kurita, Lieut.-Colonel.... 114, 126,
    179, 188, 205, 215, 263
Kuroda, Captain............ 179
Kuroki, Marshal Baron... 6, 47, 60,
    61, 63-65, 73, 89, 100,
    101, 103, 115, 124, 129,
    130, 134, 155, 173-176,
    178, 185, 186, 188, 208,
    216, 238, 242, 261, 262,
    265, 267, 268, 270-272,
    274, 284, 289, 290, 309,
    312
Kuropatkin, General.... 66, 70, 71,

Index

74, 136, 156, 172, 185, 186, 195, 209, 210, 240, 241, 261-263, 271, 292, 293, 312
Kyokahoshi 184
Kyoto, Manchuria 216
Kyurito Island 84, 89, 94
Ladysmith 66, 165
Liao River 143, 197, 263
Liaotung Peninsula 185
Liaoyang ... 97, 158, 159, 161, 173, 177, 186, 187, 189, 196, 209-211, 217, 241-244, 261, 262, 268, 270, 309, 312
Lichaputsu 199, 201, 203, 223
Lienshankuan .. 156, 157, 173, 186, 196, 197, 212, 217, 218, 221, 230, 238, 263, 264, 291
Linchatai 185
lives 16, 45, 99, 108, 137, 141, 174, 207
loopholes 111, 112, 205
Louisbourg 208
loyalty 16, 18, 168
MacDonald, Sir Claude 21
Majuba 57, 111, 228, 295
Makau 94, 95
Makumenza 194, 229, 230, 274, 280
Makurayama, Mt. ... 290-295, 297-301, 308, 309
Manchuria 8, 44, 59, 66-69, 71, 116, 142, 157, 160, 161, 179, 186, 191, 207, 208, 293, 308
Manchurian War 266
maps 6, 44, 92, 164, 263
March .. 7, 8, 13, 17, 18, 27, 40, 43, 46, 47, 51, 53, 58, 70, 72, 89, 90, 97, 99-101, 144, 146, 156, 158, 173-177, 187, 188, 192, 199, 205, 218-220, 222, 223, 225, 240, 245, 249, 256, 258, 259, 272, 273, 291, 294, 306, 309, 312
Matoriroff, Lieut.-Colonel 115, 116, 118
Matsuishi, Colonel .. 126, 162, 178, 188, 205, 245, 260
Matsumoto, Colonel 127, 179
Matsunaga, Maj.-General 125
Maxwell, Mr 143, 164
Mayapuza, ... 273
McCaul, Ethel 145
Miage, Captain 179
military bravery 221
military organisation 254
"Minstrel Boy" 176
mobility 24, 222
modesty 129
moral 17, 35, 82, 111, 117, 124, 145, 189, 206
Motienling 157, 161, 173, 183, 186, 188, 194-198, 202, 204, 207, 209, 210, 212, 214-217, 223, 224, 227, 229, 230, 232, 240-242, 264, 268-270, 272, 274, 281-285, 289
Motienling range 214, 215, 242, 268, 274
mountain guns ... 97, 105, 216, 233, 244, 246, 252, 297, 298
Mukden ... 138, 185, 193, 205, 210, 243, 262, 263, 271, 292
Nanshan 191
Napoleon III 266
Nenkyaten 261
Newchwang 69, 195, 210
Nidoboshi 187, 189
Nishi, Maj.-General Baron 100-102, 125, 129, 166-168, 196
Nodzu, General 185
Nogi, General .. 196, 208, 261, 264
officers and men ... 13, 74, 97, 117, 118, 194, 208, 221, 254
Oka, Major 187
Okahoshi 218
Okasaki, Generall ... 125, 126, 196, 223, 239, 272, 284, 300, 301, 303, 306, 307

Oku, General 136
Omdurman 8, 224
Omura, Captain 179
outposts .. 80, 83, 97, 145, 146, 148,
 194, 203, 216, 217, 219,
 222, 223, 245, 291, 308,
 309
Oyama, Lt.-General Marquis 21,
 24-28, 172, 209, 262, 312
Oyanagi, Colonel 179
Papanlin 273
patriotism 14, 16, 168, 253
Penchiho .. 243, 247, 249, 262, 292,
 294, 299, 300
Penlin 270, 272, 290-294, 301,
 303, 307
personality 125, 127
physique 14, 125, 189
picquet .. 12, 85, 198, 199, 203, 218,
 223, 295, 297, 309
picquets ... 148, 223, 296, 306, 309
Pingyang . 44, 46, 47, 50-52, 69, 73,
 87, 117
poetry 28
Port Arthur .. 26-28, 136, 158, 172,
 191, 196, 208, 261, 263,
 264
Pulienten-Shaoshiatun 156
regiments .. 155, 161, 171, 174, 219,
 223, 230, 247, 249, 279,
 292
reinforcements 26, 70, 203, 210,
 224, 299, 303, 312
religion 12, 165, 166, 168, 169
Rennenkampf, General ... 171, 271
reserves .. 89, 94, 99, 100, 148, 220,
 224, 247, 249, 252, 256,
 278, 281, 295
reticence 44, 54, 62, 196
retreat ... 82, 88, 97, 102-104, 111,
 112, 181, 201, 210, 218,
 226, 230, 232, 233, 241,
 244, 252-254, 261, 262,
 290, 294, 303, 306
rice ... 49, 52-54, 56, 115, 129, 130,
 141, 157, 183, 185, 206,
 207, 213, 264, 266, 273

Rihorei 274
Rikahoshi 197, 229
Rikwaho 52, 53
roadmaking 12
Roberts, Earl 13, 24
Rocky Hill .. 81, 224, 228, 232, 233,
 238
Ruskin 17
Russia 8, 24, 67, 68, 126, 133,
 134, 143, 144, 179, 191,
 258, 259, 292
Russian prisoners 183, 188
Saigo, Captain 43, 53
sailors 158
Saimachi .. 156, 157, 160, 168, 171,
 173, 177, 184, 185, 195,
 210, 211, 243, 247, 249
Saito, Captain 179
Sanna's Post 254
Sanseito 260
Sasaki, Maj.-General 75, 126,
 157, 294, 300-302, 306
Sassulitch, General .. 70, 72, 75, 81,
 88, 113
Satow, Colonel 43, 53
Satsuma 25
Second Army 44, 136, 147, 155,
 156, 164, 185, 205, 208-
 210, 240, 258-262
Second Division . 80, 89, 91, 94, 97,
 99-102, 125, 165, 170, 173,
 177, 180, 183, 184, 196,
 209, 216, 217, 222, 223,
 242, 244, 249, 264, 266,
 270-272, 274, 280-284,
 289, 292, 298, 301
Seisekirei 284, 289
Seisekisan 260
Sekijo 97, 100
Seoul 46, 47, 158
Seoul-Wiju 158
servant question 35
Sheechong 77, 82
Shiba, Colonel 44, 247
Shibayama, Captain 179
Shibuya, General 58
Shimonoseki 41, 42

Shinkwairei 216, 217, 223, 229, 230, 274
Shintoism 168
Shisan ... 290, 291, 293, 294, 297-300, 309
signalling ... 52, 147, 159, 160, 274
Siuyen 156, 160, 185, 187, 196, 209, 240
smokeless powder 233, 265
Smuts, General 74
Sodaiko Eikaseki 263
Sokako 188, 192, 196, 204, 263, 264
soldiers .. 10-12, 14, 17, 18, 32, 40, 52, 54, 56, 60, 63, 64, 76, 85, 87, 95, 111, 114, 115, 123, 129, 131, 132, 154, 163, 165, 167-170, 172, 182, 189, 201, 206, 212, 222, 232, 256, 296, 303, 307
South Africa .. 8, 11, 16, 45, 54, 61, 70, 74, 109, 133, 142, 168, 181, 187, 248, 256, 266, 295, 302, 308, 309
South African War .. 12, 61, 79, 109, 178, 255
spade work 111, 148
St. Aubyn, Miss 145
strategy .. 70, 71, 88, 113, 156, 196, 197
Suitechansa 274, 275, 277, 278, 282
Sukaton 164
Suminoye Maru 41-43
Suribachiyama 95, 97, 99, 100, 102, 108, 129
Swat valley 207
Tachibana, Major 245
tactics . 55, 108, 109, 111, 112, 124, 196, 256
Takubokujo 187, 261
Takushan 161, 172, 185
Talana Hill 108
Taneguchi, Maj.-General .. 127, 128, 179
Tangei, General 137, 140, 143

Taniyama, Colonel .. 217, 219, 220, 222, 252, 253, 255
Tapinrei 260
Tashihchiao 240, 260, 261
Telissu 155-157, 164, 186
temples 202, 223
Tenth Division 185, 187, 196
Teraoutsi, Lieut.-General 21, 23
Third Army 261, 263
Tiger Hill 80, 81, 86, 89, 90, 94
Tirah 170, 232, 248
To wan 283
Tokio ... 7, 9, 13, 14, 17, 21, 28, 30, 31, 35, 39-42, 47, 56, 66, 68, 73, 133, 146, 159, 160, 172
Tolstoi 303
Tori No Umi 48
Toryako 164
Towan 188, 194, 199, 201, 227, 229, 242, 268-270, 272, 280, 281, 283, 285
Towan tower 285
Tsuyenpu 183, 184
Turcheffsky, General 267, 270, 290, 301
Turkestan 258
turning march 240
Tweefontein 308
Twelfth Division 51, 65, 76, 80, 86-90, 94, 97, 98, 100, 102, 103, 105, 108, 113, 126, 160, 162, 171, 173, 177, 184, 186, 188, 194, 195, 204, 209-211, 216, 239, 241-245, 256, 261, 263, 265-267, 270, 271, 284, 290, 292, 294, 298, 301
Umezawa, General 270
valleys 7, 53, 59, 102, 137, 147, 161, 179, 184, 197, 198, 214, 218, 232, 269
Vincent, Captain .. 6, 43, 45-48, 50-52, 56, 62, 137, 140, 143, 152, 162, 163, 165, 168, 173, 183, 196, 204, 215, 238, 245, 265

Waggon Hill 279
war... 1, 3, 4, 6, 8, 9, 11-17, 21, 23, 24, 40, 42, 44-49, 52, 56, 59, 61, 62, 66, 68-71, 79, 83, 87, 96, 98, 99, 105, 109, 110, 112, 114, 115, 118, 132, 133, 142, 143, 150, 158, 163, 169, 174, 178, 182, 191, 197, 205-207, 213, 226, 245, 246, 254, 255, 266, 280, 291, 303, 308, 322
War Office..... 11, 16, 56, 66, 163
War Song........... 42, 143, 150
Waziri Expedition........... 296
Welcome Farm 295
White, Field Marshal Sir George. 11, 71
Wiju.. 55, 56, 61, 65, 72-75, 81, 87, 158, 160
Woerth................ 82, 110
women... 19, 34, 38, 140, 141, 145, 174, 208
Yalu.. 10, 41, 42, 47, 53, 55-58, 61, 62, 65, 66, 69, 71-77, 80-84, 86-90, 93, 94, 96, 98, 100, 109, 112, 113, 115, 120, 125, 126, 129, 131, 148, 150, 157, 160, 195, 197, 204, 211, 218, 219, 240, 247, 259, 271
Yamagata, Marquis........ 21, 24
Yamamoto, Baron......... 21, 23
Yamorinza Valley... 261, 268, 269, 271, 273-275, 277, 278, 282
Yongampho.............. 72, 88
Yoshi, Lieutenant 197, 199
Yoshirei.. 188, 194, 201, 241, 266-274, 277, 278, 281-285, 290, 291, 294, 312

About the Author

Sir Ian Hamilton (1853-1947) was a British staff officer, writer and diarist. After serving in multiple campaigns, including the Boer War, he was appointed to lead the British mission to the Japanese Army during the Russo-Japanese War. His military career came to an end in the First World War as a result of the disastrous Gallipoli campaign. After his retirement, he served as the Scottish President of the British Legion.

www.ingramcontent.com/pod-product-compliance
Lightning Source LLC
Chambersburg PA
CBHW050102170426
43198CB00014B/2427